Liturgies of the Future

The Process and Methods of Inculturation

Anscar J. Chupungco, O.S.B.

Paulist Press
New York *Mahwah*

Library of Congress Cataloging-in-Publication Data

Chupungco, Anscar J.
Liturgies of the future: the process and methods of inculturation/Anscar J. Chupungco.
p. cm.
Bibliography: p.
ISBN 0-8091-3095-5: $9.95 (est.)
1. Catholic Church—Liturgy. 2. Christianity and culture.
I. Title.
BX1970.C572 1989
264'.02—dc20 89-34812
CIP

Published by Paulist Press
997 Macarthur Boulevard
Mahwah, NJ 07430

Printed and bound in the
United States of America

Contents

Introduction 1

Chapter One: Sound Tradition and Legitimate Progress 3

1. The Classical Reform of Vatican II 3
2. SC 37–40: Toward a Pluriform Liturgy 8
3. Adaptation and the Competent Authority 18
4. Approaches to Adaptation: Acculturation, Inculturation, and Creativity 23
5. The Translation of Liturgical Texts 40

Chapter Two: The Future Shape of the Eucharistic Celebration 56

1. The Order of Mass in the Reform of Vatican II 56
2. Toward Alternative Forms of the Order of Mass 71

Chapter Three: The Future Shape of Sacramental Celebrations 102

1. Vatican II's Reform of the Sacramental Celebrations 102
2. The Postconciliar Revision of the Sacramental Rites 122

3. The Passage from the *Editio Typica* of the Rites of Initiation 125

4. From the *Editio Typica* to Alternative Rites of Marriage 139

5. Note on the Rite of Penance 149

6. Note on the Rite of Anointing the Sick 151

Chapter Four: The Future Shape of the Liturgical Year 163

1. Theological Premise 163

2. The Celebration of Easter Sunday 172

3. Culture and the Sunday Observance 184

4. Liturgical Feasts in the Life and Mission of the Church 195

Introduction

After the publication of my book *Cultural Adaptation of the Liturgy* a suggestion was made that I work on a sequel developing the question of adaptations in the area of the sacraments, sacramentals, the divine office, and the liturgical year. It took several years to write that sequel not only because of the enormous material it represents, but also because of the difficulty of presenting a balanced treatise on a subject that obviously needs careful handling. This book is not even complete. It does not address the question of the divine office, the sacramentals, and the blessings.

The title might appear to some readers to be provocative. For the author it sums up everything that concerns the cultural adaptation of the liturgy. But then it is probably another way of expressing wishful thinking. To be faithful to sound tradition and to foster legitimate progress at the same time is an art requiring expertise in the science of liturgy, the virtue of flexibility, and often a great faith in the wisdom of the church. The liturgies of the future are ecclesial expressions. They belong to the church, they manifest the church, they foster communion with the church.

Some parts of this book appeared in English and in Italian, French, and German translations in various publications and reviews, especially *Anàmnesis, Analecta Liturgica, Ecclesia Orans, Notitiae, La Maison-Dieu,* and *Concilium.* This book is, however, not a reprint of articles. New material has been added, and the rest has been substantially revised, updated, and sometimes modified. I admit that in the course of my research and reflection I have changed some of the views I previously held, particularly on the methods of adaptation.

I acknowledge with gratitude the encouragement and

suggestions offered by my colleagues at the Pontifical Liturgical Institute and the interest of the editors of Paulist Press in this book. I am fully aware that it has rough edges and loose ends. Nevertheless, I present it to fellow liturgists and students of liturgy in the hope of making a contribution, however modest and tentative, to their own research and study.

Pontifical Liturgical Institute
Rome

Chapter One

Sound Tradition and Legitimate Progress

The Classical Reform of Vatican II

The title of this book, with apologies to Archdale King's *Liturgies of the Past* and to Adrien Nocent's *The Future of the Liturgy*,[1] wishes to put the accent on the ongoing agenda of liturgical adaptation. Barely twenty years after the promulgation of Vatican II's Constitution on the Liturgy (SC), the principal liturgical books were revised and published. Among these are the missal and lectionary, the rituals for the celebration of the sacraments and sacramentals, the liturgy of the hours, and the Roman calendar. A striking feature of the revised liturgical books is the sustained endeavor to restore the Roman liturgy to its classical shape by eliminating, whenever timely, such elements of the Franco-Germanic culture as the Roman church adopted after the eighth century.[2]

The liturgical reform of Vatican II used as a model the classical or pure Roman liturgy. By pure is meant the shape of the liturgy that existed in Rome before it adopted Franco-Germanic elements toward the eighth century.[3] It is called classical with respect to the shape developed by the Roman pontiffs from the end of the fourth to the seventh century. The classical Roman liturgy is the accomplishment of Popes Damasus (+384), Innocent I (+417), Leo the Great (+461), Gelasius (+496), Vigilius (+555), and Gregory the Great (+604). During this period the Roman liturgy absorbed the Roman cultural traits of simplicity, sobriety, and practicality. These traits can be detected in what liturgists call the formal elements of the Roman liturgy, namely its euchology and ritual form.

The structure of the classical Roman euchology, especially the collects, is simple. Its language is sober and direct, and appeals primarily to the intellect. The collects for Christmas night, the Easter vigil, and Pentecost in the Gregorian sacramentary are perhaps some of the finest literary compositions to adorn the Roman liturgy, but they are quite devoid of human sentiments and imagery. The mystery they celebrate is expressed in words like "light," "clarity," and "splendor." Nothing is said about the manger and the song of the angels, about the violent earthquake that took place as the angel descended and rolled the stone away from the empty tomb, about the touching encounter between the risen Lord and Mary of Magdala and the two disciples on the road to Emmaus, or about the dramatic events at Pentecost.[4]

The Roman genius is evident also in the ritual form of celebration which is functional and somewhat streamlined. The first Ordo Romanus notes that the pope alone stands at the altar for the eucharistic prayer, and that at the doxology the archdeacon alone goes to the altar to raise the chalice. The songs at the entrance rite, at the preparation of gifts, and at communion are treated no more and no less than songs of accompaniment. Except for the sending of the *fermentum* to the parishes, a practice that suggests union with the pope, the classical form of the Roman mass was destitute of symbols, at least in the current understanding of the word. After gathering the eucharistic gifts the pope washed his hands, but the gesture does not appear to have any symbolic meaning.[5]

These same cultural traits made their way to the area of liturgical theology. For example, the worship of the eucharist is strikingly sober. In the same Ordo Romanus we find no external signs of veneration during and after the consecration. And the prayers after communion avoid the words "body" and "blood." Instead, they speak of the eucharist as food and drink, sacrament, sacred mystery, and heavenly gift. One can say that the classical Roman liturgy was fashioned to the cultural taste of the Roman people. It was the liturgy of the local church of Rome during its classical period.[6]

The preconciliar liturgical movement, often called classical because of its marked predilection for the classical period of the Roman liturgy, exerted a profound influence on the reform of Vatican II. It is significant that the principal framers of SC were avowed advocates of the movement.[7] Not surprisingly, the design of the conciliar document faithfully followed the blueprint of the classical reform. SC 34 is remarkable for its articulation of the movement's framework of reference: "The rites should be marked by a noble simplicity; they should be short, clear and unencumbered by useless repetitions; they should be within the people's power of comprehension and as a rule not require much explanation."

Classical restoration is at the bottom of the provision of SC 50 for the reform of the order of mass: rites are to be simplified, duplications are to be discarded, and elements that have suffered injury through accidents of history are to be restored to their pristine vigor. Along the same line SC 62 observes that "with the passage of time certain features have crept into the rites of the sacraments and sacramentals that have made their nature and purpose less clear to the people of today; hence some changes have become necessary as adaptations to the needs of our own times." As regards the divine office, SC 88 calls for the restoration of the traditional sequence of the hours "so that once again they may be genuinely related to the hour of the day when they are prayed." SC 89 trims the structure of the divine office to enable both the clergy and the laity to gain easy access to it. Lastly, SC 107 directs that the liturgical year be revised in such a way that the specific character of the sacred seasons is preserved or restored.

Thus the classical liturgical movement, like a torrent, swept every area of the liturgy. The rites of the sacraments and sacramentals, the liturgy of the hours, the liturgical year, and the norms regarding music, arts, and furnishings had, without exception, to be revised according to the classical standard set by the movement. As B. Neunheuser fittingly observed, "The Constitution *Sacrosanctum Concilium,* approved and promulgated by Pope Paul VI on December 4, 1963, can be considered—at least for now—the finishing touch of the structure put up by the Liturgical Movement for fifty or sixty years."[8]

During the council, however, classical restoration was taken to task for seemingly advocating antiquated or even obsolete models. In fact the classical liturgical movement preceding Vatican II had at times been severely criticized as a futile exercise in archeology or at best as an exhibition of some romantic inclination.[9] Accordingly a council father advised the conciliar commission not to institute liturgical changes for archeological reasons but for the pastoral purpose for which the council had been convened.[10]

The recommendation expressed the need to balance SC's option for classical shape with pastoral orientation and openness to the culture and traditions of the local churches. It is evident from the conciliar discussion that the classical restoration of the Roman liturgy was regarded as an efficacious means to promote active and intelligent participation and as the preliminary step to liturgical adaptation. The council wanted to offer to the local churches a liturgical model, an *editio typica,* marked by Roman sobriety, simplicity, and clarity. In this way they can adapt it to their culture after the example of the Franco-Germanic churches of the eighth century. These churches have the distinction of being the first to adapt the classical Roman liturgy to the culture of their people.

In a sense history must repeat itself. By bringing back the Roman rite to the classical form it once possessed the council started off today's process of cultural adaptation. In other words, the liturgical renewal envisaged by SC consists of two phases: the first is the restoration of the classical shape of the Roman liturgy, and the second, which is dependent on the first, is adaptation to various cultures and traditions.

With the publication of the *editio typica* of the principal liturgical books the first phase was completed. But these books have to be translated and above all adapted. For the *editio typica,* as these words suggest, presents a type, a model, of liturgical celebration. Unless it is adapted to concrete needs and situations, it is not usable as ritual of a local church. That is why the celebration of the liturgy as exactly and rigorously as the *editio typica* describes it, that is to say, without the necessary pastoral and cultural adjustments, can become a futile exercise in archeology for a local church. For the liturgy cannot be celebrated in a pastoral or cultural vacuum.

The liturgical reform is one of Vatican II's unfinished agenda. The local churches must begin where Vatican II left off. Because of the fluidity of cultural expressions and the growing needs of the local churches, adaptation will always be on their agenda of liturgical renewal. Their liturgies will have to be periodically reviewed, revised, and updated in order to respond "to the needs of our own times," taking account of "the modern conditions in which daily life has to be lived."[11] We can affirm that flexibility, which allows the liturgy to respond to the pastoral and cultural needs of every local church, is one of the prominent and, it is hoped, permanent gains of Vatican II.

SC 37–40: Toward a Pluriform Liturgy

Flexibility in the liturgy is the undercurrent of SC 37–40. For four centuries after the Council of Trent rigid ritualism prevailed in the liturgy for reasons that are quite understandable even for the people of today. The church was coming out of the chaotic situation of the middle ages, at least as far as the liturgy was concerned, and from the crisis brought about by the Protestant reformation. A scrupulously and minutely defined liturgy became the symbol of the church's stability in the face of unrestrained innovations.

We should not be astonished, therefore, that Pope Pius V prefaced the edition of the Roman missal of 1570 with menacing words directed at anyone who dared to change ceremonies or prayers in the said missal.[12] And we should consider it rather normal that popes discoursed on the advantages brought to the unity of the church by ritual uniformity. Pope Clement VIII, for instance, maintained that since we are one body and share in the one body of Christ, it is most fitting that we all observe one and the same manner of celebrating the mass.[13] Flexibility in the liturgy could at that point of time be easily suspected to be a sign of becoming lax and negligent or of conceding to the reformers. Above all it might bring about a liturgical pluralism that, unwittingly, could obscure the church's symbol of unity.

However, times changed. By the time Vatican II was convened, the church was addressing other major issues, including its missionary activities, where a greater flexibility was required, especially in matters involving culture. SC 37–40 or the section entitled "Norms for Adapting the

Liturgy to the Culture and Traditions of Peoples" should be read in that light. It is the fruit not only of collegial reflection and lively debate, but also of the church's missionary experience. It has opened new avenues for the liturgy and will continue to do so as long as cultures evolve and local churches feel the need for a justified change.[14]

SC 37 serves as introduction to the entire section. It affirms the church's principle of pluralism, even in the liturgy, in matters not affecting the unity of faith or the good of the whole church. The church respects and fosters the cultural heritage of every people. Sometimes in fact it admits elements of their culture into the liturgy, provided they are in keeping with the true and authentic spirit of the liturgy and are not indissolubly bound up with superstition and error. SC 40 adds that adaptations should be useful or necessary. The words "useful" and "necessary" are concerned with the furtherance of the full, conscious, and active participation of the faithful which is the primary aim of the conciliar liturgical reform.

The second part of this section is composed of articles 38 and 39. These deal with the legitimate variations within the Roman rite, or, in the words of SC 38, "provided the substantial unity of the Roman rite is preserved." As may be gathered from SC 39, substantial unity is preserved by observing "the limits set by the *editio typica* of the liturgical books." In these books the Holy See proposes to the conferences of bishops the changes which they are free to introduce into the particular rituals. The changes adopted by the conferences are confirmed by the Holy See and are then inserted into the local rituals as special features. Changes of this type do not alter the substantial unity of the Roman rite. They merely show that in the framework of that unity there is room for flexibility.

The adaptations envisaged by SC 38 and 39 include the possibility of rearranging the parts of the ritual, in accord with the provisions of the *editio typica,* and cover the area of sacraments, sacramentals, processions, liturgical language, sacred music, and liturgical arts and furnishings. To this list the liturgy of the hours and the liturgical year are to be added, as one can gather from SC 88 and SC 107 and 110.

Examples of legitimate variations can easily occur in the so-called explanatory rites or more frequently in the introductory rites. In theory the sign of welcome in the rite of infant baptism can be reexpressed in equivalent cultural forms, as also the anointing with chrism, the use of the white garment, and the giving of the lighted candle. Legitimate variations are, of course, not confined to these examples. The *editio typica,* as we shall have the occasion to discuss in the following chapters, presents instances of legitimate variations also in the liturgy of the sacrament itself, that is, in the manner of anointing the sick, in the formulation of the marriage consent, and so on.

The third part consists of article 40 which speaks of "an even more radical adaptation of the liturgy." The proposed text of this article had focused on the missions. But the conciliar commission softened the missionary thrust of the text in order not to restrict radical adaptation to the churches in the missions. The other churches also are meant to benefit from this momentous article.[15]

Radical adaptation quite simply refers to changes not foreseen by the *editio typica.* Such changes depend upon the initiative of the conferences of bishops. After a thorough study of the matter they are to submit to the Holy See for approval their proposal for radical adaptation. It is useful to note here that the adaptations listed in the *editio typica* do not exhaust all the possible legitimate variations, and hence there could be requests for adaptations that are not in themselves radical but are rather extensions of the variations allowed by the *editio typica.*

SC 37–40 is the magna charta of liturgical flexibility

and pluralism in the western church. It has successfully combined liturgical tradition and openness to liturgical progress. We can say that it epitomizes the liturgical reform of Vatican II. It is the magna charta whose breadth of vision broadens the horizons of the church as a universal community and firmly upholds the right of the local liturgies to come into being. SC 37–40 expresses the church's recognition of its own pluralistic structure, of its being Roman in tradition and international in expression, of its doctrinal unity in cultural diversity.

Indeed the experience of different local churches, especially in the missions, shows that the restored simplicity and sobriety of the Roman liturgy are not valued to the same degree by every people in the world. For some the Roman trait of simplicity might be no more than a form of inadequacy, and sobriety a synonym of ritual indigence. For others these classical qualities might appear to be not only alien but also archeological. At any rate, when a local church claims that it possesses a cultural identity sufficiently distinct from that of the classical Roman liturgy, the question of cultural adaptation must be addressed. The refusal to adapt could mean a rejection of legitimate progress.

In order to have a better grasp of SC 37–40, it is necessary to read it in conjunction with the *altiora principia* or basic principles of conciliar reform enumerated by A. Bugnini in his posthumous book *La riforma liturgica.*[16] Adaptation to the culture and traditions of peoples is above all a liturgical matter regulated by liturgical principles, criteria, and methods. Surely adaptation requires that there be a dialogue between liturgy and culture. However, there are basic liturgical principles which are indispensable for such dialogue. These, according to A. Bugnini, can be drawn by and large from the different articles of SC and may be classified as directive and operational.

Under the first category Bugnini lists six principles.

First, "the liturgy is considered as an exercise of the priestly office of Jesus Christ" (SC 7). Expressed in other words, the paschal mystery is the heart of every liturgical celebration. Second, "the liturgy is the summit toward which the activity of the church is directed; at the same time it is the fount from which all the church's power flows" (SC 10). Third, "in the reform and promotion of the liturgy, the full and active participation by all the people is the aim to be considered before all else" (SC 14). Fourth, "liturgical services are not private functions, but are celebrations belonging to the church" (SC 26). Fifth, "even in the liturgy the church has no wish to impose a rigid uniformity in matters that do not affect the faith or the good of the whole community" (SC 37). And sixth, "that sound tradition may be retained and yet the way remain open to legitimate progress, a careful investigation is always to be made into each part of the liturgy to be revised" (SC 23).

Under the second category Bugnini enumerates five operational principles. These are: the use of the vernacular (SC 36), the importance of sacred scripture in the celebration of the liturgy (SC 24), the catechetical aspect of liturgical rites and texts (SC 33–34), the place of chant in liturgical celebrations (SC 112), and the restoration of the classical shape of the Roman liturgy (SC 21 and 34).

These operational principles have, to a large extent, been observed by the Holy See in the postconciliar reform of the liturgical books. Sacramental celebrations now include a liturgy of the word or a form of it, and a reading from sacred scripture is warmly recommended for the rites of blessing. The division of the missal into the sacramentary and the lectionary and the accent on the gospel book have certainly enhanced the people's appreciation of the word of God. As regards liturgical chant, the new liturgical books carry useful indications to foster congregational singing. Especially at mass, the assembly, except in some rather peculiar instances, has taken over the role performed by the choir and orchestra during the baroque period. The catechetical aspect too is amply taken care of by the simplification and streamlining of the rites as well as by the homily and the inclusion of commentaries. We must admit that the Holy See has successfully accomplished the task assigned to it by the council. It is now up to the conferences of bishops to apply the *altiora principia* of liturgical reform to the particular rituals.

A good number of years have passed since the council formulated these principles. During that expanse of time how was the liturgical reform carried out on the level of local churches? It is obvious that some of the *altiora principia* like those concerning the chant and the classical shape will have to make allowance for the diversity of culture and traditions. However, the prospects for the genuine liturgies of the future will depend on how the local churches implement these principles. For they are the essential premises of cultural adaptation. The following points expand on the *altiora principia* of the conciliar reform.

1. The liturgy is the exercise of Christ's priesthood. This principle, articulated by SC 7, centers every liturgical celebration on Christ and the mystery of his death and resurrection. In places where the understanding and value of mediatorship are readily extended to saints, it could easily happen that Christ is relegated to the periphery of divine worship. Or where Christ in fact holds primacy in the devotion of the faithful, the devout might focus attention on an aspect of Christ's mystery that is more congenial to personal piety, like the childhood of Jesus, rather than on the mystery of his death and resurrection. In such situations there is obviously a need to redirect personal piety to the source of Christian life which is the paschal mystery.

A closely related matter is the question of popular devotions and pious exercises. Pope Paul VI sounded the alarm regarding the practice in some places of combining the mass and popular devotions like novenas into a "hybrid" celebration. He warned that this could result in turning the memorial of the Lord into a simple setting for some popular devotion. And he adds: "We wish to remind those acting in this way of the conciliar norm: popular devotions must be subordinated to the liturgy, not intermingled with it."[17]

2. The liturgy, according to SC 10, is the summit and fount of the life of the church. The entire range of church activities, from evangelization and catechesis to social concern, is directed toward the liturgy, especially of the mass, and finds meaning and inspiration in it. Since the celebration of the liturgy nourishes the life of the church, nothing must be preferred to it. This conciliar principle gives a sense of direction to the various church endeavors like catechetical instruction, prayer meetings, and social projects. Unfortunately it happens all too often that the liturgy is regarded as one of the many activities rather than the heart of all other activities. Its euchological and biblical texts, its symbols, and its feasts and seasons are not yet sufficiently inserted in the mainstream of these activities so as to effectively inspire and guide them.

3. Active participation is the right and duty of all the faithful. The principle of full, conscious, and active participation mentioned in SC 14 can be detected throughout the conciliar document. By and large the local churches have successfully implemented this principle of liturgical reform. Not only has church attendance in several places, especially in the third world, radically improved from preconciliar times, but the assembly also actively participates now through songs and responses. A good number of the laity serve in their parishes as acolytes, lectors, and special ministers of holy communion. In places too distant from the parish church lay acolytes and catechists preside at the Sun-

day liturgy in the absence of a priest, so that the community will not be entirely deprived of the word of God and holy communion. But active participation has another side, namely interiority, silence, and recollection. During liturgical celebrations a healthy balance should be kept between active participation, on which many local churches can rightly pride themselves, and prayerful interiority.

4. The liturgy is the epiphany of the church. SC 26 says that liturgical services are not private functions, but celebrations belonging to the church. SC 27 gives preference to communal celebrations, especially of the mass and the other sacraments, over a celebration that is individual and, so to speak, private. Certain factors prevailing in some local churches hastened the implementation of this principle. Because of the shortage of priests, communal celebrations are welcome reform in places where parishes have as many as eight masses on Sunday, or in several third world countries where baptism is celebrated in proportion to the high percentage of childbirth. To meet the problem a great number of parishes have scheduled communal baptism, marriage, and funeral services on specified days of the week.

In order to be the epiphany of the church the liturgy must relate to the bishop and the pastor who takes the place of the bishop. This, in short, is what we are told by SC 41–42. It is therefore necessary to foster among the faithful in attitude and in practice the liturgical life of the parish and its relationship to the bishop. Likewise efforts should be made to instill in the parish a lively sense of community, especially during the Sunday mass.

5. The new Roman liturgy requires substantial unity, not rigid uniformity. Very few pastors, including bishops, will fight tooth and nail to observe the letter of the law regarding the time, place, and certain elements of liturgical celebrations. For some years after the council many laypeople felt uneasy with the changes that priests were making,

licitly or illicitly, during the celebration of the mass. Today, thanks to an acquired spirit of tolerance and sense of spontaneity, the clergy and the laity are more inclined to accept the fact that in the liturgy there can be room for legitimate variations. The issue, however, is not confined to the substantial unity of the Roman rite. The eventual application of SC 40, which exceeds the provision of SC 38–39, will require more than just a spirit of tolerance; it will require expertise in the liturgy and related sciences without which the work of cultural adaptation cannot even be considered.

6. The question of the vernacular in the liturgy was the subject of heated debate during the council. There are still groups in some parts of the world bent on promoting the use of Latin in the liturgy. Fortunately for the local churches, especially in the missions, the shift to the vernacular not only met no opposition, but was also welcomed with gratitude by both the clergy and the laity. Behind each liturgical language, behind each liturgical book in the vernacular, there is a pioneering spirit that can fully be appreciated only by people who have worked with liturgical texts. The Instruction *Comme le prévoit* of 1969 is probably the one document that has greatly assisted translators in their monumental task. Today it continues to guide them in the new assignment to review and improve the existing translations.

7. SC 7 and SC 33 stress the importance of the word of God in the celebration of the liturgy. When the word of God is proclaimed in liturgical celebrations, it is God himself who speaks to his people, it is Christ himself who proclaims his gospel. The word of God stirs up faith, and faith is required for the celebration of the sacraments. That is why the celebration of the sacraments and sacramentals is preceded by the liturgy of the word or a reading from sacred scripture. SC 24 rightly commends a living love for God's word if it is to have an effect on the faithful. Today a great

number of local churches have a program for training lectors to perform their ministry in a manner that befits the dignity of God's word. The proclamation is normally done from the appropriate liturgical books, namely the lectionary and the gospel book, rather than from leaflets and missalettes. Moreover, the structure and decor of the lectern are now generally in keeping with the norms for liturgical arts and furnishing.

8. Active participation in the liturgy requires information and formation through liturgical catechesis. This consists of instruction on the word of God, as presented in the lectionary, and on the liturgical rites and prayers. In many countries liturgy weeks are held regularly in order to disseminate information about the liturgy. Newsletters and periodicals are published by liturgical commissions in an effort to "catechize" the pastors first. Dioceses and parishes hold liturgy seminars designed especially for lay ministers. But liturgical catechesis is an arduous undertaking which is often hampered by lack of trained personnel and funds. As a result, there are still seminaries and houses of formation that do not have professors with a formal training in the liturgy. Nevertheless, it is a consoling observation that the liturgical formation of future priests and lay ministers is now listed among the priorities of local churches.

9. SC 112 considers liturgical chant an integral part of the liturgy. It is well known that the passage from Gregorian chant to contemporary music was not smooth, and that after the council the use of native musical instruments in liturgical celebrations was even challenged. A classic example is the decision by a local ordinary that the guitar must be bolstered up by the pipe organ. There have been problems also regarding the texts to be sung. Would any religious text do, or perhaps any scriptural text or paraphrase of it, or must it be solely the text assigned by the liturgical books? Today we are becoming increasingly aware of the appropri-

ateness of strictly liturgical texts, above all in the celebration of the mass. The ease and fervor with which the liturgical assemblies in many parts of the world sing the ordinary of the mass, including the responsorial psalms, alleluia verses, and antiphons, demonstrate that the conciliar vision of active participation in liturgical chant is not an unreachable goal.

Adaptation and the Competent Authority

The question of the competent authority in matters pertaining to the liturgical adaptation was discussed at length during the council. SC 22 transmits to us the result of the conciliar debate: "Regulation of the liturgy depends solely on the authority of the church, that is, on the Apostolic See and, accordingly as the law determines, on the bishop. In virtue of power conceded by the law, the regulation of the liturgy within certain defined limits belongs also to various kinds of competent territorial bodies of bishops lawfully established." We know that the proposed text merely permitted the conferences of bishops to propose changes in the liturgy to the Holy See. The text was emended at the request of some council fathers who spoke in support of "a broader power for the conferences of bishops on this matter."[18]

SC 63b invokes this principle for the question of preparing particular rituals. In harmony with the new *editio typica* of the Roman ritual, these are to be prepared without delay by the conferences of bishops and adapted to the pastoral needs and cultural expressions of the local church. These particular rituals or collections of rites are to be submitted to the Holy See for review. Depending on the extent or type of adaptation, the Holy See will confirm or approve them. This is developed by the Instruction *Inter Oecumenici* of 1964: "The Holy See has the authority to reform and approve the general liturgical books; to regulate the liturgy in matters affecting the universal church; to approve or confirm the *acta* and decisions of territorial authorities; and to accede to their proposals and requests."[19]

The preparation of particular rituals is the right and duty of the competent, territorial ecclesiastical authority. It is the right of the conferences of bishops by virtue of their authority to preside over the liturgical life of the church committed to their care. And it is a duty they must execute without delay. For the celebration of the liturgy, as envisaged by the council, can be realized fully only on condition that the *editio typica* is adapted to the needs of the local church. The particular ritual is meant to be the actual book for the liturgical celebration of a local church. That is why it cannot be a mere word-for-word translation of the *editio typica*. SC 63b requires that it be adapted, even in regard to the language employed, to the region for which it is prepared.

Particular rituals will eventually bring about a liturgical pluralism within the Roman liturgy. This is not only to be expected; it is also to be desired, if the liturgy is to be an authentic celebration of a local church. However, pluralism is not synonymous with isolation and fragmentation. SC 63b wants the particular rituals to be in harmony with the *editio typica* of the Roman books. One reason is in order to preserve the substantial unity of the Roman rite. Another reason—and this transcends the scope of merely preserving substantial unity—is in order to securely hand on to the books of the local church the principles and criteria of the liturgical reform proposed and safeguarded in the Roman ritual. Even in those instances where radical adaptation or the creation of new formularies and rites is demanded, recourse to the Roman liturgy, which is a richly supplied storehouse of theology and spirituality, can greatly benefit the local churches.[20]

For the preparation of particular rituals or collections of rites the conferences of bishops are given much freedom by the *editio typica*. The various options are listed in the general introductions to the liturgical books under the heading "Adaptations by the Conferences of Bishops." Since they deal with the possible adaptations in the Roman ritual, they are able to forecast the future shape of the particular rituals.[21]

Going over the chief options, about which we shall go into greater detail in the next three chapters, we can observe that they are pastorally oriented and tend to foster cultural adaptation. Translations and, we may add, also the revision of existing translations are an example of such options. They have the function not only to allow the faithful to understand the meaning of the Latin text, but also to reflect the literary form proper to a language. That is why "it is not sufficient that a liturgical translation merely reproduce the expressions and ideas of the original text. Rather it must faithfully communicate to a given people, and in their own language, that which the church by means of this given text originally intended to communicate to another people in another time." We shall return to this point later in this chapter.[22]

The other options given by the *editio typica* manifest the same pastoral and cultural orientation. The conferences of bishops are free to retain distinctive elements of any particular rituals prior to the conciliar reform, provided they conform to the true and authentic spirit of the liturgy. The introductions to the liturgical books may be adapted and augmented, in order that both the ministers and the assembly may have a fuller understanding and a deeper appreciation of the liturgical celebration.[23] Furthermore, the conferences of bishops have the option to arrange the parts of the rite, following the specifications given by the *editio typica,* so that the particular rituals may respond more fully to pastoral needs. Lastly, when the Roman ritual offers optional formularies, the conferences may compose others of the same type. This applies to the composition in special circumstances of new eucharistic prayers, according to the norms to be set forth by the Holy See in each case.[24]

SC 40 wisely foresees the need for preliminary experimentation when there is a question of radical adaptation. In this connection the Instruction *Liturgiae Instaurationes* states: "Should further adaptations become necessary, in keeping with the norm of the Constitution *Sacrosanctum Concilium* art. 40, the conference of bishops is to examine the issue thoroughly, attentive to the character and traditions of each people and to specific pastoral needs." When some form of experimentation is advisable, the Holy See requires the conference of bishops to submit, besides a description of the proposed adaptation, a detailed plan of experiment before it takes place. The plan should specify the groups with which the experiment will be made. Large-scale celebrations as well as wide publicity are discouraged. The experiments themselves should be few and not last beyond a year. The unhappy experiences of some local churches, especially with regard to new eucharistic prayers, seem to justify these precautions.[25]

But changes in the liturgy may, and sometimes must, be introduced also by the minister. The option or obligation of the minister to adapt does not contradict SC 22,3 which severely forbids anyone, even if he is a priest, to add, remove or change anything in the liturgy on one's own. The law itself (and common sense which is the basic law) authorizes the minister to make the necessary adaptations. The instances are listed in the introductions to the different liturgical books under the heading "Adaptations by the Minister" and are indicated in the rubrics of each rite. Adaptations by the minister are a kind of temporary adjustments in the course of the liturgical celebration for the purpose of fostering full, active, and intelligent participation.[26] While the adaptations introduced by the conference of bishops are entered as permanent features of the particular ritual, those by the minister are transitory and are contingent upon the need of the moment.

The adaptations by the minister touch practically anything having to do with the celebration. Depending upon pastoral needs and the allowances for variations made by the liturgical norms, the minister can enjoy a sufficient latitude in the choice of biblical and euchological texts, in the use of symbols and ritual gestures, and in the formulation of suitable admonitions and commentaries. Whenever pastorally and liturgically feasible, he should involve the persons concerned in the choice of the readings and prayers for the celebration of the sacraments and sacramentals. He should make full use of the options offered by the liturgical books, in order that each celebration may indeed respond to the particular needs of the individual faithful and the assembly. The idea is to leave no option untried.

It is understood that the minister is to prepare beforehand the course of the celebration. There is nothing more injurious to the seriousness and dignity of the liturgy than unregulated improvisation and unpleasant surprises. Although improvisation was the rule more than the exception during the first three centuries, it had nothing to do with composition and performance on the spur of the moment and without any preparation. Toward the year 90 the author of the Didache was already describing the course of liturgical celebrations with written formularies, even though he allowed the "prophets" to give thanks for as long as they wished. Around the year 218 Hippolytus of Rome put into writing some liturgical practices, presumably of Rome, and offered a model of a eucharistic prayer. However, he made it clear that the minister need not recite the prayer from memory. But the fear, especially in the fourth century, that heresies might infect the liturgical texts changed the course "from freedom to formula."[27]

The reform of Vatican II has reintroduced an amount of freedom in the liturgy, but it is up to the minister to make good use of it. The golden rule is that the minister should have an accurate grasp of what the liturgical norms allow and a keen perception of the pastoral situation or, in other words, a sound practical judgment.

Approaches to Adaptation: Acculturation, Inculturation, and Creativity

During the last decade inculturation has become a familiar word in the active vocabulary of theology, missiology, and liturgical studies. The word is a neologism, but it has gained such a popularity in ecclesiastical circles that today it tends to overshadow the "official" term employed by the church in its liturgical documents: adaptation. SC does not, of course, use the word "inculturation," although in some instances we can correctly render Latin words like *aptatio* and *accomodatio* with the word "inculturation." SC 65, which allows in mission lands certain initiation elements in use among individual peoples, and SC 77,3, which empowers the conferences of bishops to draw up a completely new rite of marriage, do in fact deal with liturgical inculturation.

1. The Term "Adaptation" in SC

It is interesting to note that SC shows a certain reticence with the use of the word *aptatio.* While the word is used consistently in SC 38–40, it is dropped altogether from Chapter 3 which deals with the sacraments and sacramentals, though it reappears in Chapter 4 (SC 90), Chapter 6 (SC 120), and Chapter 7 (SC 128). The proposed text of Chapter 3 originally used the verb *aptare* throughout this section. Why the conciliar commission in charge of the section systematically changed *aptare* to *accomodare* may be explained by a desire to reach a via media or compromise so characteristic of some sections of SC.[28] Earlier a council father had complained about the frequent use of terms like "revision," "adaptation," "new composition," and "restoration" paired with such words as "radically" and "entirely." These words, he noted, smelled of the exaggerations of the liturgical movement and gave the impression that the council was out to overhaul the entire sacramental system.[29]

The use of *accomodatio* in the final text to replace *aptatio* seems to have stemmed from the perception that *accomodatio* was somewhat less radical than *aptatio.* Hence, the consistent shift to *accomodatio* in the text of Chapter 3: SC 62: "Some changes have become necessary as adaptations [*accomodare*] to the needs of our own times"; SC 63b: "These rituals are to be adapted [*accomodare*], even in regard to the language employed, to the needs of the different regions"; SC 65: ". . . to the extent that such elements are compatible [*accomodari*] with the Christian rite of initiation"; SC 67: "The rite for the baptism of infants . . . should be suited [*accomodetur*] to the fact that those to be baptized are infants"; SC 68: "The baptismal rite should contain alternatives [*accomodationes*]"; and SC 75: "The number of anointings is to be adapted [*accomodetur*]." Also the *modi* presented by the council fathers began to ignore the word *aptatio* and to employ *accomodatio,* although the relator himself, explaining the emendations made on this section, often reverted to the word *aptatio.*[30]

The hermeneutical analysis of the text of SC leads us to the conclusion that the two words were used interchangeably. The use of *accomodatio* in the section on the sacraments and sacramentals was decidedly a form of compromise, a via media meant to calm anxieties over a suspected design to overhaul the church's sacramental system. It is evident that the change in terminology did not affect the meaning intended by the framers of SC. *Aptatio* and *accomodatio* meant the same thing. In fact, once it had been made clear that these words had the same meaning, there was no further need to subject the other sections of SC to this kind of change.

The neat distinction between *aptatio,* as the competence of the conferences of bishops, and *accomodatio,* as the competence of the minister, began to evolve only with the publication of the new *editio typica* of the liturgical books. Hence, *aptatio* and *accomodatio* in SC should not be interpreted in the sense these words acquired after the council. Both words are used by SC to express Vatican II's general program "to adapt more suitably to the needs of our times those institutions that are subject to change," as read in SC 1.[31]

In other words, adaptation refers to the church's general program of aggiornamento or updating. But because adaptation is culturally neutral, it needs acculturation, inculturation, and creativity as approaches, methods, or ways of bringing about the liturgical aggiornamento proposed by the council. Today there is a tendency to discard the word "adaptation" because of its unfortunate association with the manipulation of culture in the past. However, dropping it completely from our liturgical vocabulary and employing equivalently the term "inculturation" might result in confusing a general program of renewal with one of its means, albeit the most significant.[32]

2. Acculturation: Preliminary Step to Inculturation

Besides inculturation there are other methods of adapting the liturgy. History shows that over the centuries the church employed also acculturation and creativity to develop the shape of the liturgy.[33] It was never a question of embracing one method to the exclusion of the others. Even today the method of acculturation, which is regarded at times as no more than an external juxtaposition of two or more cultures, may prove to be helpful in establishing the preliminary contact between the Christian liturgy and culture.

Acculturation operates according to the dynamics of cultural interaction. It is an initial meeting, a kind of "getting-to-know-you" encounter between two strangers each of whom has interests to protect. This phase is exemplified by the initial contact between the early Christian form of worship and the Greco-Roman culture. In Tertullian's treatise on baptism, for example, one senses a mistrust of anything pagan. He mocks the initiation ceremonies of Isis and Mithras and declares that they are extravagant but empty. We know, however, that the rites of Christian initiation are indebted to the pagan mystery rites. Clement of Alexandria who derides these rites for their corrupt practices does not hesitate to serve himself with their initiatory language. From St. Ambrose we learn that in the fourth century the church of Rome was critical of the Milanese rite of washing the feet of the neophytes on grounds that the practice was too secular to be incorporated into the liturgy.[34]

But this rather strained relationship between Christian worship and the Greco-Roman culture blossomed later into a harmonious reciprocity. By the fifth century the Roman liturgy had become emblematic of liturgical inculturation. It spoke the language of the people with an eloquence beyond compare and carried out its rituals with the noble simplicity, sobriety, and practical sense of classical Rome. In the process the Roman culture was all the richer. J. Jungmann vividly describes the role of the liturgy in the transformation of the pagan society of Rome: "Society, political life, the lives of the people, family life, the position of woman, the appreciation of human dignity, whether slave, child, or infant yet unborn—all this was transformed in a slow but sure process of fermentation: out of a pagan society a Christian society was born."[35]

Acculturation is the preliminary step to inculturation. It would indeed be somewhat unrealistic, if not presumptuous, to embark on liturgical inculturation without going through the process of acculturation. Before entering into the area of inculturation it is necessary to make a preliminary comparative study between the Christian liturgical forms and the corresponding cultural elements. The object of such a study is to discover the points of convergence on which the interaction between the liturgy and culture can operate. In the words of SC 40, the conferences of bishops "must, in this matter, carefully and prudently weigh what elements from the traditions and culture of individual peoples may be appropriately admitted into divine worship."

But sometimes the liturgy borrows cultural elements without interiorly assimilating them, that is, without allowing them to become part and parcel of its language and ritual expressions. This is surely a drawback of liturgical acculturation. A classic example is the way the liturgy was acculturated during the time of the baroque. Unable to penetrate the canonical and rubrical barriers that securely guarded the Tridentine liturgy, the culture of the baroque remained in the periphery of the liturgy. The baroque manifestations of festivity and exuberance were not absorbed by the texts and rites of the mass; there was merely an external juxtaposition of liturgical rite and cultural forms. As Jungmann aptly remarked, "at this time there were festive occasions which might best be described as church concerts with liturgical accompaniment."[36] For this reason one cannot speak of a "baroque liturgy," but of the Tridentine liturgy with the cultural expressions of the baroque at its periphery.

Liturgical acculturation is the interaction between the Roman liturgy and the local culture. It consists of studying the cultural elements that can be assimilated and of establishing the method of assimilating them in accord with the intrinsic laws that govern both Christian worship and culture. Acculturation, however, is not a permanent state of things. Interaction and external juxtaposition alone cannot fully satisfy the requirements for the genuine aggiornamento envisaged by Vatican II. Acculturation is an initial approach that needs to be completed by the process of inculturation. The dynamics of cultural interaction must develop into the dynamics of cultural insertion and interior assimilation of cultural forms. In other words, acculturation must eventually lead to inculturation.

3. What Is Liturgical Inculturation?

After Vatican II the question of inculturation has become a lively issue in the church. It has generated among theologians and liturgists a deep interest that is often mixed with anxious concern. Inculturation is with good reason regarded as something that belongs to the mystery of the incarnation. The term is a neologism, but as Pope John Paul II observed in his address to the Pontifical Biblical Commission in 1979, "it expresses one of the elements of the great mystery of the incarnation."[37]

The issue of inculturation is not only anthropological but also theological. It touches everything that touches on the relationship between God and his people, everything that the Word of God took up when he became flesh and came to dwell among us. As AG 10 explains: "If the church is to be in a position to offer to all the mystery of salvation and the life brought by God, then it must implant itself among all these groups in the same way that Christ by his incarnation committed himself to the particular social and cultural circumstances of the people among whom he lived." When SC 65 allows the churches in the missions to incorporate "initiation elements in use among individual peoples, to the extent that such elements are compatible with the Christian rite of initiation," it in fact invokes the process of inculturation which can rightly be described as incarnational.

What is liturgical inculturation? It is a liturgical neologism, but the idea is not new to the liturgy, and if the breaking of bread, baptism, laying on of hands, and anointing of the sick in the New Testament are accepted to be instances of inculturation, then the practice dates back to Christ and his first disciples.[38] But the process of inculturation did not stop there. The history of the Roman liturgy gives two fine examples of inculturation: the classical shape which flourished in Rome after the fourth century, and the Franco-Germanic form which developed during the Carolingian era on the basis of the classical Roman liturgy. Judging by their language, symbols, and rites, these liturgies belonged unmistakably to the people for whom they were developed, and whose culture and traditions they assimilated and reexpressed in cultic categories.

Liturgical inculturation may be described as the process whereby the texts and rites used in worship by the local church are so inserted in the framework of culture, that they absorb its thought, language, and ritual patterns. Liturgical inculturation operates according to the dynamics of insertion in a given culture and interior assimilation of cultural elements. From a purely anthropological point of view we may say that inculturation allows the people to experience in liturgical celebrations a "cultural event" whose language and ritual forms they are able to identify as elements of their culture.

Because of the nature of Christian worship the cultural elements to be assimilated must undergo a critical evaluation. They must not be, as SC 37 requires, "indissolubly bound up with superstition and error," but must be "in harmony with the true and authentic spirit of the liturgy." At times it is not easy to draw the line between superstition and some misguided expressions of religiosity. Moreover, there are some religious or pseudoreligious and psychic manifestations that defy classification under the category of superstition and error. On the other hand, such manifestations as trance, hypnosis, and glossolalia, although they are neither superstitious nor erroneous, are outside the scope of the liturgy which is the public worship of an hierarchically ordered community. Liturgical inculturation has to take into account not only the doctrine of faith but also the requirements of the Christian liturgy.

A question of immediate interest here is what critical evaluation involves in practice. The early church addressed this question in the light of biblical types. Baptismal anointing whose origin, according to Tertullian, is not to be traced to sacred scripture came to be regarded as an antitype of the priestly anointing of Aaron. The cultural setting of anointing is well known. The Greeks and Romans had their bodies massaged with oil for reasons like physical therapy and athletic fitness. It is quite possible that this practice made its way to the Christian liturgy in the form of the baptismal anointing mentioned by Tertullian. Besides this type of anointing, there existed in the time of Hippolytus of Rome the anointing of catechumens before baptism. Ambrose of Milan compares it to the anointing of an athlete. The candidate for baptism is anointed in order to have the strength to do battle for Christ in the arena of the present world.[39]

Another example of biblical antitype is the cup of milk mixed with honey given to the neophytes at their first communion. This, explains Hippolytus of Rome, signifies the fulfillment of the promise God made to the patriarchs regarding a land flowing with milk and honey. Having crossed the river Jordan through the water of baptism, the neophytes enter the promised land and taste its blessings. The mixed drink of milk and honey fits biblical typology rather well, though it does not figure as part of biblical tradition. However, it can be traced to the Roman custom of giving this kind of drink to newborn children as an apotropaic precaution or as a sign of welcome to the family.[40]

Thus through biblical typology cultural elements were raised to the sphere of salvation history; at the same time they became expressions of God's workings in human history. In these and other early examples of liturgical inculturation one will notice the strict observance of the canons of Christian worship: only those cultural elements that can harmonize with the nature of the liturgy are to be incorporated into the liturgy, and they should be able to communicate adequately the Christian message.

Inculturation is not unilateral. It is not a question merely of observing theological and liturgical principles. There must be reciprocity and mutual respect between the liturgy and culture. Culture has also its categories, dynamics, and intrinsic laws. Liturgy must not impose on culture a meaning or bearing that is intrinsically alien to its nature. In other words, authentic inculturation respects the process of transculturation. By this we mean that both the liturgy and culture are able to evolve through mutual insertion and absorption without damage to each other's identity. Liturgical inculturation does not debilitate culture and its inner dynamism. The assimilation of Greek, Roman, and Franco-Germanic cultures into the liturgy has certainly endowed them with superior meaning and sometimes preserved some of their elements down the centuries.

Examples of how the church inculturated the liturgy can be found in practically every area of culture: language, rituals, feasts, gestures, music and dance, sculpture, and architecture.[41] What is remarkable in these examples is that the church respected the dynamics and laws of culture. Cultural elements were inserted into the liturgy, taking account of their nature and identity. One may speak here of "connaturalness," that innate ability of culture to express the highest realities of Christianity. Liturgical inculturation does not inflict violence on culture; rather it works according to the cultural patterns whether of language and rite or of time and space. The Instruction *Comme le prévoit* of 1969 directs the translators of liturgical texts to keep in mind that each language has its proper literary form: "In the case of liturgical communication, it is necessary to take into account not only the message to be conveyed, but also the speaker, the audience, and the style."[42]

The Instruction can be extended—within certain limits—to the area of rites. In the course of the centuries the liturgy borrowed material elements and bodily gestures in use among different peoples: bread and wine, water, oil, incense, candles, immersion, laying on of hands, sprinkling with water, genuflection, prostration, and so on. In the liturgy these elements have taken the role of expressing and symbolizing with "connaturalness" the Christian realities. Thus the elements of culture and indeed culture itself, enriched by Christian faith and worship, have evolved in a transcultural process, without impingement upon their nature.

It is understood that in the process of inculturation those elements of culture that cannot be made to harmonize with the rule of Christian faith, morality, and worship will have to be left out. There is no need to repeat here that what the liturgy legitimately assimilates from culture must be accorded every respect; however, not everything can be assimilated.

A related question can be raised at this juncture. In some cultures the drinking of wine and the laying on of hands rank high among the religious and cultural prohibitions. Since the use of wine for the eucharist and the laying on of hands for ordination are of biblical origin and are essential to these sacraments, may the dynamics of transculturation in these instances be dispensed with? Will catechesis suffice to dissipate the religious and cultural objections against them? Or should the church look into the possibility of adopting some other elements that can equivalently express the meaning of these sacraments?

The effect of inculturation on theology and the liturgy has not always been exactly positive or edifying. The ordination prayers of the Sacramentary of Verona reflect a Constantinian situation that framed priestly ministry in the context of promotion, rank, dignity, and honor, although in this book these socio-political categories have been methodically entrenched in biblical typology and Christian outlook. At the *hanc igitur* of the Roman canon the sacramentary affirms that God has "promoted [the bishop] to the glory of a pontiff," while at the ordination of the presbyter it prays that God grant to the candidate "the dignity of the presbyterate." We may add another example from the Franco-Germanic liturgy of the Carolingian era. It is doubtless a classic example of inculturation, but its blessing of the instruments of ordeal even during mass and its mass formularies for cases of diabolical possession are bizarre and mar its gains.[43]

Inculturation has obviously its risks. In the third century Hippolytus of Rome was pleading with the bishops to explain carefully the meaning of the cup of milk and honey given to the neophytes at communion in order to prevent its being confused with the sacrament of Christ's blood.[44] Although prudence, even in this matter, is the mother of virtues, a certain risk will always accompany legitimate progress. And while history has something to teach about failures, it has much to tell about successful enterprise. The bottom line—to use a rather common but concrete phrase—is to take the necessary risk with prudence. And prudence is a virtue that grows on sound tradition and pastoral circumspection, while it ensures the legitimacy of progress.

4. From Inculturation to Creativity

In places where the culture of the local church remotely resembles the culture underpinning the Roman liturgy, inculturation alone might not come up to the local church's prospect for a fully updated liturgical celebration. It might be necessary to embark on liturgical creativity.[45]

By liturgical creativity we mean that new liturgical texts are composed independently of the traditional structure of the Roman euchology. The Roman structure consists normally of a simple invocation of God, a memorial of his wonderful work in creation and the history of salvation, a motivated petition based on the memorial, and the christological conclusion.[46] Textual creativity means that new models of formularies are developed in keeping with the people's linguistic pattern and rhetorical traits. The theological content will not be supplied exclusively by the Roman formulary, but can borrow from other euchological traditions or take inspiration from the conclusions of contemporary liturgical theology.

The historical development of the liturgical texts has moved from freedom to formula. Nonetheless, textual creativity, which is not the same as spontaneity or improvisation, cannot be laid aside merely for an aversion to novelty or, as we observe in the fourth century, for fear of unorthodox doctrine. Today we have an effective system of checks and balances to prevent the occurrence of errors and ambiguity in official liturgical texts. The Consilium, which prepared the Instruction *Comme le prévoit* on the translation of the Latin texts, was surely aware of risks and dangers. Yet it courageously called attention to the fact that "texts translated from another language are clearly not sufficient for the celebration of a fully renewed liturgy. The creation of new texts will be necessary."[47]

What we said regarding textual creativity applies to the preparation of new liturgical rites. The rites of marriage and funerals, even if these are inculturated, might still bear a hybrid-look about them. For this reason, as we shall discuss in the third chapter of this book, SC 77 gives to the conferences of bishops the option to draw up a completely new rite of marriage in accord with the usages of place and people.

Acculturation, inculturation, and creativity are three ways of bringing about the liturgical adaptation or aggiornamento envisioned by Vatican II. Acculturation, which is the inchoate stage of adaptation, gives way to inculturation. In the process the dynamics of transculturation are allowed to operate in such a way that both the liturgy and culture are able to develop according to the identity proper to each one. In particular instances it may be necessary to resort to creativity, but this should normally be preceded by inculturation. The observation made by the Instruction *Comme le prévoit* on textual creativity applies also to ritual creativity: "Translation of texts transmitted through the tradition of the church is the best school and discipline for the creation of new texts."

5. The Question of Method

Method is vital to the process of legitimate progress in the liturgy. In fact the three approaches we described above require a system of checks and balances. The question is whether there is a method that suits the aim of cultural adaptation. Examining narrowly the various models of acculturation and inculturation in history and modern times, we notice the constant use of dynamic equivalence whereby the Roman rite is "translated" into other patterns of thought, language, and rites.

The *terminus a quo* of dynamic equivalence is the Roman rite as presented by the new *editio typica* of the liturgical books. As *terminus a quo* the Roman rite will have to be studied in its historical, cultural, and theological context in order to determine which of its linguistic and ritual components can be replaced with equivalent native elements. On the whole dynamic equivalence has been able to produce satisfactory results. It has safeguarded the liturgical tradition contained in the Roman rite, enriched it, and integrated it with the culture of the people.

But dynamic equivalence is not a self-regulating method. The simple substitution of the Roman elements with native cultural expressions could result in a new rite whose theological content and liturgical shape are mixed in a confused way, or whose shape may even be at odds with the content. Replacing, for example, the ritual elements of the mass with rites borrowed from sacrificial ceremonies confuses the sacrificial content of the mass with its meal form. Dynamic equivalence alone cannot regulate the process of inculturation. It is necessary to elaborate a system of checks and balances in order to minimize undiscerning applications of dynamic equivalence.

SC 21 distinguishes in the liturgy the "immutable elements, divinely instituted" from the "elements subject to change." "These not only may but ought to be changed with the passage of time if they have suffered from the intrusion of anything out of harmony with the inner nature of the liturgy or have become pointless." The liturgy is a complex reality consisting of a variety of gestures, words, symbols, and material elements, and is celebrated in various circumstances of time and place covering the entire gamut of human existence. The picture becomes even more complex when one takes into account the texts and rites that developed throughout the centuries and in different cultural settings.

However, the liturgy is not an undecipherable mass. Like any other reality it is made up of an outward shape or form and an inner meaning or content. The distinction in SC 21 between the immutable elements and the elements subject to change is built on this perception of form and content. Such perception has permitted the church to affirm that Christ himself had a direct hand, even if not always explicitly declared by sacred scripture, in the determination of the content or essential meaning of the sacraments.[48]

The concepts of theological content and liturgical form spring from the definition of the liturgy as the anamnesis of the paschal mystery. In somewhat untechnical terms we may describe anamnesis as a ritual activity whereby the church commemorates the paschal mystery through the performance of appointed rites. By virtue of this activity the object being recalled becomes present in mystery or sacramental form through the working of the Holy Spirit whom the church invokes in the prayer of epiclesis. Hence, every liturgical celebration is an anamnesis of the paschal mystery and an epiclestic prayer for the bestowal of the Holy Spirit. In the liturgy the paschal mystery and the mystery of Pentecost are present and operative realities.[49]

Anamnesis allows us to distinguish in each liturgical celebration a theological content and a liturgical form. The theological content refers to the meaning of the rite, while the liturgical form refers to the ritual shape with which the content is visibly expressed. The theological content is constant and often dates back to the patristic if not the apostolic age. In the case of the sacraments the theological content or essential meaning is of divine institution. The liturgical form, on the other hand, has undergone and continues to undergo changes or modifications in the course of time because of prevailing theological and cultural factors. Although the two cannot be separated, they can be distinguished and hence studied as individual units. It is thus possible to apply dynamic equivalence to one without touching the other.

In the framework of anamnesis we may say that the memorial of the paschal mystery is the basic theological content of every liturgical celebration. The sacraments, sacramentals, divine office, and liturgical year all converge here. They all commemorate the paschal mystery; they all render it present in various degrees and under different aspects. At mass the focus is on Christ's sacrificial offering; at baptism on his burial and rising from the tomb; at confirmation on his act of sending the Holy Spirit at Pentecost. At bottom every liturgical rite contains, signifies, and celebrates the paschal mystery. But this same mystery is experienced in different ways and under different forms according to the meaning and purpose of each liturgical rite.

The liturgical form, which consists of ritual acts and formularies, gives visible or sensible expression to the theological content. Speaking of the sacraments, we may mention the recitation of the eucharistic prayer over bread and wine, the washing with water while the trinitarian formula is pronounced, the laying on of hands and anointing with chrism, and so on. Apropos of the liturgical feasts, we may mention the celebration of the mass and the divine office proper to the feast and the observance of other apposite liturgical rites. In other words, through the liturgical form the sacraments, sacramentals, and feasts are externally distinguished from one another.

But there is another consideration that has a particular bearing upon pastoral planning. The liturgical form differentiates the modes of celebrating the same sacrament, sacramental, or feast. This point is immediately evident in the case of the eucharist which can be celebrated according to various liturgical forms. What we mean here is that the Sunday mass is one form of celebrating the eucharist, while the ritual and funeral masses as well as the weekday masses are other forms of celebrating the same. This distinction has practical effect on pastoral planning.

Parish liturgists often become frustrated with the assembly's reduced participation in ritual masses, especially of marriage. The situation calls for a methodological analysis. The theological content of every mass is, of course, the same. However, ritual masses are not Sunday masses. The former concentrates on the persons who receive the sacrament or sacramental in the ambit of the eucharist, the latter on the parish community gathered together on Sunday to encounter the risen Lord in word and sacrament. Hence, the mode of participating in one differs from the other. Moreover, the Sunday assembly is normally homogeneous, whereas the assembly at ritual masses is often an heterogeneous group of people invited by the interested party for the occasion. To expect the assembly at ritual masses to participate as if it were a normal Sunday assembly of parishioners is indeed to court frustration.

Some degree of participation at all liturgical celebrations is certainly required. However, it is not necessary every time we celebrate ritual and funeral masses to aim at that full, active, and intelligent participation which we normally expect from a Sunday assembly.

A similar consideration can be made with respect to the celebration of Easter Sunday and the Sundays throughout the year. We have here two different shapes of a liturgical feast, namely a yearly anniversary of Christ's resurrection and a weekly encounter of the community with the risen Lord. To regard every Sunday as "little Easter" is like playing a piece in the wrong key. A feast that is by nature an anniversary is hardly a weekly occurrence. And as we shall have the occasion to discuss in the third chapter of this book, should we consider the rites of Christian initiation for adults the paradigm of baptism for children? In the liturgy of Vatican II these are two distinct forms of initiation with elements proper to each. Infant baptism is a liturgy in its own right and does not need to be explained and celebrated as a reduced form of adult initiation.

We conclude our discussion by recalling the implications of dynamic equivalence as a method of liturgical inculturation. They refer to two important steps which need to be made in order to apply the method correctly. The first step consists of defining the theological content of a rite and neatly distinguishing it from its liturgical form. As an example we can cite the mass whose theological content, as we shall point out in the next chapter, is Christ's paschal sacrifice, and whose liturgical form is basically the last supper. Hence, to celebrate the mass in the form of a sacrificial rite instead of a meal is to apply dynamic equivalence in the wrong place.

The second step consists of isolating the immutable elements of the sacramental celebrations from the elements that are subject to change. Some equivalent initiatory rites can take the place of baptismal elements, but the washing with water cannot be replaced with another rite. It is obvious that these two steps require a thorough inquiry on the theological content and the liturgical form of each rite. In the words of SC 23, "that sound tradition may be retained and yet the way remain open to legitimate progress, a careful investigation is always to be made into each part of the liturgy to be revised. This investigation should be theological, historical, and pastoral." There are no alternative ways of bringing about authentic and meaningful inculturation.

The Translation of Liturgical Texts

The use of the vernacular in the liturgy is undoubtedly a milestone in the reform of Vatican II. But it is an achievement that is a requirement as well. For "full, conscious, and active participation in liturgical celebrations" is possible if the people understand what is being said or read.

1. The Passage from Latin to the Vernacular

In less than twenty years after the promulgation of SC the vernacular has securely established itself in the liturgical celebrations of the local churches.[50] This extraordinary achievement of Vatican II becomes more remarkable in the light of what transpired during the council. Everyone knows that the passage from Latin to the vernacular did not come about without a struggle. Although the classical liturgical movement that preceded the council vigorously promoted the use of the vernacular, some council fathers did not share the idea. The proposed text of SC 36 had to be worded with utmost care to avoid any one-sided affirmation that could polarize the council hall.[51]

The first paragraph of the proposed text stated the general premise: Latin is to be kept in the western liturgy. The second paragraph balanced this seemingly unconditional principle by adducing the authority of Pope Pius XII who favored the use of the vernacular "in not a few liturgical rites."[52] It called for a greater use of the vernacular, especially in the readings, instructions, and in some prayers and songs. The third paragraph gave to the conferences of bishops the faculty to propose to the Holy See whether and to what extent the vernacular was to be used. The relator for the article, C. Calewaert, gives us a concise account of how the council fathers dealt with the issue: "There were eighty speakers. Some gave their approval while others expressed disapproval. Everyone presented very sensible views that are already known or else add a new aspect to the question. However, the views contradict one another."

Upon a motion made by some council fathers, the relator suggested the adoption of a via media to define the extent of the vernacular and safeguard at the same time the right of each conference of bishops to avail of the faculty granted by the article.[53] The final text acquired its definitive shape after various ammendments had been introduced according to the principle of via media, a compromise "that perhaps will please all the fathers." The expression "western liturgy" was changed to "Latin rites" in order to include the Ambrosian and the Dominican liturgies, and the clause "particular law remaining in force" was added not only to soften the statement, but also to conserve existing indults and make allowance for future ones. Furthermore, the final text defined the particular instances when the vernacular may be used. These are at mass, in the administration of the sacraments, and in the other liturgical acts, or, in other words, in every liturgical celebration.

The mass in the vernacular is one of the innovational concessions of Vatican II for the purpose of promoting active participation. The fathers of Trent acknowledged the rich catechetical content of the mass, but they decided that it was not expedient to allow the use of the vernacular. On the contrary, they condemned the statement that the mass ought to be celebrated only in the vernacular.[54] SC 36 was thus a courageous departure from a centuries-old discipline meant to preserve the purity of the mass. The departure, however, was not readily granted. Up to the last minute some *modi* presented to the conciliar commission tried to protect the mass from the onslaught of the vernacular. One *modus* petitioned that Latin be kept in the mass *modo completo et totali.* Another accepted the use of the vernacular for the sacraments but not for the mass, and a third motioned that the use of the vernacular in the canon be restricted to those words that are recited aloud.[55]

The third paragraph of SC 36 underwent an ammendment with a far-reaching effect on ecclesiology. In the final text *proponere* was changed to *statuere,* so that the conferences of bishops, instead of merely submitting proposals to the Holy See, would be empowered to decide whether and to what extent the vernacular is to be used. The role of the Holy See would be to confirm the decision reached by the local authority regarding this matter. As the relator perspicuously explained, "the law legitimately established by the local authority is acknowledged and perfected by the superior authority. Thus the via media is obtained when the local authority establishes the law and the superior authority adds to it a new juridical force."[56] In other words, within the limits set by law the local churches determine their rule of life, create their traditions, and develop their form of worship. The Holy See confirms them, that is to say, puts on them the seal of universal approval.

Soon after the promulgation of SC the work of translating the liturgical books into the vernacular began. Today the great majority of the local churches are in possession of approved translations.[57] But there are questions requiring further consideration. The principal reason for translating the liturgical texts is to foster intelligent and active participation. How far can translated texts accomplish this? How well can a translated text communicate the same message that the original text communicated to the people for whom it was composed? If the translation neglects the cultural genius of the Latin text, will the substantial unity of the Roman rite suffer?[58]

2. Translation Implies Cultural Adaptation

On January 25, 1969 the postconciliar Consilium for the implementation of the Constitution on the Liturgy issued the Instruction *Comme le prévoit,* on the translation of liturgical texts.[59] The Instruction has three parts. The first gives an outline of the principles of liturgical translations. Their purpose "is to proclaim the message of salvation to believers and to express the prayer of the church to the Lord." The translator is reminded that one is dealing here with spoken words, and that "a liturgical text, inasmuch as it is a ritual sign, is a medium of spoken communication." The second part of the Instruction offers particular considerations, and the third part recommends the formation of committees for translating.

It is not possible to analyze here the various points raised by the Instruction. It is, however, necessary to call attention to the fact that the work of translating liturgical texts cannot prescind from cultural adaptation in general and from inculturation in particular. The Instruction clearly points out that "in the case of liturgical communication, it is necessary to take into account not only the message to be conveyed, but also the speaker, the audience, and the style. Translations, therefore, must be faithful to the art of communication in all its various aspects, but especially in regard to the message itself, in regard to the audience for which it is intended, and in regard to the manner of expression."[60]

Translation implies cultural adaptation. This requires the translator to have an adequate knowledge of the *terminus a quo,* which is the Latin text, and of the *terminus ad quem,* which is the vernacular language. As Pope Paul VI reminded translators of the liturgical texts: "Those dedicated to this work must know both Christian Latin and their own modern language."[61]

In order to establish the authentic meaning of a liturgical text, "the translator must follow the scientific methods of textual study as used by experts." These scientific methods imply a certain amount of familiarity with the various cultures that influenced the liturgical texts, namely the biblical, the Greco-Roman, and the medieval. Without some familiarity with these cultures the translator might miss the message of the text which is normally expressed in the cultural categories proper to each period. The use of the scientific method of textual study ensures that the translation will faithfully communicate to a given people and in their own language the message which the church, through the Latin text, intended to communicate to another people in another time.

Translations are the church's instrument for conveying to the people of today the message contained in the original Latin texts. Translations are part of the process of Christian tradition. In this they differ from textual creativity which communicates the message of faith independently of existing liturgical texts, although it draws its material from the revealed word and the Church's living tradition.

The English text of the Instruction discusses at length various Latin terms that should be considered in the light of their historical, cultural, and liturgical uses. It also offers suggestions on how they may be translated into English. Examples are: *devotio, oratio, pius* and *pietas, salus, caro, tentatio, iustitia, mysterium,* and such expressions as *locus refrigerii* and *terrena despicere.* It will be to the advantage of language groups, especially those outside the ambit of the European languages, to develop a lexicon of key Latin liturgical terms with their equivalents in the modern or contemporary languages.[62]

The task of the translator is to express Latin concepts in contemporary idiom, to bridge the cultural gap between the Latin text and the liturgical audience.[63] The translator is thus expected to be conversant with the *terminus ad quem,* which is not confined to the question of oral and written language. The *terminus a quem* includes an appreciation of the values, rituals, and traditions of one's own culture. For language contains, reveals, and expresses everything that touches the history, traditions, and life of a people.

The complexity of the matter demands the interdisciplinary collaboration of cultural anthropologists, sociologists, and linguistic experts. Translations cannot be the exclusive work of one person, because the *terminus ad quem* embraces the entire gamut of a people's cultural experience.

They cannot be a mere word-for-word rendering of Latin terms, because communication takes place in a cultural setting. And this is an area that needs the assistance of various experts. The cultural factor, however, is not everything. The translator is exhorted to take the greatest care "that all translations are not only beautiful and suited to the contemporary mind, but also express true doctrine and authentic Christian spirituality." For through the liturgical texts the church transmits what it believes and celebrates as a worshiping community.[64]

The need to give careful attention to the cultural aspect of translations becomes evident when we consider the liturgical text as a "linguistic fact" designed for celebration.[65] Liturgical texts are meant primarily for celebration, not for private reading. They are read aloud, proclaimed, or sung in the assembly. Hence, the translator must take into account the different forms used by the people to express acclamation, supplication, proclamation, and dialogue. The Instruction notes that "the literary genre of every liturgical text depends first of all on the nature of the ritual act signified in the words—acclamation or supplication, proclamation or praying, reading or singing. Each action requires its proper form of expression."[66]

In some cultures oral communication is accompanied by a body language that often includes swaying and dancing, especially on solemn occasions. For this reason, the scope of translating cannot be confined to the area of the written words. The translator must consider the words also as the spoken medium of communication. Every time words are spoken or sung, culture is at work. Some words, unaccompanied by gestures, fall flat; others, deprived of images taken from nature and human experience, arouse no response. Liturgical texts are formulas meant to be spoken. They transmit the message not only through written words but also through the art of communication which is a composite of cultural elements that make up or accompany the spoken language. The work of translating the liturgical texts is indeed a service to the church whose task is to proclaim the message of faith and to human culture whose highest fulfillment is to express and communicate the reality of God.

Notes

[1] A. King: *Liturgies of the Past,* London 1959; A. Nocent: *L'Avenir de la Liturgie,* Paris 1961.

[2] The conciliar preparatory commission pointed out the need for classical restoration in connection with the missal, *praesertim cum ritus romanus in Gallia assumptus et ex indole gallico-germanica in formam novam redactus est, quam Ecclesia romana postea adoptavit. Schema Constitutionis de Sacra Liturgia,* henceforth *Schema,* Emendationes VI, Vatican City 1963, p. 32. See A. Bugnini: "Ordo Missae," *La riforma liturgica (1948–1975),* Rome 1983, pp. 332–88.

[3] It should be noted, however, that earlier the Roman liturgy assimilated also Oriental elements such as "Agnus Dei" (introduced by Pope Sergius I at the end of the seventh century) and the feasts of the "Hypapante" and the Nativity of Mary. See P. Jounel: *Le renouveau du culte des saints,* Rome 1986, pp. 100–01 and 179–80.

[4] J. Deshusses: *Le Sacramentaire grégorien* I, Fribourg 1971, no. 36, p. 99 (for Christmas night); no. 377, p. 189 (for Easter vigil); no. 520, p. 225 (for Pentecost after baptism) and no. 526, p. 227 (for Pentecost Sunday).

[5] M. Andrieu (ed.): *Les Ordines Romani du haut moyen âge* II (Les textes), Louvain 1971, pp. 67–108. See J. Jungmann: "Fermentum," *Colligere Fragmenta,* Beuron 1952, pp. 182–90; A. Nocent: "La comunione nel rito romano," *Anàmnesis* 3/2, Casale Monferrato 1983, pp. 265–66; R. Cabié: "La participation

du peuple," *L'Eucharistie, L'Église en prière* II, Paris, 1983, pp. 62–64.

[6] For a description of the classical shape of the Roman liturgy see E. Bishop: "The genius of the Roman rite," *Liturgica Historica,* Oxford 1918, pp. 1–19; T. Klauser: *A Short History of the Western Liturgy,* Oxford 1969, pp. 59–68; B. Neunheuser: "Storia della liturgia. La liturgia romana classica," *Nuovo Dizionario di Liturgia,* ed. D. Sartore–A. Triacca, Rome 1984, pp. 1461–65.

[7] See the list of the members of both the preparatory and conciliar commissions in A. Bugnini: *La riforma liturgica,* pp. 903–06.

[8] B. Neunheuser: "Il movimento liturgico: panorama storico e lineamenti teologici," *Anàmnesis* I, Turin 1974, p. 29. Throughout this work the English translation of SC and other liturgical documents is taken from *Documents on the Liturgy,* henceforth *DOL,* published by ICEL, Collegeville 1982.

[9] B. Neunheuser: "Il movimento liturgico," pp. 22–29; J. da Silva: *O Movimento Litúrgico no Brasil,* Petropolis 1983, pp. 163–99. See also T. O'Meara: "The Origins of the Liturgical Movement and German Romanticism," *Worship,* 59/4 (1985) pp. 326–42.

[10] *Schema,* Modi II, p. 8.

[11] SC 62, 88, 107, and 110.

[12] *Apostolic Constitution "Quo primum"* of July 19, 1570, *Missale Romanum,* Rome 1962, p. viii: *Neque in Missae celebratione alias caeremonias, vel preces, quam quae hoc Missali continentur, addere vel recitare praesumant.*

[13] *Apostolic Letter "Cum sanctissimum"* of July 7, 1604, *ibid.,* p. ix: *Sane omnino conveniens est, ut qui omnes unum sumus in uno corpore, quod est Ecclesia, et de uno corpore Christi participamus, una et eadem celebrandi ratione, uniusque officii et ritus observatione in hoc ineffabili et tremendo sacrificio utamur.*

[14] A.J. Chupungco: *Cultural Adaptation of the Liturgy,* New York 1982, pp. 42–57. See A.G. Martimort: "Adaptation liturgique," *Mens Concordet Voci,* Paris 1983, pp. 338–48.

[15] See *Schema,* Emendationes IV, p. 16. As the conciliar relator, C. Calewaert, explained *Ex Patribus alii quoque contendebant*

eo suppremendam esse mentionem de Missionibus, quod eaedem conditiones alibi easdem solutiones postulent; sed cum dicitur "praesertim", clare indicatur Missiones non esse solas regiones in quibus aptatio necessaria evadat.

[16] "Altiora Principia," *La riforma liturgica,* pp. 50–59. See also B. Fischer–P.M. Gy: "De Recognitione Ritualis Romani," *Notitiae,* 2 (1966) 220–30.

[17] *Apostolic Exhortation "Marialis Cultus,"* no. 31, *DOL,* p. 1220.

[18] Apropos of SC 37–40 C. Calewaert explained that the pair of words *recognitio-probatio seu confirmatio* has a special meaning: *Nam hac locutione ostenditur ius quod ab auctoritate inferiore legitime statuitur et ab auctoritate superiore agnoscitur ac completur. Inde via media obtinetur, cum auctoritas inferior ius condat et auctoritas superior novam vim iuridicam addat. Schema,* Emendationes IV, p. 15. See A.G. Martimort: "La Constitution sur la Liturgie de Vatican II. Esquisse historique," *La Maison-Dieu* 157 (1984) pp. 45–58; K. Seasoltz: *New Liturgy, New Laws,* Collegeville 1980, pp. 169–81.

[19] No. 21; *DOL,* p. 93. A *modus* presented to the conciliar commission asked that *accomodationes fiant a S. Rituum Congregatione vel a Sancta Sede.* The answer was: *Ad mentem art. 63b, accomodationes conficiuntur a competenti auctoritate territoriali, actis ab Apostolica Sede recognitis, at adhibentur de iudicio Ordinarii. Schema,* Modi III, p. 13.

[20] A. Bugnini: "Rituale romano," *La riforma liturgica,* pp. 566–69; A.G. Martimort: "Le nouvel esprit de la législation liturgique," *L'Église en prière* I, Paris 1983, pp. 134–36. For the history and list of medieval particular rituals see C. Vogel: *Medieval Liturgy. An Introduction to Sources,* trans. and revised by W. Storey and N. Rasmussen, Washington, D.C. 1986, pp. 257–65.

[21] Cf. *Ordo Initiationis Christianae Adultorum,* Vatican City 1972, General Introduction IV, nos. 30–33, *DOL,* pp. 724–25; *Ordo Confirmationis,* Vatican City 1973, Introduction IV, nos. 16–17, *DOL,* p. 775; *Ordo Paenitentiae,* Vatican City 1974, Introduction VI, nos. 38–39, *DOL,* p. 968; *Ordo Unctionis Infirmorum,* Vatican City 1975, Introduction IV, 38–39, *DOL,* p. 1060; *Ordo Celebrandi Matrimonium,* Vatican City 1972, Intro-

duction, nos. 12–18, *DOL,* pp. 923–24; *Ordo Exsequiarum,* Vatican City 1969, Introduction, nos. 21–22, *DOL,* pp. 1072–73; *Ordo Lectionum Missae,* Vatican City 1981, Introduction IV, nos. 111–25; *De Benedictionibus,* Vatican City 1984, General Introduction V, no. 39.

[22] Consilium, *Instruction "Comme le prévoit,"* no. 6, *DOL,* pp. 284–85.

[23] In particular instances it is advisable to compose special introductions to particular rituals, in order to enrich the *editio typica* and explain the adaptations that have been introduced. An example of this is ICEL's *Order of Christian Funerals,* Washington, D.C. 1985, which adds an introduction that is truly remarkable for its theology and pastoral usefulness.

[24] See Congregation for Divine Worship, *Circular Letter "Eucharistiae participationem,"* no. 6; *DOL,* p. 625.

[25] Cf. Congregation for Divine Worship, *Instruction "Liturgicae instaurationes,"* no. 12, *DOL,* pp. 166–67; see also Consilium, *Letter "Le renouveau liturgique,"* no. 4, *DOL,* p. 119.

[26] K. Seasoltz: *New Liturgy, New Laws,* pp. 202–11.

[27] A. Bouley: *From Freedom to Formula,* Washington, D.C. 1981; A. Nocent: "Dall'improvvisazione alla fissazione delle formule e dei riti," *Anàmnesis* II, Genoa 1978, pp. 131–35. See also A. Vööbus: *Liturgical Traditions in the Didache,* Stockholm 1968; J. Hanssens: *La liturgie d'Hippolite. Documents et études,* Rome 1970.

[28] The spirit of via media can be seen in the modifications introduced by the conciliar commission into the text of SC. Examples are the addition of phrases like *pro opportunitate* and *ex more,* the elimination of strong expressions like *funditus* and *ex integro,* and the softening of some words like *admittatur* to *admitti liceat. Schema,* Emendationes VII, pp. 9–10.

[29] In the words of Cardinal Ferretto: *Quae verba . . . aliquantulum sapiunt sic dictum "liturgismum exaggeratum," qui omnes ritus Ecclesiae immutare conari censetur. Acta et Documenta,* Concilio Oecumenico Vaticano II Apparando, Series II,3, Sessio V, Vatican City 1961, pp. 291–92. In response the relator Archbishop Hallinan reported: *Quaedam expressiones huius Capitis III [=II] Schematis ablatae sunt quia non sunt necessariae, ex. gr.,*

"funditus" recognoscantur, "ex integro" recognoscantur . . . Schema, Emendationes VII, p. 9.

[30] *Schema,* Emendationes VII, pp. 12–15.

[31] See: C. Valenziano: "Per l'≪adattamento≫ culturale della Liturgia dopo il Vaticano II. Appunti metodologici," *Ho Theologos,* nuova serie, III,2 (1985) pp. 179–202.

[32] G. Arbuckle strongly suggests that "because of the theological, anthropological and historical connotations of the term 'adaptation,' it should be dropped from theological and liturgical use" and substituted with the term "inculturation" which was invented to express the evangelical implications of local church theology. "Inculturation Not Adaptation: Time to Change Terminology," *Worship* 60/6 (1986) p. 519.

[33] See J. Jungmann: *The Early Liturgy to the Time of Gregory the Great,* London 1966, pp. 122–63; A.J. Chupungco: "Greco-Roman Culture and Liturgical Adaptation," *Notitiae* 153 (1979) pp. 202–18; idem: "A Historical Survey of Liturgical Adaptation," *Notitiae* 174 (1981) pp. 28–43.

[34] Tertullian: *De Baptismo,* ed. R. Refoulé, *Sources Chrétiennes* 35 (1952) pp. 65–66; Clement of Alexandria: *Protrepticus,* ed. O. Stählin, *Die griechische christliche Schriftsteller* I, Leipzig 1905, pp. 1–86; St. Ambrose: *De Sacramentis* III, 5 (ed. B. Botte), *Sources Chrétiennes* 25bis (1961) p. 94.

[35] *The Early Liturgy,* p. 165. See T. Klauser: *A Short History of the Western Liturgy,* Oxford 1969, pp. 18–72.

[36] See J. Jungmann: "Mass and Baroque Culture," *The Mass of the Roman Rite,* New York 1961, pp. 111–17; idem: "Liturgical Life in the Baroque Period," *Pastoral Liturgy,* London 1962, pp. 80–89.

[37] Pontificia Commissione Biblica: *Fede e cultura alla luce della Bibbia,* Turin 1981, p. 5.

[38] For the meaning of inculturation in general, see A. Crollius: "What is New about Inculturation? A Concept and its Implications," *Gregorianum* 59 (1978) pp. 721–38; M. Azevedo: *Inculturation and the Challenge of Modernity,* Rome 1982. See also M. Dumais: "The Church of the Acts of the Apostles: a Model of Inculturation?" *Inculturation,* Vol. X: Cultural Change and Liberation in a Christian Perspective, Rome 1987, pp. 3–4. The series

Inculturation. Working Papers on Living Faith and Cultures, edited by A. Crollius, Rome, offers a number of articles pertinent to the question of liturgical inculturation. See also R. González: "Adaptación, inculturación, creatividad. Planteamiento, problematicas y perspectivas de profundización," *Phase* 158,27 (1987) pp. 129–52.

[39] Tertullian: *De Corona* III,1; IV,4, *Corpus Christianorum Latinorum* II, Turnholt, 1954. What Tertullian affirms on the subject is significant: *Hanc [unctionem] si nulla scriptura determinavit, certe consuetudo corroboravit, quae sine dubio de traditione manavit.* III,1, p. 1042. St. Ambrose: *De Sacramentis* I, 4, p. 62: *Unctus es quasi athleta Christi, quasi luctam huius saeculi luctaturus, professus es luctaminis tui certamina.* See J. Daniélou: *The Bible and the Liturgy,* London 1964, pp. 19–69; B. Botte: "Le symbolisme de l'huile et de l'onction," *Questions Liturgiques* 4 (1981) p. 196; A. Chupungco: "Greco-Roman Culture and Liturgical Adaptation," pp. 202–18.

[40] Hippolytus of Rome: *La Tradition Apostolique,* ed. B. Botte, Münster 1963, p. 54. Tertullian mentions the same practice in the rite of Christian initiation in Africa: *Inde suscepti lactis et mellis concordiam praegustamus.* The term *susceptio* or *munus susceptionis* was a juridical term that signified, among other things, a father's official recognition of a new-born child. *De Corona* III, 3, pp. 1042–43. See Pauly-Wissowa: *Real-Encyclopedie* XXX (1920), pp. 1570–71; VII (1931), pp. 974–75.

[41] Besides the classic work of J. Jungmann, *The Early Liturgy,* the following books may be consulted: C. Andronikof et al.: *Gestes et paroles dans les diverses familles liturgiques,* Rome 1978, especially the articles of C. Andronikof: "La dyamique de la parole et la liturgie," pp. 13–29, of W. Rordorf: "Les gestes accompagnant la prière d'après Tertullien et Origène," pp. 191–203, and of E. Theodorou: "La danse sacrée dans le culte chrétien et plus spécialement dans la famille liturgique byzantine," pp. 285–300; E.O. James: *Seasonal Feasts and Festivals,* New York 1961; J. Van Goudoever: *Biblical Calendars,* Leiden 1961; C. Vogel et al.: *Culto cristiano. Politica imperiale carolingia,* Todi 1979.

[42] No. 6, *DOL,* p. 285.

[43] For the ordination prayers, see C. Mohlberg (ed.): *Sacramentarium Veronense,* Rome 1966, nos. 942–54, pp. 118–22; D. Power: *Ministers of Christ and his Church,* London 1969, pp. 58–73. For the ordeals, see C. Vogel (ed.): *Le Pontifical romano-germanique du dixième siècle* II, Vatican City 1963, pp. 380–94. The new Book of Blessings does not consider it proper to bless instruments of war: *De Benedictionibus,* no. 1245, p. 478.

[44] Hippolytus of Rome: *La Tradition Apostolique,* p. 56.

[45] Cf. A. Pistoia: "Creatività," *Nuovo Dizionario di Liturgia,* pp. 314–32.

[46] M. Augé: "Ermeneutica liturgica," *Anàmnesis* I, Genoa 1974, p. 172.

[47] No. 43, *DOL,* p. 291. A. Echiegu's *Translating the Collects of the Solemnities of the Lord in the Language of the African,* Vol. I, Münster 1984, is a remarkable work of textual creativity in the Igbo language. Although the model translations he proposes take both the content and the rhetorical qualities of the Roman collects into account, they are in fact not mere translations but new creations. On the subject of translation and improvisation see A.-G. Martimort: "Essai historique sur la traductions liturgiques," *Mens concordet voci,* Tournai 1983 pp. 72–94; A. Nocent: "Dall'improvvisazione alla fissazione delle formule e dei riti," *Anàmnesis* 2, Casale Monferrato 1978, pp. 131–35; A. Bouley: *From Freedom to Formula,* Washington, D.C. 1981.

[48] E. Schillebeeckx: *Christ the Sacrament of Encounter with God,* London 1971, pp. 137–63.

[49] O. Casel: *Das christliche Kultmysterium,* Regensburg 1960, pp. 25–74; S. Marsili: "Verso una teologia della Liturgia," *Anàmnesis* I, Turin 1974, pp. 47–84; idem: "Il 'tempo liturgico' attuazione della storia della salvezza," *Rivista Liturgica* 57/2 (1970) pp. 207–35; idem: "Memoriale-anamnesi nella preghiera eucaristica," *Notitiae* 9/6 (1973) pp. 225–27.

[50] "Investigatio de usu linguae latinae in Liturgia Romana et de Missa quae ≪tridentina≫ appellari solet," *Notitiae* 17 (1981) pp. 586–611.

[51] *Schema,* Emendationes IV, p. 24.

[52] *Mediator Dei, Acta Apostolicae Sedis* 39 (1947) p. 545.

[53] *Schema,* Emendationes IV, p. 12.

[54] *Concilium Tridentinum,* Sessio XXII, can. 9, *Enchiridion Symbolorum,* Rome 1976, no. 1759: *Etsi Missa magnam contineat populi fidelis eruditionem, non tamen expedire visum est Patribus, ut vulgari passim lingua celebraretur.* The council proposed as alternative that the pastors explain to the faithful, especially on Sundays and feasts, what is read during the mass. See Th. Freudenberger: "Die Messliturgie in der Volksprache im Urteil des Trienten Konzils," *Reformatio Ecclesiae. Festschrift für E. Iserloh,* Paderborn 1981, pp. 679–98.

[55] *Schema,* Modi I, p. 24.

[56] *Verbum enim "probatis," de se genericum, specificatur seu explicatur verbo "confirmatis." Nam hac locutione ostenditur ius quod ab auctoritate inferiore legitime statuitur et ab auctoritate superiore agnoscitur ac completur. Inde via media obtinetur, cum auctoritas inferior ius condat et auctoritas superior novam vim iuridicam addat. Schema,* Modi I, p. 15.

[57] J. Gibert: "Le lingue nella liturgia dopo il Concilio Vaticano II," *Notitiae* 15 (1979) pp. 387–520.

[58] P. Grelot: "Heurs et malheur de la traduction liturgique," *Étude* (Octobre 1971) pp. 449–60; A. Kavanagh: "Liturgical Business Unfinished and Unbegun," *Worship* 50 (1976) pp. 354–63; P. Garret: "The Problem of Liturgical Translations. A Preliminary Study," *St. Vladimir's Theological Quarterly* 22 (1978) pp. 83–114; idem: "The Problem of Liturgical Translation. An Addendum," *ibid.,* pp. 37–50. See also A.-G. Martimort: "Essai historique sur les traductions liturgiques," *La Maison-Dieu* 86 (1966) pp. 75–105.

[59] *Notitiae* 5 (1969) pp. 3–12; *DOL,* pp. 284–91. See J. Gelineau: Quelques remarques en marge de l'Instruction sur la traduction des textes liturgiques," *La Maison-Dieu* 98 (1963) pp. 156–62.

[60] *Comme le prévoit,* no. 7, *DOL,* p. 285.

[61] *Address,* November 10, 1965, *DOL,* p. 273.

[62] *Comme le prévoit,* nos. 11–24, *DOL,* pp. 285–86. ICEL has made an excellent compilation of Latin terms and their English equivalents.

[63] S. Marsili: "Des textes liturgiques pour l'homme moderne," *Concilium* 42 (1969) pp. 47–62; A. Dumas: "Pour mieux

comprendre les textes liturgiques du Missel Romain," *Notitiae* 6 (1970) pp. 194–212; idem: "Cum in forma Dei esset . . . *ibid.* 7 (1971) pp. 299–303; G. Venturi: "Problemi della traduzione liturgica nel cambio di strutture linguistiche e di visione del mondo," *Salesianum* 40 (1978) pp. 73–118.

[64] *Comme le prévoit,* no. 24, *DOL,* p. 287.

[65] *Ibid.*, no. 27, *DOL,* p. 287.

[66] *Ibid.*, no. 26, *DOL,* p. 287.

Chapter Two

The Future Shape of the Eucharistic Celebration

The Order of Mass in the Reform of Vatican II

The cultural adaptation of the order of mass is an arduous task ahead of local churches. It is arduous not only because of the fair amount of work it requires but also because of a certain reluctance on the part of some members of the clergy and the laity to introduce changes in the order of mass "out of a profound veneration for the eucharist." There are also those who are averse to modifying its celebration for a different consideration which we may call scholarly: the present order of mass is the result of "countless studies of scholars" and of conciliar deliberation.[1] It did not come about on the spur of the moment but at the end of a long process of theological and pastoral discernment. Any call for additional changes in its order of celebration will evidently meet with reserve.

It took five long years to revise the order of mass. In his posthumous book *La riforma liturgica* A. Bugnini describes in great detail the various phases of the revision from the first meeting of the study group in April 1964 to the publication of the new *editio typica* on April 3, 1969.[2] Several years have elapsed, but the new order of mass has not totally replaced the Roman missal of Pius V which stood unchallenged and practically unchanged for four hundred years. In spite of this distressing turn of events, we may affirm that the Roman missal of Paul VI is surely a breakthrough in liturgical renewal. Nevertheless, the breakthrough must become a milestone to indicate not only the achievement but also the new horizons. The breakthrough cannot turn the new missal into the monolith that has become of its predecessor: it must become a living tradition.

1. SC 50 and the Revision of the Order of Mass

Article 50 of the Constitution on the Liturgy gives two reasons why the order of mass needed revision. The first is in order to restore it to its pristine clarity; the second is in order to foster active participation. The proposed text asked that the order of mass be revised completely, "in order to be more clearly understood and make easier the active participation of the faithful."[3] The idea of a complete revision "of both the general outline and the individual parts" of the Roman missal did not meet with the unanimous approval of the council fathers. There were those who felt that a complete revision could give the impression that the entire Tridentine order of mass had been a mistake and therefore was in need of a thorough correction.[4] Due to such misgiving the conciliar commission proposed the following text which the council fathers readily approved: "The order of mass is to be revised in a way that will bring out more clearly the intrinsic nature and purpose of its several parts, as also the connection between them, and will more readily achieve the devout, active participation of the faithful." Except for the matter regarding complete revision, both the proposed and the final texts agree on the reasons for revising the order of mass, namely ritual clarity and active participation.

We should note at this juncture that the revision contemplated by SC 50 is not an application of the provision in SC 37–40 for cultural adaptation. In fact SC 40 is cited only in SC 54 in connection with a more extended use of the vernacular within the mass. The absence of any significant reference to SC 37–40 indicates that the cultural adaptation of the order of mass was not in the council's list of priorities or probably was not entered into its agenda at all. What the council explicitly wanted was revision, not cultural adaptation. And revision had a very precise meaning in the mind of those who shaped the Constitution.

Early on the preparatory commission had suggested that the work of revision should focus primarily on those Franco-Germanic elements that the Roman order of mass assimilated when it was introduced into Gaul toward the eighth century.[5] Beneath the recommendations given by the preparatory commission to simplify, shorten, and omit several medieval mass elements, we can feel the strong current of the classical liturgical movement. In effect, revision meant eliminating the Franco-Germanic ingredients from the Roman order of mass in order to restore it to its classical shape.

It was not the first time the issue of the classical restoration of the liturgy was raised in the Roman church. Adhering to Pope Gregory VII's reformist principle of "imitating the ancient fathers," the Roman liturgists of the twelfth century discarded a considerable amount of Franco-Germanic elements from the tenth-century Romano-Germanic pontifical. Rites not considered congenial with the Roman taste for sobriety, like exorcism, excommunications, and ordeals, were excluded from the revised Roman pontifical.[6]

After the Council of Trent Pope Pius V made an unsuccessful attempt to restore the divine office to its former shape according to "the ancient rule of praying" as handed down by the popes, especially Pope Gelasius and Pope Gregory the Great.[7] Likewise he tried, with little success, to revise the order of mass according to the "ancient rule and rite of the holy fathers."[8] In reality, his order of mass differed very little from the Roman missal of 1474, which in turn followed faithfully the one used at the time of Pope Innocent III. The absence of critical editions of the ordines and sacramentaries did not allow the revisors to make any adequate research into the "tradition of the fathers." To preserve the existing liturgical practices of the Roman church, then being assailed by the Protestant reformers, Pope Pius V preferred to introduce only very slight changes in the order of mass.[9]

In the eighteenth century the edition of several patristic and liturgical sources greatly facilitated the return to the classical shape of the Roman liturgy. The Synod of Pistoia in 1786 presided over by Bishop S. dè Ricci is remarkable for its endeavor to return to the sources. Its decrees reforming the celebration of the mass have much in common with SC 50. They heralded the classical reform of Vatican II. Unfortunately, besides being entrapped in Jansenism and the political gambit of the duke of Tuscany, the synod did not gather the support of both the clergy and the faithful. Its Jansenist errors were condemned by Pope Pius VI in 1794. The Synod of Pistoia was yet another unsuccessful attempt to return to the classical shape of the Roman liturgy.[10]

In 1909 the Gregorian principle of "imitating the ancient fathers" was resuscitated by the classical liturgical movement ushered in by the Congress of Malines. The movement agreed with the Synod of Pistoia on several points like the use of the vernacular, active participation through songs and responses, the reading of a more representative portion of sacred scripture in the course of the year, and communion from the altar rather than from the tabernacle. For the movement and the synod classical restoration, which meant bringing greater clarity to the order of mass and fostering fuller participation, was the obvious way of giving shape to the principle of "imitating the ancient fathers."

The Synod of Pistoia was condemned, but the movement did not suffer the same fate, even if for some fifty years it had to contend with those who opposed the principle. In the end the movement won, and its principle is now solemnly enshrined in SC 50: "Elements that have suffered injury through accident of history are now, as may seem useful or necessary, to be restored to the vigor they had in the tradition of the fathers."

The second paragraph of SC 50 leaves no doubt as to the council's intention of revising the order of mass in the spirit of classical restoration. The article lays down three operational principles which clearly echo the recommendations of the preparatory commission.[11] First, the rites are to be simplified without injury to their substance. Second, elements that came to be duplicated or were introduced with but little advantage are now to be discarded. Third, the traditional elements that disappeared from the order of mass in the course of time should be restored to their former vigor, as may seem useful or necessary.

In connection with the first two principles, the preparatory commission suggested that the number of gestures like making the sign of the cross, kissing the altar, genuflecting, and bowing be reduced. Likewise, the number of the prayers at the foot of the altar should be decreased, and the rite itself should be simplified. Apropos of the third principle the preparatory commission, relying on the studies by contemporary scholars on the classical shape of the Roman mass,[12] made the following recommendations: sacred scripture is to be proclaimed facing the people; the offertory procession should be commended on Sundays and solemn feasts; the prayer over the gifts is to be restored to its former importance; the treasury of prefaces should be recovered; the principal parts of the canon, including the embolism of the Lord's prayer, are to be recited aloud and the assembly should respond to the final doxology; the rites of the breaking of bread and the exchange of peace need to be restructured; the restriction on the communion of the faithful in some masses should be abolished; the formula for distributing holy communion is to be shortened; and the mass should conclude with a blessing and the formula *Ite, missa est.*[13]

Simplicity and sobriety of rites, practical sense, and adherence to the tradition of the fathers are the inherent qualities of the classical Roman liturgy that SC 50 proposed to recover. However, reviving them in the twentieth century for a church embracing many and diverse cultural traditions could easily be misinterpreted as an archeological exercise that neglects the present reality. As one council father dutifully reminded the conciliar commission, "the reason for reforming the rites should be pastoral rather than archeological."[14] The conciliar commission, directing the attention of the council fathers to the provision of SC 23 and SC 33–36, assured them that classical restoration does not disregard pastoral needs.

The above-mentioned articles keep a perfect balance between classical restoration and the reality of the pastoral and cultural pluralism existing in the church today. SC 23 speaks of retaining sound tradition while keeping the way open to legitimate progress. Classical reform does not ignore "the experience derived from recent liturgical reforms and from the indults conceded to various places."

The remaining articles deal with the norms based on the teaching and pastoral character of the liturgy. The noble simplicity, brevity, and clarity of the liturgical rites are meant to improve the quality of active participation. The norms concerning the use of Latin not only do not exclude the use of the vernacular, they also recognize that it "frequently may be of great advantage to the people." In fact SC 54 has explicit provision for the extended use of the vernacular within the mass. In short, the restoration of the classical shape of the order of mass was not calculated to retard the progress of the liturgical aggiornamento. Its ultimate aim, according to the conciliar commission, is to "more readily achieve the devout, active participation of the faithful."

The proposal to revise the order of mass received contrasting reactions from the council fathers. Those who were in favor cited the pastoral benefit of active participation and the liturgical advantage of restoring the Roman rite to its original splendor. Those who were against expressed the fear that the proposed changes might cause scandal among the faithful, impair the sanctity of the mass, and eventually do away with this "very ancient rite" and "supreme work of art" inspired by the *romana vetus sobrietas,* the sobriety of ancient Rome. Some strongly recommended moderation when introducing changes, especially in the canon of the mass, while others sought a compromise solution that would allow changes in the liturgy of the word but not in the rest of the mass.[15]

The objection to SC 50 is understandable considering the veneration given by the Roman church to the Roman missal of Pius V. In the preface to its first edition the pope threatened *sub indignationis Nostrae poena,* "under pain of Our wrath," anyone who dared to add to, subtract from, or change anything whatsoever in the said missal.[16] Except for the minor changes introduced by Pope Pius X in 1911, the Tridentine missal remained practically intact for four hundred years. For Catholics it stood as a dogmatic statement against Protestants on the issues concerning the sacrificial character of the mass, the ministry of ordained priests, and the enduring real presence in the eucharistic species. Revising it was therefore perceived as an enterprise that could endanger the faith. However, the conciliar commission held its ground. By inserting into the text of SC 50 Pope Pius V's venerated phrase *ad pristinam sanctorum Patrum normam,* "in keeping with the pristine rule of the holy fathers," it allayed fears and gave the assurance that the proposed revision was nothing more than a return to the tradition of the fathers.

The foregoing discussion makes it clear that the immediate concern of SC 50 was to restore the classical form of the order of mass and thereby foster the active participation of the faithful. Unlike SC 65 and SC 77, which address the question of cultural adaptation and open wide the door to the alternative rites of Christian initiation and marriage, SC 50 wanted to revise the Tridentine missal without promoting alternative orders of mass. The terse declaration of the preparatory commission in this connection is significant: "The present order of mass, which developed over the centuries, is to be kept."[17]

When SC 50 was being discussed, a council father suggested that "the faculty be granted to choose or vary [the order of mass] according to the liturgical year."[18] What he was requesting in effect was that the council sanction the development of various orders of mass suited to the different moments of the liturgical year. One could wish, for instance, that the order of mass on weekdays be different from the order of mass on Sundays. The same thing could be desired for high feasts like Christmas, Easter, and Pentecost. Except for the sequence and, in some places, the renewal of baptismal vows, the order of mass for Easter day has, in fact, the same plan as the order for the other Sundays of the year.

Unfortunately we do not have any recorded account of how the mass was celebrated in the Roman parishes during the classical period. Reporters at that time, as in our day, were more interested in what took place during the papal masses than in what happened in an ordinary parish church.

The fact that the papal order of mass and, from the thirteenth century, the missal of the Roman curia became the standard rite for celebrating the eucharist does not mean that the Roman church has always had one order of mass. J. Jungmann makes an illuminating distinction between the episcopal collective service that developed into the *missa sollemnis* and the presbyteral mass that survived in the form of the *missa cantata*.[19]

In answer to the petition for different orders of mass the conciliar commission pointed to articles 30, 35, 51, 53, 107, and 109 of SC. To the mind of the conciliar commission these articles provided enough room for variations, without there being a need to have more than one order of mass. Article 30 asks that the people be encouraged to participate by means of acclamations, responses, psalmody, antiphons, and songs, as well as by actions, gestures, and bearing. Articles 35, 51, and 53 recommend that the readings from scripture be more varied and apposite, that the homily be drawn from the scriptural and liturgical sources, and that the prayer of the faithful or intercessions for the church, civil authorities, and the needs of all be restored. Articles 107 and 109 speak of "the traditional customs and usages of the sacred seasons," especially Lent, that should be preserved or restored to suit the conditions of modern times.

If these options are fully made use of, they can satisfy, at least in part, the need for variations within the order of mass. However, it seems obvious that they do not address the basic question, namely, must there be a single order of mass for every day of the year, regardless of whether it is Sunday, high solemnity, or ordinary weekday? At present, except for the hymn of the Gloria, the Creed, and the number of readings which may be reduced to two on Sundays, there is nothing in the order of mass to mark the difference between one liturgical day and another. The question, therefore, is about different ritual structures of the order of mass rather than the possible variations within the same structure.

Why the reluctance to have more than one order of mass? At the time of the council the idea of alternative orders of mass was surely regarded as a deviation from the long-standing tradition of the Roman rite. In 1604 Pope Clement VIII justified a uniform celebration of the eucharist, invoking the principle of church unity. Pope Paul VI himself explained that "St. Pius V offered it [the *editio princeps* of the Roman missal] to the people of Christ as the instrument of liturgical unity."[20] Of no other sacramental rite has a similar affirmation ever been made.

But times, even for the church, have changed. After the council the experience of local churches in the area of cultural adaptation, especially in the missions, has instilled into consciousness that church unity does not have to be anchored exclusively on the uniform observance of the liturgical rites. Even if SC 50 does not deal directly with cultural adaptation, its program of classical restoration has opened new horizons for cultural adaptation. By advocating the restoration of the classical form it unwittingly recreated an eighth-century situation. In short, it has given to the local churches the occasion, or one might say a perfect excuse, to do with the new order of mass what the Franco-Germanic churches did with the order of mass they received from Rome in the eighth century.

2. The Postconciliar Revision of the Order of Mass

Pope Paul VI's Apostolic Constitution *Missale Romanum* and the General Instruction of the Roman missal are documents that not only define the nature and shape of the new order of mass but also pave the way for the alternative orders of mass. It is evident from the *Missale Romanum* that the pope's chief concern was to keep to SC's principles of revision, namely the restoration of the classical form and the active participation of the faithful. The document affirms that SC 21, 50, 51, and 57, which are the pertinent articles for that matter, guided the work of revision. SC 21 and 50 are particularly relevant, since they deal explicitly with the question of recovering the noble simplicity and clarity of the Roman rite and the need to promote active participation.

With regard to the sources used for the elaboration of the new order of mass, Pope Paul VI writes: "No one should think that this revision of the Roman missal has come out of nowhere. The progress in liturgical studies during the last four centuries has certainly prepared the way."[21] Pope Pius V had attested that the ancient manuscripts in the Vatican library and elsewhere helped greatly in revising the Tridentine missal. We know for a fact, however, that the more important sources were discovered or critically edited only after the sixteenth century, and the forerunner of liturgical science, St. Giuseppe Tomasi, began his scholarly activity a century after the publication of the Tridentine missal.[22]

Apropos the General Instruction does point out that the Vatican manuscripts mentioned by Pope Pius V provided some verbal emendations, but they seldom allowed research to extend beyond the examination of a few liturgical commentators of the middle ages. "Today, on the other hand, countless studies of scholars have enriched the 'tradition of the fathers' that the reviewers of the missal under St. Pius V followed." In support of this the General Instruction enumerates the theological, spiritual, and liturgical gains of modern scholarship.[23]

In short, the two documents affirm that the new order of mass has achieved what the Roman missal of Pius V, given the difficult situation of the time and the limited access to the sources, was unable to realize. In the words of the General Instruction, "when the more profound elements of this tradition are considered, it becomes clear how remarkably and harmoniously this new Roman missal improves on the older one." And again, "the liturgical norms of the Council of Trent have been completed and improved in many respects by those of Vatican Council II."[24]

Throughout the various phases of the postconciliar reform we can observe how the program of renewal designed by the liturgical movement was carried out with unflinching resolve. The results are palpable. We must admit that active participation is one of the chief achievements of the new order of mass. Perhaps in no other period of liturgical history has active participation by the assembly received as much attention. Reading through the description of the papal mass in the Ordo Romanus I before the eighth century, that is, at the height of the classical period, one will be disappointed with the assembly's participation. One does not get the impression that the assembly took part in the acclamations, responses, and songs, unless the reporter did not bother to write on the subject.[25]

The new order of mass, on the other hand, was designed with active participation especially in mind. The General Instruction names several elements introduced into the new order of mass with the express intention of fostering among the faithful "a participation in body and spirit that is conscious, active, full, and motivated by faith, hope, and charity." Among these elements the following may be mentioned: the use of the vernacular; the obligatory homily on Sundays and holidays; the permission to interpose some commentary during the celebration; communion from the same sacrifice, that is, from the altar instead of from the tabernacle; communion under both kinds; the ritual and votive masses directed expressly to the needs of our time; and the revision of some euchological texts to suit modern conditions.[26]

The concrete instances of active participation abound. The General Instruction mentions them in detail: in the penitential rite, the profession of faith, the general intercessions, and the Lord's prayer; through responses and acclamations; through songs like the Gloria, Alleluia, and Sanctus; through movements and postures; and through prayerful silence.[27]

The other feature of the postconciliar order of mass is its preferential option for the classical form. It goes without saying that the revisors executed in earnest the directives of SC 50. Rites once perplexingly elaborate were simplified; duplications, which tended to become tiresome repetitions with little effect, were eliminated from the rites of offertory, breaking of bread, and communion; and the traditional elements that disappeared or lost their importance in the course of time, like the homily, the prayer of the faithful, and the penitential rite, were reintroduced.[28]

The work of revision, however, was not confined to the ambit of the classical Roman liturgy. By citing the progress in eucharistic theology brought about by the study of the Ambrosian, Spanish, Gallican, and Oriental traditions the General Instruction wanted to give a broader interpretation to the "tradition of the fathers." The scope of this tradition is not exclusively Roman, but embraces all the ways in which the Christian faith has been expressed by the different liturgical traditions. With such interpretation the General Instruction intended to justify the inclusion of non-Roman elements in the new order of mass. However, except for the adoption of some Ambrosian formularies and the Oriental inspiration that can be traced in some new compositions, the new order of mass is very much a Roman product.

The work of revision did away with or reduced to the minimum several Franco-Germanic and other medieval accretions, and thus streamlined the order of mass according to the specifications of classical reform. The flow of the celebration is now certainly smoother and the connection between the parts is now much clearer. But beneath what can be regarded as a successful undertaking there lurk some unsettling questions. Is the classical shape the ideal shape for the eucharistic celebration of a church that is culturally pluralistic? Must there be only one order of mass in the entire Roman church? Do the documents *Missale Romanum* and the General Instruction make provision for the cultural adaptation of the order of mass?

The answer to the last question is that Pope Paul VI's *Missale Romanum* does not make even a vague allusion to the issue of cultural adaptation. On the other hand, the General Instruction, which officially interprets *Missale Romanum* and executes the conciliar program of revision, admits that "the single faith has been expressed in the quite diverse human and social forms prevailing in Semitic, Greek, and Latin cultures."[29] According to this document, diversity in cultural expressions was partly responsible for the diversity in liturgical forms. Among the people of God, it declares, "prayers and rites differ so greatly." In other words, in the history of the order of mass cultural adaptation cannot be regarded as a closed book. That is why the General Instruction had to sponsor the most innovative decision made by the postconciliar renewal: "In accord with the Constitution on the Liturgy [SC 37–40], each conference of bishops has the power to lay down norms for its own territory that are suited to the traditions and character of peoples, regions and various communities."[30]

We should note that the General Instruction cites not only SC 38–39 but also SC 40. The conclusion seems obvious: the General Instruction endorses the radical adaptation of the order of mass to the culture and traditions of various peoples. By endorsing radical adaptation, which necessarily leads to alternative orders of mass, it dispenses with the old tradition of a single order of mass within the Roman rite.

3. Conclusion

The foregoing discussion allows us to draw four important considerations concerning the cultural adaptation of the order of mass.

1. SC 50's program of classical restoration has in a sense recreated a situation similar to what existed before the Roman order of mass migrated to the Franco-Germanic territories. Because of its simplicity, sobriety, and brevity the Roman rite will always be vulnerable to the compelling influence of other cultures. SC 50 has set the stage by restoring the order of mass to its classical shape. It provided the local churches with an ideal *terminus a quo* of cultural adaptation.

2. SC 50 and indeed the entire conciliar document gave an unequaled priority to full, active, and conscious participation. The order of mass was revised having in mind this fundamental principle of the liturgical movement and Vatican II. In the final analysis every liturgical adaptation is directed to the promotion of active participation.

3. The General Instruction explicated what at most was only a vague allusion to cultural adaptation in SC 50. The revised order of mass, like the other sacramental rites, can admit suitable elements of culture and traditions. Inculturation is an integral part of the council's vision of an updated eucharistic celebration. Since the General Instruction cites all four articles of SC on cultural adaptation, we may conclude that the variations in the order of mass are not confined to what is pastorally convenient.

4. Inculturation logically leads to the drawing up of particular orders of mass for local churches whose cultural setting differs radically from the one in which the classical Roman liturgy took shape. Considering the complex nature of the eucharistic celebration, the passage from the Roman order of mass to new alternative forms is a tremendous task ahead for the local churches. The new order of mass, which

is itself a passage from the older one, lays down the fundamental norms that must be observed when making the passage to the alternative forms of the eucharistic celebration, namely fidelity to sound liturgical tradition, a sense for creativity tempered by prudence, and respect for culture and traditions.

Toward Alternative Forms of the Order of Mass

1. The Question of Method

In matters relating to the adaptation of the order of mass, we can never be too scrupulous about the validity or soundness of the method we use. It is, of course, true that adaptation will always be accompanied by a certain tentativeness. What must be guarded against is instituting changes in the order of mass without liturgical criteria or a clear theological perception of the eucharistic celebration. This is indeed to plunge rashly into a difficult enterprise. Liturgical adaptation is a process, a method that requires various steps and accurately defined operations. The question is: How do we get off the ground?

In the preceding chapter of this book we discussed the method of cultural adaptation with accent on dynamic equivalence, and defined the constituent parts of the *terminus a quo,* namely the theological content and the liturgical shape. Before we apply that method to the adaptation of the order of mass we should say something about its theological content and liturgical shape. A great deal has been written on these aspects, but in particular the work of J. Jungmann, *The Mass of the Roman Rite,* and the one of S. Marsili, "Teologia della celebrazione dell'eucaristia," deserve to be cited.[31] Although recent scholarship on the history of the mass modifies some of Jungmann's affirmations, his work is a classic.

Elaborated in four parts, it traces the development of the eucharistic celebration through the centuries and offers a detailed historical account of the different parts of the order of mass. As in his other work, *The Early Liturgy,*[32] the author discusses the cultural factors that lie beneath each historical development, thereby calling attention to the cultural relativity of certain elements of the mass.

S. Marsili's work, on the other hand, is a masterpiece of liturgical theology. He proposes a theological method whose sustaining element is the anamnesis or memorial of Christ's paschal sacrifice. Seen in this light the supper of Jesus should be regarded not as the memorial of the ancient passover, but as the ritual anticipation of the new covenant in his blood.[33] The eucharistic celebration of the church, on the other hand, is "the sacrament of Christ's sacrifice" or, in other words, "the sacramental celebration of Christ's paschal sacrifice."[34]

With S. Marsili we can say that, while the last supper was the ritual anticipation of Christ's sacrifice on the cross, the church's eucharist, shaped according to the basic plan of the last supper, is its ritual memorial and hence its sacramental celebration. The last supper and the church's eucharist contain the mystery of Christ's cross and resurrection, the former in anticipation, the latter in anamnesis, but both in the shape of a meal.

With this premise we may approach the subject of adapting the order of mass by distinguishing the theological content of the eucharistic celebration from its liturgical shape. The theological content, if it refers to the substance of the sacrament, cannot obviously be the subject of change, although it can be reexpressed in ritual forms and linguistic style that suit the culture of the local church. Moreover, we should bear in mind that in the mass the sacrifice of Christ is celebrated as a sacrament, that is, in the form of a ritual meal. Hence, from a purely methodological consideration it would be a grave mistake to assign to the eucharistic celebration the external shape of a sacrificial rite. The mass indeed contains the sacrifice of Christ, but its outward shape as sacrament is in the form of a ritual meal.

Because we are so accustomed to use such theological short-cuts as "the mass *is* the sacrifice of the cross" in place of the fuller statement "the mass is the *sacrament* of Christ's sacrifice on the cross," and "the bread *is* the body of Christ" instead of "the bread is the *sacrament* of Christ's body," the possibility of confusing the theological content with the liturgical shape is not too remote even in our day.

The ninth century mass commentator, Amalar of Metz, inspired probably by Theodore of Mopsuestia and Narsai, explained the rite of the mass allegorically in the context of Christ's life and above all his passion. He was correct in affirming that the passion of Christ is present in the sacrament of bread and wine, but he was wrong in trying to give evidence of the passion in the various elements of the mass. In his *Expositio Missae* he interprets the preface as the hymn at the last supper; the different parts of the canon as Christ's prayer at Gethsemani, his being raised on the cross, and his crying out with a loud voice as he breathed his last; and the recitation of the Lord's prayer as Christ's burial.[35]

The confusion between the theological content and the liturgical shape has, in liturgical practice, led many to regard the eucharistic table as altar of sacrifice and the president of the assembly as priest. No doubt the table, by theological association with the sacrifice, is called altar, but it should not lose thereby the appearance of table for the eucharistic meal. The president of the assembly, inasmuch as he acts in the person of Christ, must be an ordained presbyter, but his visible function at mass is to preside. The real danger occurs when bloody rites, like peace pacts, are incorporated into the mass to heighten its character as a sacrifice for peace!

The liturgical shape of the mass is ritual meal with

accent on ritual; hence, it can be highly stylized. Its components of assembly, presiding minister, bread and wine, eucharistic prayer, and communion give it the shape of a meal, but do not necessarily make it a dinner by candlelight. The celebration of the eucharist in the dining room to create the semblance of a meal misses the point about the mass being a meal without being a dinner.

The liturgical shape of the Order of Mass is defined for us by the General Instruction of the Roman missal: "The Mass is made up as it were of the liturgy of the word and the liturgy of the eucharist. . . . There are also certain rites to open and conclude the celebration."[36] For purposes of adaptation, it is useful to keep in mind the dynamics present in all four parts of the eucharistic celebration, particularly in the liturgy of the word and in the liturgy of the eucharist. In so many words the General Instruction describes the liturgy of the word as a ritual dialogue between God and the assembly: God proclaims his word, the president explains it, and the people, having been fed by this word, make their petitions in the prayer of the faithful. The readings from sacred scripture, the homily, and the general intercessions are thus the three integral elements of the liturgy of the word. Together they constitute the ritual dialogue.[37]

Because of its dialogical plan the liturgy of the word readily lends itself to cultural adaptation. Cultural groups possess their own set of time-honored ritual gestures, symbols, and formularies as well as regulations on the time and place for holding dialogues. Together these ritual elements constitute the integral plan of a dialogue. When adapting the liturgy of the word, it is necessary to bear in mind this integral plan. The idea is to avoid making adaptations in pieces, that is, elaborating one element according to a particular dialogical structure but leaving the rest untouched according to the plan of the Roman liturgy. It is not expedient to adapt piecemeal, when one is dealing with something like a dialogue whose dynamics require a smooth flow from one element to another, that is, from speaking and listening to responding.

The elements of the liturgy of the word that can be reviewed from the point of view of a dialogue are its structural outline, the place and furnishings for the reading, the manner of proclamation, the form of the homily and the intercessions, the external appearance of the books, and the bodily posture of the assembly. In the Roman liturgy the dialogue begins somewhat abruptly, that is, when the reader goes to the lectern to read. For some cultural groups abruptness is synonymous with lack of social refinement. It is true that the introductory rites prepare the assembly for the entire celebration and hence also for the liturgy of the word. But the apposite rites to introduce the word of God, as we find in the Oriental liturgies, do not exist in the Roman rite.

In some places, also the traditional Roman pattern of listening needs to be reviewed. Reading or speaking while everyone listens in silence is a behavioral pattern that is alien to a people for whom listening involves audience participation through interjections of approval and appreciation. In a way, the insertion of the memorial acclamation and responses into the texts of the eucharistic prayer has served to interrupt this "long prayer," as St. Justin describes it. Probably this was the idea behind the medieval practice of repeating the conclusion "Through Christ our Lord" at several parts of the Roman canon.

Regarding the liturgy of the eucharist the General Instruction explains that "the church has planned the celebration of the eucharistic liturgy around the parts corresponding to the words and actions of Christ" at the last supper. These words and actions refer principally to what he did when he took the bread and the cup, said the prayer of blessing and thanksgiving, and distributed the sacred elements to his disciples. Accordingly the liturgy of the eucharist has three corresponding parts: the preparation of the gifts, the eucharistic prayer, and the breaking of bread and communion.[38]

It may take some effort to recognize the elements of the last supper in the actual shape of the liturgy of the eucharist. The various rites for the preparation of the gifts and the formulary of the eucharistic prayer have become so stylized that their resemblance to what took place at the last supper is not immediately apparent. Nevertheless, it is not impossible to detect in the three parts of the liturgy of the eucharist the presence of a ritual meal designed according to the plan of the last supper.

If the liturgy of the word lends itself to cultural adaptation because of its dialogical form, the liturgy of the eucharist does so because of its meal structure. Apropos we can think of two methodological considerations that affect the work of adapting the meal structure.

The first consideration concerns the liturgical shape of the celebration. It must relate to the last supper. Its structural plan or arrangement has to be such that it is able to evoke what Jesus did on the night before he died: he took the bread and the cup, he gave thanks, and he gave the bread and the cup to his disciples. Regardless of the meal-shape it assumes from other cultures, the liturgy of the eucharist must always project the supper of the Lord.

The second consideration is with respect to the type of meal on which the celebration of the last supper must be modeled, namely a meal of a ritual kind. By this we exclude such forms of meal as breakfast and lunch or the regular midday meal between breakfast and dinner. Their ordinariness does not represent the special character of the last supper. Needless to say, choosing the suitable type of ritual meal can be rather tortuous. Can the liturgy of the eucharist be arranged according to the ritual plan of funeral meals or of sacrificial banquets? Is the model of socio-religious meals like the thanksgiving dinner—if it is possible at all to identify its ritual elements—appropriate? Can these types of meal project the last supper aspect of the eucharist? It is obvious that the meal approach will present many loose ends. But as a method it is sound and, unlike the approach that seeks to incorporate sacrificial rites into the mass, it does not run the risk of confusing the theological content with the liturgical form of the eucharistic celebration.

Although some texts of the mass, above all the eucharistic prayer, contain theological affirmations regarding the sacrificial character of the mass, the plan of the liturgy of the eucharist follows the basic shape of the last supper. Hence, the work of adaptation should not ignore the meal aspect of the preparation of gifts, the recitation of the eucharistic prayer, and the rite of communion. The same observation applies to the arrangement of the sanctuary, the appearance of the eucharistic table and its furnishings,[39] and the manner of presenting the gifts and of setting them on the table.

The question of greater or lesser ritualization is a matter that belongs in large measure to cultural patterns. The revised order of mass eliminated practices connected with the eucharistic prayer, like ringing the sanctuary bell, bringing in more candles at the Sanctus, and incensing the sacred species at the elevation. These forms of ritualization, so dear to the Catholics of the baroque period, heightened the solemnity of the consecration and proclaimed the Church's faith in the real presence. By simplifying the rites the General Instruction wishes to put the accent on the words being recited: "The eucharistic prayer calls for all to listen in silent reverence, but also to take part through the acclamations for which the rite makes provision."[40]

Listening in silent reverence, however, does not have to be interpreted as the total absence of ritual accompaniment. Although the assigned acclamations are considered the most appropriate mode of participating in the eucharistic prayer, there are surely other ways of fostering this in consonance with the religious culture of the people. Humming in unison or in voices the tune of the words of consecration as these are sung by the president of the assembly can be, for the assembly, a very moving and meaningful experience.

But something needs to be said about the text of the eucharistic prayer. In the letter approving the twelve points of adaptation presented by the bishops of India, the postconciliar Consilium made it known that "the proposal to compose a new Indian anaphora in collaboration with experts in different fields is most welcome. When completed, copies should be sent to the Consilium for study. It might help if this were not publicized too much."[41]

In 1973 the Congregation for Divine Worship issued the Circular Letter *Eucharistiae participationem* on the eucharistic prayers. In this letter the congregation made it clear that the Holy See reserves to itself the right to regulate the discipline of the eucharistic prayers. However, "the Apostolic See will not refuse to consider lawful needs within the Roman rite and will accord every consideration to the petitions submitted by the conferences of bishops for the possible composition in special circumstances of a new eucharistic prayer and its introduction into the liturgy."[42]

Within a couple of years a number of new eucharistic prayers and prefaces were approved for use in individual countries or regions. The indult to compose new eucharistic prayers stemmed in a measure from the need of some local churches for liturgical texts that suit their cultural expressions. The eucharistic prayers in the Roman missal are not always able to meet such a need. The Roman canon, in particular, "has its distinctive style, deeply imbued with the Roman taste for a certain gravity and for a simultaneous redundance and brevity." Due to this cultural trait "its unity and the logical sequence of its ideas are not immediately or readily perceptible. It leaves the impression of discrete, merely juxtaposed prayers; it requires a degree of reflection for a grasp of their unity."[43]

The Congregation for Divine Worship restricts the use of original eucharistic prayers to the places for which permission has been granted.[44] The restriction is not a purely disciplinary matter. If a eucharistic prayer is composed having in mind the particular thought and language pattern of the people as well as their literary tradition and life experience, it will surely not be usable elsewhere. And the question does not depend on whether one is dealing with one or several languages. For the same language may be spoken in different countries and continents, but the images that the words produce will be conditioned by the history, traditions, climate, actual experience, and above all the particular character of each people. In this sense the eucharistic prayer for the use of a local church can hardly be the product of a joint international venture.

We should note at this juncture that for the composition of original eucharistic prayers there are, besides the juridical regulations that we mentioned in the first chapter of this book, also liturgical norms regarding the content and the shape of a eucharistic prayer. The General Instruction enumerates the following chief elements making up the eucharistic prayer: thanksgiving which is expressed especially in the preface; acclamation or Sanctus; consecratory and communion epiclesis; institution narrative with the words of consecration; anamnesis of Christ's passion, resurrection, and ascension; memorial offering; intercessions for the church and all its members, both living and dead; and final doxology.[45]

These elements can be appreciated better in the light of what the Consilium declared to be the essentials of the eucharistic prayer. According to it, the eucharistic prayer is made up of a central core and its further elaborations. The central core "is the narrative-reactualization of what Jesus did at the last supper, leaving out only the breaking of the bread and the communion, which come at the final part of the mass." This core consists of the following: the hymn of thanksgiving and praise to the Father; the narrative of Jesus' actions and the words he spoke when he instituted the eucharist; the prayer of supplication addressed to the Father, asking that he make the narrative effective by transforming the bread and wine into the body and blood of Christ; the prayer with which the holy gifts are offered in memory of Christ's paschal mystery; and the doxology to which the people reply: Amen. This central core is further elaborated by three elements, namely the Sanctus, the intercessory prayers, and the commemoration of the saints.[46]

There is one last point about the eucharistic prayer that needs to be considered. Because of its immediate link with the last supper and the words of consecration, it has a well-defined scope and plan. It is not a prayer for all occasions nor can it be used as a compendium of all the dogmatic and moral statements of the magisterium. In it "it is not always or easily possible to achieve a precise adaptation to the different groups or circumstances and a complete expression of its catechetical function. These are to be achieved in those parts and formularies of the liturgical service that allow or require variations."[47]

The other parts of the order of mass, namely the introductory rites and the concluding rite, have a secondary role. The General Instruction explains that the purpose of the introductory rites "is that the faithful coming together take on the form of a community and prepare themselves to listen to God's word and celebrate the eucharist properly."[48] The concluding rite, on the other hand, consists basically of the blessing and dismissal of the assembly, whereby "each member is sent back to doing good works, while praising and blessing the Lord."[49]

While the introductory rites of the revised order of mass have an elaborate layout, especially on solemn occasions, the concluding rite is the paradigm of Roman simplicity and brevity. The main thing about them, however, is not how they are planned or how long it takes to perform them, for structure is easily influenced by culture, and time-length can be a very relative matter among some peoples. The chief consideration is what their names indicate: they introduce and conclude the eucharistic celebration. This point is sometimes overlooked, when in reality it is the methodological consideration with which to begin and pursue the work of adapting these rites.

The future shape of the introductory rites will depend to some extent upon the social rituals or traditions of each cultural group. While some have the propensity for solemn or even dramatic introductory rites, others prefer a simple opening speech. The entrance rite of the papal mass described by the first *Ordo Romanus* was carried out in the full splendor of an imperial court. We do not know what the entrance rite looked like in the Roman parishes at that time, but it surely kept the traditional sobriety and simplicity of the Roman liturgy.

Something similar may be said in connection with the concluding rite. In some cultures leave-taking takes a considerable amount of time because of the social graces, assurances of friendship or respect, and the advice and blessing by the elders. These rituals normally accompany leave-taking which, for this reason, could go on endlessly. This is an aspect that should be taken into consideration when adapting the plan of the concluding rite. The length of time is not the decisive element here, but the cultural form which gives to the eucharistic celebration a fitting conclusion.

The principle of right proportion, in the sense of assigning respectively a longer or a shorter period of time to the principal or subsidiary parts of the mass, is by no means absolute. The importance and value of a thing cannot be reckoned on this score alone. The eucharistic prayer, which is the heart of the entire eucharistic celebration, takes a short time to recite and has a relatively sober ritual. The preparation of gifts, on the other hand, is made up of elaborate rites and on solemn occasions may be embellished by the use of incense. In fact, a feast that lasts but a couple of hours may require preparations extending for several days. The bottom line is what function we give to each part of the order of mass. So long as the assembly can perceive the meaning and the function of the introductory and concluding rites, the question of elaborate structure or length of time is quite academic.

2. The Passage from the Roman Order of Mass

Cultural adaptation may be described as a movement from the *terminus a quo* to the *terminus ad quem,* from the Roman order of mass to new alternative forms. It is obvious that anyone who embarks on cultural adaptation must possess an adequate knowledge of the Roman order of mass, especially of its cultural traits. The recommendation given by SC 23 cannot be repeated ad nauseam: "That sound tradition may be retained and yet the way remain open to legitimate progress, a careful investigation is always to be made into each part of the liturgy to be revised."

Early on we made the observation that the revised order of mass is in large measure the product of the liturgical movement which untiringly worked for the restoration of the classical forms. In the new order of mass some ancient euchological texts have, of course, been modified "so that the style of language would be more in accord with the language of modern theology and would faithfully reflect the actual state of the church's discipline." Others have been adapted to contemporary needs and circumstances. The revised order of mass is, however, not an exclusively classical production. It has newly composed texts, many of which draw on the doctrine and even use the expressions of the conciliar documents *Lumen Gentium* and *Gaudium et Spes.*

The General Instruction admits that "many expressions, drawn from the church's most ancient tradition and become familiar through the many editions of the Roman missal, have remained unchanged."[50] Hence, a good number of euchological texts in the new *editio typica* reflect what E. Bishop has called the "genius of the Roman rite." They retain their original clear-cut outline, sobriety of expression, and doctrinal content. In keeping with the Roman cultural traits of simplicity, directness, and sobriety, the new formularies have been composed in the style of the classical ones. Thus, even if the corpus of the liturgical texts in the revised Roman missal represents sources dating from ancient, medieval, and modern times, its formularies share, in varying degrees, the same literary style. Hence, in spite of its complex nature it does not, as a whole, constitute an unwieldy *terminus a quo* of cultural adaptation. In this connection one can find practical help in the studies of A. Dumas and J. Johnson-A. Ward on the collects and prefaces of the new missal.[51]

Another aspect of the *terminus a quo* is ritual simplicity and practical sense. We noted in the preceding chapter that these traits date back to the classical era of the Roman rite. The original Roman order of mass was developed in accord with a culture that was not particularly keen on dramatic and symbolic expressions. The exceptional occurrence of symbolic gestures during the papal mass which the first Ordo Romanus so minutely describes were at best borrowed from the liturgical usage of the eastern churches. Examples of these are facing the east at the singing of the Gloria and at the recitation of the collect and making the sign of the cross three times over the chalice at the rite of commixtion.[52] Even the practice of sending the *fermentum* to the parishes, an eloquent symbol of eucharistic unity with the bishop of Rome, is said to have been introduced by Pope Melchiades who was an African by birth.[53]

As we pointed out earlier, the revision of the order of mass was guided by SC 21, 34, and 50 which in turn had been influenced by the classical liturgical movement. There is no need to go over the new order of mass or to compare it with the previous one to prove that the work of classical revision has taken the necessary steps to make the texts and rites easier to understand and to eliminate useless repetitions and duplications. Yet it is precisely this classical form of the revised order of mass that has been assailed time and again for having caused the eucharistic celebration to become so anemic and arid. In a sense the criticism is founded. But then the *editio typica* cannot be faulted by those who have taken the *terminus a quo* for the *terminus ad quem.*

What value should we then attach to the classical character of the new order of mass? Although its shape is defined by the cultural qualities of the classical Roman rite, its orientation is decisively pastoral. Simplicity, for example, has a definite pastoral purpose, namely to make the meaning of the texts and the rites easily accessible to the assembly. That is why the passage from the *terminus a quo* cannot neglect entirely the cultural genius of the Roman rite. To dismiss the Roman quality of simplicity in favor of an intricacy that leads to confusion is to move in the wrong direction. Intricacy is not synonymous with a carefully worked out elaboration of a simple text or rite.

Repetitiousness, on the other hand, is not the same as a well-balanced repetition or duplication for the sake of emphasis. SC 34 does not speak against repetition as such but against the tiresome effect of useless repetitions. Roman simplicity simply means that "the intrinsic nature and purpose of the various parts of the order of mass, as also the connection between them," are clearly defined and can be easily understood. The plainness of the eucharistic celebration or its embellishment is often a matter of a people's cultural taste and predisposition. What is important is that by their clarity—a quality which does not exclude repetition and elaboration—the texts and rites can be grasped easily by the liturgical assembly.

Another aspect of the *terminus a quo* is the doctrinal content of the formularies. The remark is often made that the Roman euchology appeals more to the intellect than to the human sentiment. This is particularly true of several collects and prefaces authored by theologians like Pope Leo the Great and Pope Gregory the Great. How much theology the assembly learned as collects and prefaces were solemnly pronounced in the Roman basilicas is difficult to ascertain, but one can assume that that type of scholarly discourse must have greatly pleased its listeners. Today we tend to favor the kind of prayer that speaks not only to the mind but also to the heart, and uses not so much the rational categories as the images taken from our daily experience of God, people, and nature.

Nevertheless, the doctrinal content of the Roman formularies belongs to the church's theological heritage. As such it is one of the elements of the *terminus a quo* that should not be allowed to disappear in the process of cultural adaptation. To ensure this, it is necessary to identify the theological content of each formulary and to distinguish it from the literary form in which it is expressed. The famous Leonine collect for Christmas, for example,[54] is composed according to the rhythmical disposition of the *cursus* and adorned by figures of rhetoric like periphrasis, pleonasm, epanaphora, paronomasia, and parallelism. Beneath this impressive literary form we can perceive an equally impressive doctrinal content: God created us in the dignity of human nature and now makes us sharers in the divine nature of his incarnate Son. We probably have no use for the

Latin rhetoric, but the doctrine is not something we should dismiss.

If we fail to identify the content and distinguish the literary form, we run the risk of dismissing the entire corpus of Roman euchology as irrelevant because of its particular literary form. As a result, the theological and spiritual riches contained in the Roman corpus will be irretrievably lost to the local churches. Cultural adaptation, therefore, does not mean breaking from the Roman *terminus a quo* in order to espouse a totally new creation; rather it means taking a step forward in liturgical tradition.

3. The Passage to Alternative Orders of Mass

The General Instruction of the Roman missal speaks of two types of adaptation: one by the minister in the course of the celebration,[55] and the other by the conferences of bishops. Regarding the second type the General Instruction mentions several ways of adapting to the cultural expressions and to the various needs of each local church the order of mass and the furnishing for the eucharistic celebration. Over the years a number of conferences of bishops have issued concrete norms on the matter. We confine ourselves to the enumeration of what the General Instruction allows.

First, the conferences of bishops may adapt the actions and postures described in the revised order of mass to the customs of the people. Second, they approve the text of the songs to be sung in place of those found in the *Graduale Romanum* or the Simple Gradual. Third, they may determine, in accord with the culture and customs of the people, the form that the sign of peace should take. Fourth, they may substitute the traditional practice of kissing the eucharistic table and the gospel book with some other sign in harmony with the traditions or the culture of the region. Fifth, they have the discretion to introduce, in place of natural stone, the use of some other solid, becoming, and well-crafted material for fixed altars. Sixth, they decide on the kind of materials for sacred furnishings in keeping with the genius and traditions of each people. Seventh, they judge the suitability of the materials to be used for chalices and other vessels. And eighth, they may determine and propose to the Holy See adaptations in the design, materials, and color of vestments in accord with the needs, usages, and culture of the region.[56]

Twenty-three days after the publication of the General Instruction the postconciliar Consilium approved the twelve points of cultural adaptation in the order of mass presented by the conference of bishops of India. We can distinguish two types: one referring to gestures and material elements, the other to the structure of the order of mass.

With reference to the first type we can mention the following points: adopting for both the priest and the faithful the posture of sitting on the floor; making the profound bow known as *anjali hasta* instead of genuflection; kneeling and touching the floor with the forehead in the manner of *panchanga pranam* at the penitential rite and, as sign of adoration, at the conclusion of the eucharistic prayer; touching sacred objects with the fingers or the palm of the hand and bringing the hands to one's eyes or forehead as a sign of respect; doing the *anjali hasta* to express the sign of peace; using an incense bowl with handle in place of the thurible; using the tray known as *thali* or *thamboola thattu* for the corporal; and adopting the single tunic-type chasuble called *angavastra* with a stole.

The second type includes the following points: modifying the entrance rite so as to incorporate into it the presentation of gifts, the Indian rite of welcoming the celebrant, the ceremony of lighting the lamp, and the exchange of the sign of peace; permitting some spontaneity with regard to the structure and formulation of the prayer of the faithful; and incorporating into the offertory rite and the conclusion of the eucharistic prayer the Indian form of worship consisting of a double or triple *arati* of flowers, incense, and light.[57]

One will observe that the twelve points include ritual elements and postures borrowed from Hindu social and religious ceremonies. In his commentary D.S. Amalorpavadass gives the assurance that such elements are "universally accepted in the country and involve or affect no doctrinal principles."[58] They are, according to him, "a first, modest, step to give to our liturgy a more Indian setting and complexion." Although to his mind "most of them are little more than an intelligent interpretation of the present rubrics," they represent in reality the first significant attempt after the council to adapt the order of mass.

The attempt acquires a greater significance in the light of its methodological approach. Besides replacing traditional Roman rites with equivalent native elements, it develops in detail some parts of the order of mass. The *panchanga pranam* and the double or triple *arati* at the end of the eucharistic prayer are examples of how the assembly's response to the prayer of sacrifice can be culturally enriched. But it is the structural elaboration of the entrance rite—however trivial it might have seemed at that time—that has a far-reaching repercussion on the adaptation of the order of mass. Two new elements, namely the rite of welcoming the priest and the ritual lighting of the lamp, are added to the entrance rite. Moreover, the presentation of the eucharistic gifts and the sign of peace are transferred here from the traditional place they occupy in the Roman order of mass.[59]

In the early 1970's these changes were considered radical. They showed that not only such external elements as posture, incense holder, and vestments, but also the structure of the Roman order of mass can be adapted and modified. For different reasons the realization of the twelve points suffered a setback. However, the attempt signaled for the Roman church the first official passage to alternative orders of mass.[60]

Another attempt, this time with better results though not with less vicissitude, is the *Missel Romain pour les diocèses du Zaïre.* The project was begun in 1970 with the blessing of the Congregation for Divine Worship. Its aim was to give to the Roman order of mass an African and Zaïrean cultural form. Three years later, the conference of bishops presented the project to the Holy See for authorization to make the preliminary experiments. What elapsed between 1973 and April 30, 1988, when the project was officially approved by the Holy See,[61] is an interesting chapter in the history of liturgical adaptation.[62]

The plan of the celebration follows the Roman order of mass, except for the penitential rite and the sign of peace, which have been relocated to the liturgy of the word after the homily or the creed. This new arrangement, according to the dossier presented by the bishops to the congregation, was inspired by the structure of the *palabre africaine* centered on the words of the elder and by the fundamental truth that God's word calls us to conversion and reconciliation. Hence, the basic outline consisting of the proclamation of the word of God, repentance, and sign of peace.[63]

The entire celebration itself focuses on the presence of the sacred, of God, and the world of spirits and ancestors with whom the assembly is asked to commune in an attitude of humility and awe. That is why not only the saints but also the "ancestors of righteous heart" are invoked during the entrance litany: V: "You, our ancestors of righteous heart." R: "Be with us." The conference of bishops explains that by becoming a Christian an African does not sever all relationship with the ancestors. Invoking them in Christian worship is consequently a pastoral and liturgical imperative. The conference argues further that the ancestors of righteous heart are, through the merits of Christ, in communion with God and hence can be invoked in the liturgy just as Abel, Abraham, and Melchizedek are remembered in the Roman liturgy.

This line of argumentation will not allay all apprehensions about the acceptability of invoking during mass the presence of ancestors who lived outside the ambit of the old and new covenants. To remember the ancestors before God is one thing; to address them directly and call on them to be present during the liturgy is another. But in places where ancestral veneration is deeply rooted in the religious culture of the people, the church, which has learned a hard lesson from the Chinese rites controversy, can ill afford to refuse the invocation of ancestors in liturgical worship.[64]

The other changes in the *editio typica* are of elaborative nature. The following are some notable examples. At the entrance rite introductions are made by an "announcer" whose role can be described as a cross between the function of a tribal herald and that of a liturgical commentator. The president of the assembly, with arms extended in V-form, venerates the eucharistic table by touching its four sides with his forehead. At the singing of the Gloria, the assembly is invited to perform the traditional rhythmic movements, while the president of the assembly and the other ministers "dance" around the altar. The sign of peace may be done by the assembly by washing the hands in the same basin. At the liturgy of the word the reader receives the blessing, and the gospel book is enthroned. Incense is burnt during the general intercessions "so that the smoke may rise up together with the prayer of the faithful." At the presentation of gifts a brief dialogue is held between one of the offerers and the president of the assembly. Tam-tam accompanies the chants, and the gong the narration of the institution. The shape and color of the chasuble, dalmatic, and tunic are those proper to Zaïre.

As one can observe, these Zaïrean adaptations have been inspired by both Christian and native usages. Some of them, like the sign for venerating the altar and the sign of peace, are dynamic equivalents of the traditional Roman practices. Others, like the dance and the use of incense, elaborate on the different parts of the mass. Several elements belong to the African culture, but their transcultural quality renders them easily accessible to the people of other cultures.[65]

The eucharistic prayer is an interesting example of euchology for a local church. Drawn up in accord with "the biblical values, the nature of the Catholic liturgy, and the religious genius and cultural heritage of Africa and Zaïre," it displays something so Roman and yet so Zaïrean. Its outline, from the initial dialogue and preface to the final doxology, follows faithfully the Roman model: preface and Sanctus, consecratory epiclesis, institution narrative, anàmnesis and memorial offering, communion epiclesis, intercessions, and final doxology. In content it does not differ from the other eucharistic prayers in the Roman missal.

However, the composition is Zaïrean. To foster active participation the preface, intercessions, and final doxology have been worked out in such a way that the assembly can easily respond or, in typically African tradition, interject at appropriate moments. The text was originally composed in Lingala and was translated later into French. Obviously a translation, however good it might be, cannot capture the images, nuances, and idioms present in the original text. The Zaïrean bishops assure us, however, that a great effort was exerted to incorporate into the original text the traits of the African language, namely its sonority, its inclination to repeat words, and its facility to use images, enigmatic expressions, and allusions.[66]

The mass for Zaïre and the twelve points concerning the order of mass for India are two pioneering models of cultural adaptation. They not only opened new horizons but also gave concrete example of how the passage from the Roman order of mass to new alternative forms can be achieved. In both models we observe that the Roman form was the *terminus a quo* of the long and arduous process. We observe too that they have faithfully guarded the theological and spiritual treasures of tradition and have even enriched this tradition with new textual and ritual forms derived from the culture and customs of the people. The effects they have on the faithful are, according to the report of the bishops of Zaïre, "a more lively participation" in the celebration of the eucharist and "a deeper understanding of the mystery of Christ the Redeemer."[67] Surely the appearance of these new orders of mass is a major step forward in liturgical tradition, a legitimate progress based on sound tradition.

A third model, submitted to the Congregation for Divine Worship in 1976, is the *Misa ng Bayang Filipino* or the order of mass for the Philippines. Originally composed in Tagalog, it was translated into English for study purposes. The *Misa* closely follows the plan of the Roman mass, including the eucharistic prayer.[68] Since to date it has not received the blessing of Rome, it is gradually disappearing from the parish scene where it made its debut in 1976.[69]

The chief features of the *Misa* are the incorporation of Filipino religious practices, which mean Catholic baroque traditions, and the elaboration of texts according to the speech pattern of the Tagalogs. The baroque elements can be recognized throughout the celebration, but especially at the eucharistic prayer. At the start of the eucharistic prayer church bells are rung and candles are lit, and at the end, as the priest raises the consecrated bread and wine, the assembly sings a eucharistic doxology while church bells are rung festively. One might object to such baroque manifestations of eucharistic piety at a time when the conciliar reform has eliminated most of them from the mass. For the Filipino

Catholics, however, the baroque is a living culture which is deeply ingrained in native religious sentiments and traditions. The special focus on baroque ritual elements was meant to bring the eucharistic celebration closer to the ambit of a religious culture richly adorned with baroque manifestations.

As regards the texts, a considerable effort was made to incorporate into the eucharistic prayer some of the elements of the Tagalog language, especially idiomatic expressions and those words and phrases that evoke Filipino values or conjure up images from daily life.[70] The preface, for instance, is wrapped in typical Filipino modesty or unassuming behavior in the presence of a person of higher status. It humbly admits that "our tongues fail us when we speak of your power and boundless mercy." The Tagalog text has the idiomatic expression *kapos ang dila namin* (literally, "our tongues do not measure up") which is used to preface a formal speech to praise and thank a personage.

There is also an attempt to capture in Tagalog words certain theological concepts like epiclesis and anamnesis which can prove to be the stumbling block of translators. For both the consecratory and communion epiclesis the text uses the word *lukuban* which calls to mind the action of a bird brooding its eggs. We read at the communion epiclesis: "Father, grant us your Holy Spirit. May he look upon us with favor and take us lovingly under his wing (*lukuban*)." The Tagalog word is a graphic description of the vivifying and transforming action of the Holy Spirit on the eucharistic elements and on the assembly. The concept of anamnesis, on the other hand, is expressed by the phrase *tandang-tanda pa namin* (literally, "we still clearly remember") which introduces the institution narrative. The phrase is used when relating past events of great significance. Here it means that the church is a witness of what happened at the last supper, remembers its details with freshness, and now narrates the event as part of its living tradition.

Another feature of the eucharistic prayer is the translation of the Sanctus. This acclamation presents linguistic difficulties for Tagalog, as it probably does for other languages. The repetition of the word three times does not conform to the Tagalog grammar and pattern of speech. The solution reached was to retain the triple Sanctus while elaborating it each time: "Holy are you, Almighty Father, holy is your name, holy is your kingdom. Heaven and earth resound with praise for your glory."[71] This translation, meant originally for the *Misa ng Bayang Filipino,* was adopted by the official Tagalog translation of the Roman missal, the *Aklat ng Pagmimisa sa Roma* approved by the Holy See in 1981.[72]

Although the text of the *Misa* begins to gather dust and the celebrations are now a rare occurrence, at times in the interest of promoting the use of the Tagalog language, the work cannot be said to have been in vain. In its own way it contributes to the process of bringing about alternative forms of the eucharistic celebration. Unlike the Indian model, which is adapted to the rites and language of the Hindu religion, and the Zaïrean, which is shaped largely according to native cultural patterns, the *Misa ng Bayang Filipino* is framed in the Catholic traditional practices, especially of the baroque type, and in a religious language that developed through four centuries of contact with Christianity. The Filipino situation is not an isolated case, if one considers the local churches in Latin America and even some remote parts of Europe. At least for the church in the Philippines the *Misa* was able to uncover the hidden treasure of Filipino Catholic rites, symbols, and linguistic expressions and to suggest that these elements need not be alienated from the celebration of Christ's paschal mystery.

Notes

[1] *Institutio Generalis Missalis Romani*, henceforth *IGMR*, *Missale Romanum*, Vatican City 1975, Introduction, no. 8, pp. 22–23; *DOL*, p. 467.

[2] "Ordo Missae," *La riforma liturgica*, Rome 1983, pp. 332–88. For the background of the new Roman Missal see idem: "Il nuovo Messale romano," *ibid.*, pp. 389–400. See also R. Cabié: "L'«Ordo Missae» de Paul VI," *L'Église en prière* II, Paris 1983, pp. 205–37.

[3] *Schema Constitutionis de Sacra Liturgia*, henceforth *Schema*, De Sacrosancto Eucharistiae Mysterio, Emendationes VI, Vatican City 1963, p. 26: *Ordo Missae ita recognoscatur, sive in generali dispositione sive in singulis partibus, ut clarius percipiatur et actuosam fidelium participationem faciliorem reddat.*

[4] *Ibid.*, p. 15.

[5] *Schema*, Emendationes VI, p. 32: *Inter singulas vero partes Ordinis Missae, illae potissimum recognoscendae videntur quae in initio, ad Offertorium, ad Communionem et in fine accesserunt, praesertim cum ritus romanus in Gallia assumptus et ex indole gallico-germanica in formam novam radactus est, quam Ecclesia romana postea adoptavit.*

[6] In his *Regula Canonica* Pope Gregory VII observed: *Romani autem diverso modo agere coeperunt, maxime a tempore quo Teutonicis concessum est regimen nostrae Ecclesiae. Nos autem et ordinem romanum et antiquum morem investigantes, statuimus fieri nostrae Ecclesiae sicut superius praenotavimus, antiquos imitantes patres.* G. Morin: "Études, textes, découvertes," *Analecta Maredsolana*, Paris 1913, pp. 459–60. See M. Andrieu: *Le Pontifical Romain au moyen-âge* I, *Studi e Testi* 86, Vatican City 1972, pp. 3–19; C. Vogel: *Medieval Liturgy*, trans. and revised by W. Storey and N. Rasmussen, Washington, D.C. 1986, pp. 249–51.

[7] *Apostolic Constitution "Quod a nobis"* of 1568: *Quae divini Officii formula . . . a Summis Pontificibus, praesertim Gelasio ac Gregorio Primo constituta, a Gregorio autem VII reformata, cum diuturnitate temporis ab antiqua institutione deflexisset, necessaria visa est, quae ad pristinam orandi regulam revocaretur.* See R. Taft:

The Liturgy of the Hours in East and West, Collegeville 1986, pp. 307–17. For bibliography see: A.-G. Martimort: "La prière des heures," *L'Église en prière* IV, Paris 1983, pp. 168–71.

[8] *Apostolic Constitution "Quo primum"* of 1570: *ad pristinam Missale ipsum sanctorum Patrum normam ac ritum restituerunt. Missale Romanum,* Rome 1962, p. viii.

[9] See *IGMR,* Introduction, no. 7, *DOL,* p. 467.

[10] For the decrees of the Synod see: J. Mansi: *Sacrorum Conciliorum Nova et Amplissima Collectio* 38, Graz 1960–62, pp. 989–1282. See C. Bolton: *Church Reform in the 18th-Century Italy (The Synod of Pistoia, 1786),* The Hague 1969, pp. 55–114.

[11] *Schema,* Emendationes VI, p. 32. See A. Bugnini: "Ordo Missae," *La riforma liturgica,* pp. 334–35.

[12] The Preparatory Commission declared: *Nonnulla tamen [Ordinis Missae] passim recognoscenda et aliquatenus emendanda videntur, ope studiorum quae, nostra aetate, peracta sunt sive circa originem sive circa evolutionem singulorum rituum Missae. . . . Schema,* Emendationes VI, p. 32. Pope Paul VI's Apostolic Constitution *Missale Romanum* and *GIRM,* Introduction, no. 8, affirm the same thing.

[13] These recommendations can be traced back to liturgical scholars who wrote on the subject before the council, like: E. Bishop: *Liturgica Historica,* Oxford 1918; J. Jungmann: *Missarum Sollemnia,* New York 1961; A. Mayer: "Altchristliche Liturgie und Germanentum," *Jahrbuch für Liturgiewissenschaft* 5 (1925) pp. 80–96; T. Klauser: "Die liturgischen Austauschbeziehungen zwischen der römischen und der fränkisch-deutschen Kirche vom 8. bis zum 11. Jahrhundert," *Historisches Jahrbuch* 53 (1933) pp. 169–87; C. Vogel: "Les échanges liturgiques entre Rome et les pays francs jusqu'à l'époque de Charlemagne," *Le Chiese nei regni dell'Europa occidentale e i loro rapporti con Roma sino all'800,* Spoleto 1960, pp. 185–295.

[14] *Schema,* Modi II, no. 9, p. 8.

[15] *Schema,* Emendationes VI, pp. 14–16.

[16] *Apostolic Constitution "Quo primum": Huic Missali Nostro nuper edito, nihil umquam addendum, detrahendum, aut immutandum esse decernimus, sub indignationis Nostrae poena, hac Nostra perpetuo valitura constitutione statuimus et ordinamus.* A similar

warning was issued by Pope Clement VIII and Pope Urban VIII. See A. Nocent: *La Messe avant et après Pie V,* Paris 1977; R. Cabié: "Les origines médiévales de l'«Ordo Missae» de 1570," *L'Église en prière* II, pp. 166–88.

[17] *Schema,* Emendationes VI, p. 32.

[18] *Schema,* Modi II, no. 10, p. 8.

[19] *Missarum Sollemnia,* pp. 147–56. See: C. Vogel: "Excursus: The 'Private Mass,' " *Medieval Liturgy,* pp. 156–59.

[20] *Apostolic Constitution "Missale Romanum," Missale Romanum,* Vatican City 1975, p. 16; *DOL,* p. 460. See Pope Clement VIII's *Apostolic Letter "Cum Sanctissumum": Sane omnino conveniens est, ut qui omnes unum sumus in uno corpore, quod est Ecclesia, et de uno corpore Christi participamus, una et eadem celebrandi ratione, uniusque officii et ritus observatione in hoc ineffabili et tremendo sacrificio utamur. Missale Romanum,* Rome 1962, p. ix.

[21] *Apostolic Constitution "Missale Romanum,"* p. 12; *DOL,* p. 458.

[22] For a list of publishers from the sixteenth to the eighteenth century see C. Vogel: *Medieval Liturgy,* pp. 17–20. See I. Scicolone: *Il Cardinale Giuseppe Tomasi di Lampedusa e gli inizi della scienza liturgica,* Rome 1981.

[23] *IGMR,* Introduction, nos. 7–8, p. 22; *DOL,* p. 467.

[24] *Ibid.,* Introduction, no. 6, p. 22; *DOL,* p. 467; no. 15, p. 26; *DOL,* p. 469.

[25] *Ordo Romanus I,* ed. M. Andrieu: *Les Ordines Romani du haut moyen âge* II, Louvain 1971, pp. 68–108.

[26] *IGMR,* Introduction, nos. 13–15, pp. 24–26; *DOL,* pp. 468–69.

[27] *Ibid.,* Chapter I, nos. 14–23, pp. 30–33; *DOL,* pp. 472–75.

[28] *Apostolic Constitution "Missale Romanum,"* p. 14; *DOL,* p. 459. These revisions correspond almost entirely with the recommendations of the preparatory commission. See: *Schema,* Emendationes VI, p. 32.

[29] *IGMR,* Introduction, no. 9, p. 29; *DOL,* p. 467.

[30] *Ibid,* Chapter I, no. 6, p. 28; *DOL,* p. 471.

[31] J. Jungmann: *The Mass of the Roman Rite,* New York

1961, 552 pp.; S. Marsili: "Teologia della celebrazione dell'eucaristia," *Anàmnesis* 3/2, Casale Monferrato 1983, pp. 11–186.

[32] London 1966.

[33] On the supper of Jesus, S. Marsili writes: *Cristo nel fare la sua "eulogía-eucharistía" aveva lo spirito rivolto non agli avvenimenti antichi di cui conosceva il ruolo profetico, ma a quelli promessi "nuovi" dal profeta (Is 43, 19) e che in lui s'erano andati compiendo (Lc 4, 21); non all'alleanza del Sinai, ma alla "nuova alleanza" annunciata da Ger 31, 31, e che egli avrebbe realizzata tra poco nel suo sangue versato sulla croce.* "Teologia della celebrazione dell'eucaristia," p. 153.

[34] *Ibid.*, p. 121.

[35] For the complete works of Amalar see: J. Hanssens (ed.): *Amalarii Episcopi Opera Liturgica Omnia*, 3 vols., *Studi e Testi* 138–40, Vatican City 1948–50. See: S. Marsili, pp. 91–93, and J. Jungmann, pp. 66–70.

[36] *IGMR*, Chapter II, no. 8, p. 29; *DOL*, p. 471.

[37] Chapter II, no. 33, p. 35; *DOL*, p. 477. See: R. Cabié: "L'≪Ordo Missae≫ de Paul VI," pp. 213–19; A. Nocent: "Storia della celebrazione dell'eucaristia," *Anàmnesis* 3/2, pp. 208–23.

[38] Chapter II, no. 48, p. 38; *DOL*, p. 480. See R. Cabié: "L'≪Ordo Missae≫ de Paul VI," pp. 219–35; A. Nocent: "Storia della celebrazione dell'eucaristia," pp. 225–70.

[39] *IGMR*, Chapter V, nos. 258–70, pp. 75–77; *DOL*, pp. 518–19.

[40] *Ibid.*, Chapter II, no. 55, p. 40; *DOL*, p. 483.

[41] Text in D.S. Amalorpavadass: *Towards Indigenisation in the Liturgy*, Bangalore 1971, p. 33.

[42] *Circular Letter "Eucharistiae participationem,"* no. 6, *DOL*, p. 625.

[43] Consilium: *Guidelines "Au cours des derniers mois,"* no. 5; *DOL*, p. 617.

[44] *Declaratio circa Preces eucharisticas et experimenta liturgica*, no. 2, *Notitiae* 261 (1988) pp. 234–35.

[45] *IGMR*, Chapter II, no. 55; p. 40; *DOL*, pp. 482–83.

[46] *Guidelines "Au cours des derniers mois,"* no. 2; *DOL*, p. 615.

[47] *Circular Letter "Eucharistiae participationem,"* no. 12; *DOL,* p. 627.

[48] *IGMR,* Chapter II, no. 21, p. 32; *DOL,* p. 475.

[49] *Ibid.,* no. 57, p. 42; *DOL,* pp. 484–85.

[50] *IGMR,* Introduction, no. 15, p. 25; *DOL,* p. 469.

[51] A. Dumas: "Les sources du nuoveau Missel romain," *Notitiae* 60 (1971) pp. 37–42; 61 (1971) pp. 74–77; 62 (1971) pp. 94–95; 63 (1971) pp. 134–36; idem: "Les Oraisons du nuoveau Missel romain," *Questions Liturgiques* 52 (1971) pp. 263–70; idem: "Les Préfaces du nouveau Missel," *Ephemerides Liturgicae* 85 (1971) pp. 16–28. See also: C. Johnson–A. Ward: *The Sources of the Roman Missal* I: Advent and Christmas, *Notitiae* 240–42 (1986); idem: *The Sources of the Roman Missal* II: Prefaces, *Notitiae* 252–54 (1987). A. Echiegu made an excellent study of the collects of the solemnities of the Lord in the Missal of Paul VI. He has published the collects of Christmas and Epiphany. See *Translating the Collects of the Solemnities of the Lord in the Language of the African,* Münster 1984.

[52] *Ordo Romanus I,* no. 53, pp. 84–85 (for facing the east); no. 95, p. 98 (for commixtion). See F. Dölger: "Die christliche Gebetsrichtung nach Osten," *Sol Salutis,* Münster 1972, pp. 136–49; C. Vogel: "Versus ad Orientem. L'Orientation dans les Ordines Romani du haut moyen âge," *La Maison-Dieu* 70 (1962) pp. 67–99; J. Jungmann: *The Early Liturgy,* pp. 134–35.

[53] U. Prerovsky (ed.): *Liber Pontificalis* II, Rome 1978, p. 46.

[54] *Sacramentarium Veronense,* ed. C. Mohlberg, Rome 1966, no. 1239: *Deus, qui in humanae substantiae dignitate et mirabiliter condedisti et mirabilius reformasti: da, quaesumus, nobis Iesu Christi filii tui divinitatis esse consortes, qui humanitatis nostrae fieri dignatus est particeps.* See A. Echiegu: *Translating the Collects of the Solemnities of the Lord,* pp. 171–79.

[55] *IGMR,* Chapter VII, nos. 313–24, pp. 85–88; *DOL,* pp. 526–30.

[56] *IGMR,* in sequence: Chapter II, no. 21, p. 32 (*DOL,* p. 474); no. 26, p. 33 (p. 475); no. 56b, p. 41 (p. 483); Chapter IV, no. 232, p. 67 (p. 510); Chapter V, no. 263, p. 76 (p. 518); Chapter VI, no. 288, p. 81 (p. 523); no. 290, p. 81 (p. 523); nos. 304, 305 and 308, pp. 83–84 (pp. 524–25). See SC Divine Wor-

ship: *Instruction "Constitutione Apostolica,"* no. 8, *DOL,* p. 535: "Assisted by the respective bishops' committees and liturgical institutes, the conferences of bishops have the further responsibility of making the necessary decisions on matters that the General Instruction of the Roman missal leaves up to them." These are: the faithful's movements, standing, kneeling, and sitting during mass; the reverences made to the altar and the gospel book; how the sign of peace is to be given; the permission to have only two readings on Sundays and holydays; and the permission authorizing women to proclaim the scriptural readings before the gospel.

[57] Text in: D.S. Amalorpavadass: *Towards Indigenisation in the Liturgy,* pp. 31–33.

[58] "A Commentary on the First Stage of Adaptations in the Liturgy," *Ibid.,* pp. 33–53.

[59] *Ibid.,* pp. 41–42.

[60] The new order of mass for India has two versions. Both include the option to read Indian scriptures before reading the Christian canonical books. The first version presents a short and a long form of a new eucharistic prayer, while the second gives its own which is different from the other two. At the IV All India Liturgical Meeting held at Bangalore on December 2–8, 1973 it was decided that the second version, presented by Cardinal Joseph Parecatil, be adopted by the National Liturgical Commission as the official text. See *New Orders of the Mass for India,* Bangalore 1974.

[61] Congregation for Divine Worship: *Decree "Zairensium Dioecesium," Notitiae* 264 (1988) p. 457.

[62] The text of this new order of mass and the explanatory notes are found in the dossier presented to the Congregation: Conférence Épiscopale du Zaïre: *Rite zaïrois de la célébration eucharistique,* Kinshasa, August 1985, pp. 1–21. See also: J. Evenou: "Rencontre au Zaïre avec la Conférence Épiscopale," *Notitiae* 247 (1987) pp. 139–42; idem: "Le Missel Romain pour les diocèses du Zaïre," *Notitiae* 264 (1988) pp. 454–56; R. Moloney: "The Zaïrean Mass and Inculturation," *Worship* 62 (1988) pp. 433–42.

[63] *Rite zaïrois de la célébration eucharistique,* pp. 42–43. In a sense this outline limits the effect of the proclamation of God's

word to repentance. One can think of other effects such as thanksgiving, praise, and trust.

[64] The dossier reads: *Dans le contexte de l'Église universelle, associer la vénération de nos ancêtres au coeur droit à celle des saints reconnus par l'Église, exprime la volonté d'ouverture des chrétiens d'Afrique aux ancêtres d'autres peuple dans la foi. . . . Par conséquent, leur intégration au culte chrétien doit être comprise au plan pastoral et liturgique, comme la volonté d'adhésion de soi-même tout entier au Christ. Ibid.*, pp. 32–38. The general presentation of the approved order of mass further explains: *Dans la même perspective, se justifie l'invocation des ancêtres au coeur droit, qui sont, en vertu des mérites du Christ, en communion avec Dieu, de même que la liturgie romaine évoque depuis l'antiquité Abel le juste, Abraham, Melkisédek. Notitiae* 264 (1988) p. 459.

[65] "Le Missel pour le diocèses du Zaïre," *Notitiae* 264 (1988) pp. 458–64.

[66] *Ibid.*, pp. 53–54.

[67] *Rite zaïrois de la célébration eucharistique*, p. 7.

[68] The project was approved by the conference of bishops in 1976. The text, in Tagalog and English, is printed in: A. Chupungco: *Towards a Filipino Liturgy,* Manila 1976, pp. 96–139. See also: idem (ed.): *Liturgical Renewal in the Philippines,* Quezon City 1980.

[69] The *Misa* was celebrated as part of the activities of the International Mission Congress held in Manila in December 1979.

[70] A. Chupungco: "A Filipino Adaptation of the Liturgical Language," *Eulogia*, Miscellanea for B. Neunheuser, Rome 1979, pp. 45–55.

[71] The Tagalog text reads: *Banal ka, Poong Maykapal! Banal ang iyong pangalan! Banal ang iyong kaharian! Langit, lupa'y nagpupugay sa iyong kadakilaan.*

[72] *Aklat ng Pagmimisa sa Roma,* Manila 1981.

Chapter Three

The Future Shape of Sacramental Celebrations

Vatican II's Reform of the Sacramental Celebrations

1. The General Principles of the Conciliar Reform

"For well-disposed members of the faithful, the effect of the liturgy of the sacraments and sacramentals is that almost every event in their lives is made holy by divine grace that flows from the paschal mystery of Christ's passion, death, and resurrection, the fount from which all sacraments and sacramentals draw their power." With these words SC 61 defines the role of the sacraments and sacramentals in the life of the church. Their celebration assures the faithful of the abiding presence of the paschal mystery which accompanies and sanctifies them at every important moment and at every turning point in life. "It is therefore of the highest importance," says SC 59, "that the faithful should readily understand the sacramental signs."

Unfortunately, at least at the time of the council, the sacramental signs often lacked clarity. SC 62 candidly admits that "with the passage of time certain features have crept into the rites of the sacraments and sacramentals that have made their nature and purpose less clear to the people of today." The proposed text of this article went so far as to claim that this unhappy state of things has had "a detrimental effect on the faithful."[1]

The intent to recover the classical clarity of the Roman liturgy dominates the entire chapter of SC on the sacraments and sacramentals consisting of twenty-three articles.[2] Throughout this chapter one can recognize the call for classical restoration in SC 34: "The rites should be marked by a noble simplicity; they should be short, clear, and unencumbered by useless repetitions; they should be within the people's powers of comprehension and as a rule not require much explanation." To heed this call the proposed text of SC 61 recommended a thorough revision of the liturgical structure, texts, and rites of every sacrament and sacramental.[3]

The recommendation proposed by SC 61 was left out from the final text, probably because its wording tended to be somewhat radical. But that did not hamper its entry into the articles dealing with the celebration of the sacraments. In these articles the word "revision" is repeated like a refrain: "the rites for the baptism of adults are to be revised" (SC 66); "the rite for the baptism of infants is to be revised" (SC 67); "the rite of confirmation is also to be revised" (SC 71); "the rite and formularies for the sacrament of penance are to be revised" (SC 72); "the prayers that belong to the rite of anointing are to be revised" (SC 75); "both the ceremonies and texts of the ordination rites are to be revised" (SC 76); and "the marriage rite now found in the Roman ritual is to be revised" (SC 77).

Unlike the chapter on the eucharist, the chapter on the other sacraments does not confine its scope to the revision of the rites. It draws out the full implication of the classical revision. The liturgy of the sacraments is to be restored to its pristine simplicity, sobriety, and clarity in order to foster active participation and set down the *terminus a quo* of cultural adaptation. This inference is supported by SC 62 which admits that in the rites of the sacraments "some changes have become necessary as adaptations [*accomodare*] to the needs of our own times." We pointed out early on that in the third chapter of SC the words *aptare* and *accomodare* mean the same thing. Both should be read in the light of SC 37–40. SC 65, for example, refers to "art. 37–40 of this Constitution as the norm" to be followed for the question of admitting native initiatory rites into the baptismal liturgy. From the outset SC's chapter on the sacraments was firmly resolved to espouse the idea of cultural adaptation including the radical type.

SC 62 gives historical and pastoral reasons why it advocates the updating of the sacramental rites to the present-day needs. The history of some sacramental rites shows that not every adaptation yielded positive results. In the course of time, particularly during the middle ages, the sacramental rites assimilated practices that tended to obscure the nature and meaning of the sacraments. The evolution of the anointing of the sick into extreme unction or sacrament for the dying is a typical example. The proposed text of SC 62 could very well have alluded to this as a detrimental feature of the sacrament. Surely there have been pastorally useful adaptations even in the middle ages. Several examples concerning the initiation of children, especially in the Ordo Romanus 11, can be adduced here. The adaptations in the number of scrutinies, symbols, and prayers reveal a genuine pastoral spirit. They at least took account of the fact that those to be baptized were children who did not go through the process of the catechumenate.[4] However, such adaptations, conditioned by a particular historical situation, do not always correspond with "the needs of our own times."

The council wanted urgently to restore the rites of the sacraments to their classical shape. In this way the nature and purpose of the sacraments will be clearly and easily understood by the people. Active participation rests on this premise. But as we observed earlier, the conciliar reform of the sacramental rites was not confined to the restoration of the classical shape. The simplicity, clarity, and practical sense of the restored rites are the qualities that should make up the suitable *terminus a quo* for cultural adaptation. An intricate model with a perplexingly elaborate interweaving of parts will be an impossible *terminus a quo.* The classical reform was thus a necessity. We should recall that ultimately the aim of cultural adaptation is to infuse a better quality into the participation of the faithful in the celebrations of Christ's mystery. The faithful will appreciate more deeply the meaning of the sacraments if they are able to recognize the sacramental language, rites, and symbols as belonging, or at least conforming, to their own culture and traditions.[5]

But there could be instances when cultural adaptation, however radical it might be, falls short of the goal set by the council for a truly renewed and updated sacramental liturgy. SC 77 recognizes such an eventuality for the rite of marriage. This article not only proposes the revision of the Tridentine marriage rite and the retention of praiseworthy traditions of local churches, but also grants to the conferences of bishops the faculty to draw up a completely new rite "suited to the usages of place and people." This conciliar text has really nothing revolutionary about it. It merely reiterates a long-standing practice of the Roman church to make allowances for the development of local marriage rites. Hence, besides revision and cultural adaptation there is the option to compose a new rite. Marriage is for now the only sacramental rite that enjoys such a wide range of options for its aggiornamento.

The reform of the sacramental rites as envisaged by the council also revolves around the question of language and the preparation of the particular rituals. Today we take it for granted that the sacraments are celebrated entirely in the vernacular. This was not the case during the council. After a protracted debate regarding the use of the vernacular in the liturgy, SC 36 was finally approved. However, its practical application to the sacramental celebrations aroused another round of debate.[6] In the spirit of via media or compromise the text of SC 63 presented for the approval of the council fathers was moderate and restrained: "In the administration of the sacraments and sacramentals the vernacular may be used, but Latin is to be kept for the form of the sacraments, except marriage and, with express approval, also the other sacraments."[7]

An overwhelming majority approved the text against a few who supported a more limited use of the vernacular. But not all those who approved did so unconditionally. In the *modi* accompanying their vote a total of 601 council fathers advocated that the restriction concerning the sacramental form be eliminated from the text. In fact the wording of the text was clearly at odds with the intent of the council to promote active and intelligent participation. The meaning of the sacraments, expressed above all in the sacramental form, should not be veiled from the understanding of the faithful by Latin words.[8] Accordingly the text was reformulated thus: "With art. 36 as the norm, the vernacular may be used in administering the sacraments and sacramentals." The restrictive clause was struck off from the text so as to permit the use of the vernacular also for the form of the sacraments.

Summing up, we can identify five operational principles set down by the third chapter of SC for the aggiornamento of the sacramental celebrations. They are: the revision of the rites according to their original classical shape; the adaptation of these rites to the needs of our own times; the creation, when timely, of a new rite of marriage by the conferences of bishops; the unlimited use of the vernacular in the celebration of the sacraments; and the preparation of the particular rituals.

2. The Conciliar Provision for the Reform of Sacramental Rites

SC devotes fifteen articles for the reform of all the sacramental rites, namely Christian initiation which includes the adult catechumenate and confirmation (SC 64–71), penance (SC 72), anointing of the sick (SC 73 and 75), continuous rite for the dying (SC 74), holy orders (SC 76), and marriage (SC 77–78). In these articles the words "revision" and "adaptation" recur with great regularity, because they are key to the council's program of sacramental renewal.

Revision refers to the work of correcting, improving, or updating, when necessary, the liturgical texts and rites of the sacraments. This phase of the conciliar reform has been largely conditioned, as we noted elsewhere, by the liturgical movement's strong attachment to the classical form of the Roman liturgy. Adaptation, on the other hand, refers to the work of finding the appropriate response to the needs of the local churches, especially in the missions, and of the individual faithful who ask for the sacraments in different life situations. The needs are in most instances directly pastoral, but they often reveal a cultural underpinning. In the final analysis, what is pastoral is inseparably tied to the cultural reality in which the sacraments are celebrated. That is why the adaptation of the sacramental rites for purposes that are immediately pastoral cannot ignore the cultural question.

To appreciate the meaning and purpose of the provision of the articles in question it is necessary to review what the council had in mind when it set off to institute changes in the celebration of the sacraments. The principal aim of the classical revision is to express more clearly the nature and effect of the sacraments and the obligations connected with them. The predilection of SC for the classical shape derives, as we have insisted time and again, not so much from its veneration of antiquity as from the liturgical and pastoral convenience that can be gained, if the sacramental rites are clear and simple. There is no doubt that the nature and effect of the sacraments can be more easily understood by the faithful if the rites possess the catechetical clarity and noble simplicity of the classical Roman liturgy. Regardless, therefore, of the particular cultural setting in which the sacraments are celebrated, clarity remains an indispensable requirement for intelligent and active participation. Clarity, which is an essential quality of the liturgy, is a universal value.

The provision of SC 64–78 for the reform of the sacramental rites is markedly pastoral in orientation. Disputed theological questions are passed over, while the doctrinal statements on the nature and effects of the sacraments are turned over to the responsibility of the postconciliar commission in charge of the liturgical books. The paramount concern of this entire section of SC is pastoral. For pastoral reason the rites of the sacraments are to be revised "so that they more clearly express the nature and effect of the sacraments." For pastoral reason new rites are to be drawn up, like a shorter rite of baptism for use in the missions, the rite for welcoming baptized children to the church, the rite for receiving baptized Christians into full communion, the rite of marriage—if a new one is needed—and the continuous rite for the dying. For pastoral reason the rite of baptism for children and the anointing of the sick are to be revised so that they correspond to the varying conditions of both the children and the sick. For pastoral reasons the praiseworthy customs and traditions observed by the local churches when celebrating the sacrament of marriage are to be retained.

This is not to say that the theological, historical, and cultural premises have been entirely ignored. The norm regarding the fitting time to receive the sacrament of anointing is based on historical and theological reasons. And so is the provision for the laying on of hands by the bishops present at the episcopal ordination. On the other hand, the faculty to assimilate native initiatory elements is drawn from cultural considerations. We may safely affirm that any other valid reasons that sustain and promote the basic pastoral principle *sacramenta sunt propter homines* have a rightful, though subordinate, place in the scheme of the conciliar reform.

With these considerations we tried to present in clearer light the conciliar provision for the sacraments. They explain the underlying reasons for the changes introduced by SC and consequently also the reasons that should motivate both the revision of the *editio typica* and the preparation of the particular rituals. But what provision has the council set for each sacrament and what are the supporting reasons for it?

1. The intent to restore the adult catechumenate as a general practice in the church is conspicuous in SC 64. In the years immediately preceding the council the Holy See had granted to local churches the indult to reestablish the catechumenate. The experience proved satisfactory, and bishops were keen on having the catechumenate restored as a normal practice, though adapted to the conditions of modern times. In response SC 64 decrees that "the catechumenate for adults, divided into several stages, is to be restored and put into use at the discretion of the local ordinary." SC 66 gives effect to this provision by calling for the revision of the rites for the baptism of adults, "not only the simpler rite, but also the more solemn one, with proper attention to the restored catechumenate."[9]

The solemn form of the initiation of adults shall thus include the different stages of the catechumenate with rites celebrated at successive intervals of time. The intention is to lead the candidates to the water of baptism through the gradual process of conversion. The length of time needed for this will depend on several factors, though gradualness is a pertinent consideration in this regard. The restoration of the catechumenate has reestablished the solemn form of initiation as the normal practice. For this reason, the use of the simple rite, which dispenses from the usual process of the catechumenate, is celebrated only "in extraordinary circumstances when the candidate has been unable to go through all the stages of initiation."[10] Even then the solemn form should not be entirely neglected. One or another of the elements of the catechumenate or the period of purification and enlightenment can be inserted into the simple rite in order to enrich its celebration and signify, though in an abridged form, the process of conversion.[11]

As regards the rite of baptism for children SC 67 rules that "it should be suited to the fact that those to be baptized are infants." Until the council the Tridentine rite for the baptism of children had formulas and ceremonies which were originally intended for adult candidates. It was in reality the shorter form for the baptism of adults. In spite of this the preparatory commission suggested that the Tridentine rite be retained with some emendations like omitting references to the stages of the catechumenate and stressing the role of parents and godparents.[12] Nonetheless, the revised rite contemplated by SC 67 should not be regarded as an abbreviated form of the Rite of Christian Initiation of Adults. The basic elements of the two rites are the same, but the subjects and the course of the celebration of each one are so different that we have to speak here of two distinct rites. Hence the work of adapting the rites of Christian initiation for adults and for children has to set off from the respective *terminus a quo* of these rites. From a methodological point of view it seems untenable to consider the former the paradigm of the latter.[13]

The remaining articles of SC on the subject of initiation deal with practical pastoral situations. For occasions when a very large number of children are to be baptized together SC 68 directs that the baptismal rite should contain alternatives to be used at the discretion of the local ordinary; otherwise, as one council father remarked, "there is danger that due to exhaustion the minister will administer the sacrament in a mechanical way."[14]

To meet the pastoral needs, especially in the missions, a shorter rite is to be drawn up for use by catechists and by the faithful in general when there is danger of death and neither a priest nor a deacon is present. The shorter rite contemplated here is different from the one used in situations of emergency. As a norm, the shorter rite should have as integral components the liturgy of the word and the liturgy of the sacrament, though in an abbreviated or simplified form.[15]

For welcoming children who have been baptized by the short rite and converts who have already been validly baptized SC 69 ordains that new corresponding rites be drawn up. Such rites should respectively show that the supplementary ceremonies are not for validity but for the integrity of the baptismal liturgy. Moreover, the celebration of the reception of converts into full communion with the Catholic Church should not cast any doubt on the validity of the sacrament of baptism celebrated by the other churches.

Lastly, regarding the blessing of the baptismal water SC 70 suggests that "except during the Easter season, baptismal water may be blessed within the rite of baptism itself." Through frequent blessing the conciliar commission hoped to achieve two things, namely to avoid the use of stagnant water, and to restore to the baptismal rite its integral shape and, through the formula of blessing, also its catechetical dimension. Earlier the preparatory commission, when discussing the subject, deplored "the miserable and indecorous condition of the baptismal water found very often in smelly baptismal fonts, especially in warm climates." For this reason as well as for the liturgical and catechetical integrity of the rite the commission recommended the frequent blessing of the baptismal water.[16]

This then is how SC envisaged the reform and updating of the rites of Christian initiation. The underlying reasons for each provision are decisively pastoral, although liturgical, historical, and ecumenical considerations are not ignored. They refer directly to the work of revising the *editio typica*, but they certainly apply also to the work of shaping the particular rituals of Christian initiation. Cultural adaptation possesses a pastoral, liturgical, historical, and ecumenical latitude.

2. SC 71 ordains that "the rite of confirmation is also to be revised in order that the intimate connection of this sacrament with the whole of Christian initiation may stand out more clearly." The proposed text, which remained unchanged in the final form except for some verbal emendations, suggested that confirmation be conferred within mass, when convenient, and that the candidates renew the baptismal promises before they are confirmed. In this way the traditional plan of Christian initiation consisting of baptism, confirmation, and eucharist in that order could somehow be evoked.[17]

Concerning the renewal of the baptismal promises a council father expressed the fear that the practice could raise in the mind of the faithful some confusion between baptism and confirmation. The conciliar commission answered that since the two sacraments have been celebrated separately for many centuries now, there is no real ground for such confusion. What is to be regretted, the commission said, is that the faithful of the Latin rite have difficulty in seeing the connection between baptism and confirmation, not to speak of the three sacraments of initiation.[18]

It is outside the scope of this book to address the question regarding the place of confirmation in the Christian initiation of children. It has become a liturgical practice to follow a peculiar plan which inverts the order of confirmation and eucharist and inserts the sacrament of penance before first communion. In effect the sequence of the sacraments is this: baptism, penance, eucharist, and confirmation. There are surely genuine reasons for this liturgically odd arrangement, like its pedagogical value and pastoral convenience. However, one cannot help but be skeptical of the value of any theological reflections drawn a posteriori from such arrangement. The word "initiation" used in this connection is not coterminous with the word used in liturgical tradition.[19] One is dealing here with another concept and another praxis. At any rate, the disruption in the plan of these sacraments, especially with the insertion of penance, has rendered theological discussions on the Christian initiation of children moot and academic.[20]

It is important at this point not to lose sight of the council's vision of an integral process of initiation consisting of the three sacraments arranged according to their tradition sequence and excluding the sacrament of penance which is not an initiatory rite. Notwithstanding the current pastoral practice, the particular rituals, whose *terminus a quo* is the *editio typica,* should continue to follow the normal sequence, even if pastoral notes regarding the reordered sequence and the insertion of penance have to be added for the convenience of the minister.

3. To the sacrament of penance SC 72 devotes one short sentence: "The rite and formularies for the sacrament

of penance are to be revised so that they more clearly express both the nature and effect of the sacrament." Wishing to refrain from discussing the nature of penance, the conciliar commission confined the reason for revising the rite to the need to project a clearer picture of its sacramental effect. Several council fathers thought differently. While the revised rite need not present the dogmatic aspect of the sacrament, it should not pass over in silence its social and ecclesial character which is an integral part of its nature.[21] The conciliar commission accepted the emendation and added to the text the word "nature." The word is actually a shorthand for the many ideas expressed by the council fathers. The text, as it stands, requires a considerable effort, indeed the art of hermeneutics, for anyone to read into the word "nature" all the social and ecclesial implications of penance.

For signifying the effect of penance the preparatory commission stressed the importance of the laying on of hands. This gesture "signified, according to St Cyprian, reconciliation and communion through penance with the church, for sin breaks the bonds of life with the church. It signified reconciliation through the Holy Spirit."[22] The commission recommended that the laying on of hands on the head of the penitent be restored "to make it known that the rite consists of the laying on of hands, even without physical contact." This is an improvement on the Tridentine ritual which directed the priest to raise his right hand toward the penitent at the words of absolution. In contrast the Ambrosian ritual prescribes the laying on of hand on the head of the penitent.[23]

What emerges from the historical examination of SC 72 is that beneath its strikingly brief sentence there lies a whole program of conciliar reform. The rite of penance should be revised so that its celebration will clearly signify the social and ecclesial aspects of the sacrament as well as the reconciliation of the penitent with the church through the working of the Holy Spirit.

We cannot conclude this section without posing some questions. To signify the effect of the sacrament the preparatory commission insisted on recovering the full impact of the laying on of hands. In places where this gesture is at odds with the cultural pattern of behavior which regards it as a social taboo, can one or another dynamic equivalent be used instead to express sacramental reconciliation? The council attached great importance to the social and ecclesial character of the sacrament. It is unfortunate that the rites and texts of the new *editio typica* seem to have given it scarcely any attention. Has this something to do with the perennial problem of translating theory into ritual praxis, especially when the prevailing concern is of another nature, like individual penitential discipline and juridical norms?

4. The provision for the rite of anointing is contained in three articles, namely SC 73, 74, and 75. Originally there were four articles. The first dealt with the name and nature of the sacrament, the second with the norms for its administration, the third with the liturgical rites, and the fourth with the faculty to have it repeated in the course of the same sickness. The conciliar commission supported this last article with historical and pastoral reasons: "Repeating anointing during the same illness was practiced by the churches until the thirteenth century. For obviously the sick, especially those with prolonged illness, more frequently need spiritual comfort."[24] But these historical and pastoral reasons did not alter the fact that from the time of Trent the sacramental discipline of the church forbade the practice.[25] By an explicit vote of the council fathers the article was suppressed, "lest the council be dragged into a disputed question." However, the idea was not definitively discarded. The new rite published in 1972 resolved the question by accepting the practice under the following terms:

"The sacrament may be repeated if the sick person recovers after being anointed or if during the same illness the person's condition becomes more serious."[26]

The article dealing with the name of the sacrament underwent considerable modifications. The proposed text was firm and incisive: "The sacrament which is commonly called extreme unction shall henceforth be called anointing of the sick; for it is not in itself a sacrament for the dying, but for those who are seriously ill [*graviter aegrotantium*]. Hence the fitting time to receive it is as soon as the faithful falls into serious illness [*gravis morbus*]."[27] The final text is conciliatory: "Extreme unction, which may also and more properly be called anointing of the sick, is not a sacrament for those only who are at the point of death. Hence, as soon as any of the faithful begins to be in danger of death [*periculum mortis*] from sickness or old age, the fitting time for that person has certainly already arrived."

As the relator noted, there are two major changes in the text: one regarding the name, the other the fitting time to receive the sacrament. The strong views expressed by two council fathers prompted the commission to keep the name "extreme unction," while declaring that the name "anointing of the sick" is more appropriate, especially "for countering the practice of priests and faithful who interpret 'extreme' to mean that the sacrament ought to be received only at the point of death."

In connection with the other change the conciliar commission admitted that to ask for the sacrament at the last moment is indeed an abuse. However, it decided to abandon the disputed phrase "serious illness" [*gravis morbus*] in favor of the current discipline according to which the fitting time to receive the sacrament is when there is danger of death [*periculum mortis*] from sickness or old age.[28]

The conciliar provision for the rite of anointing did not touch disputed theological questions nor did it entertain casuistry. The conciliar commission explained that the scope of the provision is to keep to the existing norms of the magisterium without, however, closing the door to legitimate progress and the particular needs of the local churches. Thus, "as the texts stand, they can admit a broader interpretation."[29] The bounds of this broader interpretation will be defined by the nature of the sacrament, the pastoral needs of local churches, and the people's traditions connected with sickness and healing. It is within these bounds that the revision of the *editio typica* and the preparation of particular rituals are expected to be realized.

5. For the rites of ordination SC 76 provides two paragraphs whose intent is manifestly to restore the tradition and classical simplicity of the Roman rite. The preparatory commission reported that "several suggestions have been made on how to adapt the rite of this sacrament so that its meaning may be more easily understood by the people."[30] The commission itself proposed that the revision and adaptation of the liturgy of ordination should aim toward the simplification of the rites, the updating of the allocutions in order to stress the obligations inherent in each sacred ministry, the adaptation of obsolete formulas to contemporary situations, the reform of the rite of handing the ministerial instruments and vestments, and the use of the vernacular at the allocutions for the sake of the faithful. All this is summed up by the first paragraph of SC 76: "Both the ceremonies and texts of the ordination rites are to be revised. The address given by the bishop at the beginning of each ordination or consecration may be in the vernacular."

The second paragraph, which allows all the bishops present at episcopal ordination to take part in the laying on of hands, was added by the conciliar commission at the recommendation of one of its members. The practice "is part of the sound tradition of the church and was in use until the end of the middle ages." Hippolytus of Rome is an early witness to this tradition.[31]

6. The revision and adaptation of the rite of marriage and the faculty to draw up a new rite are treated in SC 77 and SC 78. The main thrust of these articles came from the comments and proposals sent by the bishops and prelates to the antepreparatory commission. We can say that these articles are truly synodal: they were authored by no less than the pastors of the local churches the world over. The principles they articulate and the wide range of possibilities they offer meet amply the expectations for the aggiornamento of the rite of marriage.

SC 77 gives clear and effective utterance to the principles of the conciliar reform. It is laid out in three paragraphs. The first paragraph asks for the revision and enrichment of the Roman ritual "in such a way that it more clearly signifies the grace of the sacrament and imparts a knowledge of the obligations of spouses."[32] It is obvious that if the *editio typica* is to serve as the *terminus a quo* of adaptation, it must exhibit the qualities of an adequate model or type. Its structure must be flexible, its theology and spiritual doctrine rich, and its orientation truly pastoral.

Before and during the council pastors were unanimous in their assessment of the Roman rite promulgated by Pope Paul V in 1614. In spite of the modifications introduced by Popes Benedict XIV, Pius IX, Leo XIII, Pius XI, and Pius XII, it did not succeed to express clearly and sufficiently the grace of the sacrament and the obligations of the spouses. Its prevailing concern seems to be juridical, that is, to obtain the valid consent of the contracting parties. Its celebration was too short and too sober to have an impact or leave a lasting impression. During the discussions prior to the council several bishops deplored the brevity and ritual poverty of the Roman rite. As one bishop quipped: "With this rite the sacrament of marriage can be expedited in two minutes!"[33]

The second paragraph of SC 77 is quoted verbatim from the Council of Trent: "If any regions follow other praiseworthy customs and ceremonies when celebrating the sacrament of marriage, the council earnestly desires that by all means these be retained."[34] It will be recalled that the Tridentine rite of marriage was never made obligatory for the entire Latin church. The Council of Trent, though a staunch exponent of uniformity in the liturgy, guaranteed the right of every local church to keep its particular marriage rite. However, after the publication of the Roman rite in 1614 a great number of the local churches eventually adopted it to the detriment of local traditions.

What were the praiseworthy customs and ceremonies mentioned by the Council of Trent? The council had probably in mind such practices as the giving away of the bride, the exchange of rings, the giving of arrhae and precious jewels, the wrapping of the hands of the spouses with the priest's stole, the crowning or veiling of the bride, the blessing of bread and wine, and the blessing of the matrimonial bed or chamber.[35] These local customs and ceremonies, if they are still part of a people's living tradition, should by all means be preserved. SC 77 pledges that the new *editio typica* not only will not suppress what still remains of them, but also will vindicate their rightful place in the particular rituals.

The third paragraph of SC 77 gives to every conference of bishops the faculty "to draw up, in accord with art. 63, its own rite, suited to the usages of place and people." This was written taking into account the request made by the bishops in the missions, namely that they be permitted to insert into the particular ritual those indigenous marriage ceremonies that are "good and honorable and are neither superstitious nor contrary to Catholic faith." The provision of this paragraph actually grants more than what was originally requested. For what is contemplated here is the creation of new marriage rites, not mere adaptation of the *editio typica* to local marriage traditions. Some council fathers wanted to confine the use of this faculty to the missions, but the conciliar commission saw no reason for it.[36]

This paragraph shows great liberality and flexibility. Its provision does not only desist from the normal procedure which takes off from the *editio typica*, but also limits the requirements to the bare minimum. All that is needed for validity is that the new rite "always conform to the law that the priest [or duly appointed witness] assisting at the marriage must ask for and obtain the consent of the contracting parties." This juridical requirement merely reaffirms the decree *Tametsi* of 1563 and Canon 1095 of the old code whose chief concern was to ensure the validity of the marriage contract and suppress the practice of clandestine marriages.[37]

But we may not forget that the liturgy has also its requirements. Chief among them is the necessity to imbue the indigenous marriage traditions with "the true and authentic spirit of the liturgy." Throughout history the church has sought to reinterpret in the light of salvation history the cultural elements it incorporates into the liturgy. Through the system of biblical typology it has succeeded in making them bearers of the message of faith. Moreover, it is important that the new rite is accepted by the faithful as their particular way of celebrating the sacrament of marriage. The similarity between the native marriage ceremonies and the new rite could cause a certain uneasiness among the faithful. In a situation like this there is clearly no substitute for catechesis.

SC 78 complements the preceding article. It lays down

four operational principles for the revision of the *editio typica* of the rite of marriage: first, the sacrament is normally to be celebrated within mass; second, the nuptial blessing, duly emended, is to remind the spouses of their equal obligation to remain faithful to each other; third, if the sacrament is celebrated apart from mass, the liturgy of the word is to precede it; fourth, the nuptial blessing is always to be given to the spouses.

The provision of SC 78 reflects the *consilia et vota* or the wishes expressed by the bishops during the antepreparatory consultation.[38] The implementation of this provision is expected to enrich the ritual form and the doctrinal content of the *editio typica.* The celebration of marriage within mass is meant to manifest the relation between the two sacraments. Marriage as the sacrament of covenant between man and woman has its source and finds meaning in the covenant sacrifice which the church celebrates in the eucharist. The nuptial blessing, originally intended for the bride alone, now expresses the church's teaching on the equality or reciprocity between husband and wife as well as the obligation of mutual fidelity.[39] The liturgy of the word gives form to the liturgical theology of Vatican II: the word of God leads to faith and the celebration of the sacrament; the sacrament in its turn ritualizes the word and nourishes faith. Lastly, the norm requiring that the nuptial blessing be always imparted intends to offset with the rich doctrinal content of this liturgical formulary the juridical character of the marriage contract.

Although the immediate objective of SC 77–78 is the aggiornamento of the *editio typica,* the doctrinal, ritual, and pastoral gains of the reform should be transmitted also to the particular rituals. Apart from the resources of liturgical tradition and the principles of the conciliar reform, cultural adaptation or creativity is destined to produce a rite of marriage that espouses theological and liturgical destitution. Surely a marriage rite that is inculturated in accord with the existing norms can be raised to the dignity of a sacrament. What the law actually requires is so little. However, the juridical element alone cannot satisfy all the requirements for a meaningful liturgical renewal and valid cultural adaptation.

The Postconciliar Revision of the Sacramental Rites

The actual shape of the sacramental rites constitutes the *terminus a quo* of cultural adaptation. The introduction to each *editio typica,* especially the section on adaptation, the texts, the gestures, and the rubrical indications give a clear view of the principles and methods of preparing the particular ritual or *terminus ad quem* of cultural adaptation.

The program for the revision of the *editio typica* by the postconciliar Consilium is laid out in the document *De Recognitione Ritualis Romani.*[40] According to this document, the revised Roman ritual serves as the *norma et typus,* the norm and model, for the preparation of the particular rituals contemplated by SC 63b. As norm it gives the specific instances of legitimate variations "within the substantial unity of the Roman rite." The document notes that since the council did not define the limits of the adaptations which the *editio typica* should allow, it is left to the responsibility of the Consilium to decide on the matter as the situation may require.[41]

In effect the legitimate variations proposed by the present *editio typica* of the sacramental rites represent the work of the Consilium and subsequently of the Congregation for Divine Worship. This implies that the kind of changes allowed by the *editio typica* is often determined by their perception of what is essential to the substantial unity of the Roman rite and what can be dispensed with. It is evident that in the world of liturgical scholarship the perception will differ from one school of thought to another. For instance, the *editio typica* permits the omission of the postbaptismal anointing, which is a traditional element of the Roman rite, when the number of the children to be baptized is very great.[42] On the other hand, it would seem to be more in keeping with the Roman tradition to use the triple profession of faith in place of the present declarative formula for baptism. The triple profession is alluded to by Justin Martyr in his *First Apology,* is explicitly mentioned by Hippolytus of Rome, and was kept by the Roman church until the ninth century.[43]

The document formulates the general and particular principles for revising the Roman ritual. Regarding the general principles the document states that "the basic norm and specific method of the entire work are those contained in art. 23 of the Constitution."[44] It will be recalled that this article urges that sound tradition be retained, though keeping open the way to legitimate progress, and that any innovations be avoided which are not genuinely and certainly required by the good of the church. The article enumerates the specific ways of achieving this. First, changes should be preceded by a theological, historical, and pastoral investigation of the liturgical elements to be revised. Second, the general laws governing the structure and meaning of the liturgy should be studied in conjunction with the experience derived from recent liturgical reforms and special indults. Third, the new forms should grow organically from forms already existing. And fourth, as far as possible, marked differences between the rites used in neighboring regions should be avoided.

In addition to SC 23, the document mentions SC 27, 30, 32, 34, and 35. They articulate the main thrust of the conciliar liturgical reform. On the basis of these articles the document individuates seven particular principles for the revision of the *editio typica.* The first principle refers to the preference to be given to the communal celebration especially of the mass and the sacraments over a celebration that is individual and, so to speak, private. The second deals with active participation. The third eliminates special honors paid in the liturgy to any private persons, whether in the ceremonies or external display. The liturgy makes distinction, however, between persons because of sacred order or liturgical function, and provides for due honors to be given to civil authorities. The fourth principle is the quintessence of the classical reform: the rites should be simple, short, clear, and unencumbered by useless repetitions. The fifth decrees that there be more reading from sacred scripture and that it be more varied and apposite. The sixth deals with the ministry of preaching which should be fulfilled with exactitude and fidelity. And the last directs that within the rites themselves provision be made for brief comments, when needed, by the priest or a qualified minister.

It is important to bear in mind that the foregoing principles invoked by the document for the revision of the *editio typica* are by and large the pertinent principles also for the preparation of the particular rituals. They give concrete shape to "the true and authentic spirit of the liturgy," or, simply stated, they define what is good liturgy. The method, which consists principally of the theological, historical, and pastoral investigation of the *terminus a quo,* applies also to the work of cultural adaptation. It permits us to distinguish with some certainty and confidence between the liturgical form and the doctrinal content of the sacramental rites, between one historical period and another, in short, between what is immutable and what is subject to change.

The Passage from the Editio Typica *of the Rites of Initiation*

1. The Methods of Adapting the Rites of Initiation

The question of adapting the rites of Christian initiation tops the agenda of liturgical renewal in local churches where the catechumenate flourishes. By local churches we mean not only those in the missions, but also those in situations sometimes referred to as the post-Christian era. In places where infant baptism progressively declined over the years because of religious indifference the need for adult catechumenate began to be felt with nervous urgency. In many ways such a situation displays a similarity with the experience of the early church before infant baptism became common or with the circumstances of the churches in the missions. Today the word mission is no longer a confined word in the active vocabulary of the church.

The instances when the conferences of bishops may adapt the rites of Christian initiation are indicated in three places: the general introduction named *Christian Initiation,*[45] the introduction to the *Rite of Baptism for Children,*[46] and the introduction to the *Rite of Christian Initiation of Adults.*[47] The general introduction addresses matters pertaining to the rites both for children and for adults. Its section on adaptation is arranged in four numbers (30–33) corresponding to the four principal methods of adapting the *editio typica,* namely the preparation of the particular rituals, the admission of certain initiation ceremonies in use among some peoples, the composition of new formularies, and the composition of musical settings for the liturgical texts. We shall dwell at some length on the first three methods.

1. The future shape of the particular rituals depends upon the conferences of bishops which are directed by SC

63b to prepare them. If they carry into effect what is allowed or suggested by the *editio typica,* the particular rituals will have a reasonably local shape. Like the *editio typica* they can include a section on adaptations to explain the meaning of the changes and specify how and when they are carried out. The list of what may be done is obviously incomplete, but it does offer a leverage for the preparation of the particular rituals.

From among the adaptations allowed by the general introduction in connection with the preparation of particular rituals, we single out five types. The first type refers to the admission of "elements of a people's distinctive traditions and culture" into the rite of baptism.[48] These elements include the pertinent linguistic, ritual, and artistic expressions that can contribute immensely to a better understanding of the sacramental celebration. If they are employed as dynamic equivalents they can illustrate, for example, the rite of welcoming the candidate for baptism or the meaning of the explanatory rites of anointing, clothing, and giving of the lighted candle. The dynamic equivalents need not be drawn directly from ceremonies which are specifically initiatory, like those in use among fraternities and sororities. They can be elements of daily observance connected with family and social life, or else traditional rites set apart by society to mark significant occasions. The important thing is that they should possess the quality of "connaturalness" for signifying certain aspects of the sacramental reality such as conversion, light of faith, and admission to the priestly community. In other words, they should be able to frame Christian initiation in the context "of a people's distinctive traditions and culture."

The second type of adaptations concerns the question of retaining the distinctive elements of existing local rituals of baptism.[49] This type extends to Christian initiation the Tridentine decree regarding the retention of praiseworthy marriage customs and traditions of local churches. Some local churches using the Roman baptismal rite since the Tridentine reform have developed and conserved particular usages related to the sponsors, the baptismal garment, the lighted candles, the ringing of church bells, Marian devotion, and so on. They have become distinctive elements of the particular ritual. It is understood that these elements must meet the requirements of the liturgical reform, that is to say, they must "conform to the Constitution on the Liturgy and correspond to contemporary needs." The practice of placing a napkin-like piece of white cloth on the breast of the child as a token of the baptismal garment is an example of what should not be retained. Provided the distinctive elements suit the purpose of the liturgical reform and do not smack of archeologism or anachronism, there is no reason why they should not be retained at least in a modified form.

The third type proposed by the general introduction deals with the translations of the texts of the baptismal rite.[50] Translations are to be prepared taking into consideration "the characteristics of various languages and cultures." Many initiatory words are borrowed from the Greco-Roman culture. Are there equivalent words in the current usage of a language that can aptly render the meaning of these words? The idea is to translate the key words and phrases of the baptismal liturgy, like "order of the catechumenate," "period of enlightenment," "exorcism," "initiation," and "mystagogy," in such a way that they not only make sense to the people but also respect the particular trait of each language. Evidently the question becomes somewhat more complicated when one is dealing with the translation of the sacramental form, probably not so much for baptism as for confirmation.[51]

The fourth type attends to the question of preparing the introductions to the particular ritual. The *editio typica* may be adapted and augmented, "so that the ministers may fully understand the meaning of the rites and carry them out effectively."[52] Normally the liturgical texts, especially those that accompany gestures, give a clear explanation of what the rite is all about. This is particularly true of the texts for the explanatory rites of baptism. The meaning of these rites, however, can be understood even better if in the introduction to the particular ritual they are explained in their historical, theological, and cultural setting and possibly in the context of the people's culture. Something similar was done in the tenth century by the compilers of the Romano-Germanic pontifical, although the idea did not please the Roman liturgists of the twelfth century who expunged the explanatory notes from the book.[53] The risk of falling into allegorism, subjectivism, pietism, or plain banality when interpreting the rites cannot be entirely discounted, but a timely appeal to modern liturgical scholarship can surely help to minimize it.

The fifth type refers to the rearrangement of the material in the *editio typica,* so that the particular ritual "may be best suited for pastoral use."[54] The editorial layout of the ritual has a specific objective: the convenience of those who will use the book. The *editio typica* indicates the general plan of the celebration and offers the pertinent texts and rubrics. The norm requires that the translation of the *editio typica,* including the optional texts, decrees, and introductions, be complete.[55] The material may, of course, be augmented or, at any rate, must be adapted. But its actual arrangement is a pastoral decision that concerns the local church.

2. Besides using the *editio typica* as *terminus a quo* for particular rituals the local churches in mission countries may employ another method. The conferences of bishops in these countries "have the responsibility to judge whether certain initiation ceremonies in use among some peoples can be adapted for the rite of Christian baptism and to

decide whether these ceremonies are to be incorporated into it."[56]

For this faculty the general introduction invokes the corresponding articles of the conciliar Constitution, namely SC 37–40 and SC 65. It will be recalled that in SC 37 the council affirms that the church admits the elements of a people's culture and traditions into the liturgy itself, provided they are in keeping with the true and authentic spirit of the liturgy. In SC 40 the council entrusts the realization of this principle to the competent, territorial ecclesiastical authority which "must, in this matter, carefully and prudently weigh what elements from the traditions and culture of individual peoples may be appropriately admitted into divine worship." All this finds a concrete expression in SC 65 which declares that "it is lawful in mission lands to allow, besides what is part of Christian tradition, those initiation elements in use among individual peoples, to the extent that such elements are compatible with the Christian rite of initiation."

What are these initiation ceremonies? Already during the antepreparatory phase of the council some bishops in the missions were broaching the possibility of admitting into the liturgy those indigenous ceremonies that can be cleansed from superstition. Examples of these are the rites connected with marriage, birth, new year, sowing, and harvesting. These, the bishops claimed, are in themselves good and noble. "All that is needed is to purify them of some stains of superstition before incorporating them into the sacred ritual of the church."[57]

Apropos we should note that all too often initiatory rites, though they are chiefly of a social nature, are tied to the pagan cult. Since it is no easy task—indeed one might even find it impossible—to distinguish at all times between what is purely social and what is a purely cultic ingredient, a rule of thumb is to ask whether these initiatory rites are able to receive a Christian interpretation and to express the mystery of rebirth in the water and the Holy Spirit. At any rate, there is no clear evidence that SC 65 and the general introduction exclude cultic initiatory elements from the list of what can be admitted into the liturgy.

This method operates within the framework of the *editio typica*. It does not advance the idea of creating a new rite. Its scope is confined to the question of incorporating indigenous initiatory elements into the liturgy. By way of a proposal, suitable initiation ceremonies could be placed side by side with some parts of the baptismal rite for purposes of illustration, or, better yet, they could replace those parts, provided they qualify as dynamic equivalents. This proposal refers above all to the rites of the catechumenate and the explanatory rites of baptism. Moreover, taking account of the development of the Christian initiatory language, especially during the Greco-Roman period, we may presume that the proposal holds in the case of the technical terms used in indigenous rites of initiation. We could affirm that as long as they equivalently express the meaning of the traditional Christian words, they could be assimilated into the liturgical usage.

3. The third method envisaged by the general introduction is of a creative type: "When the Roman ritual for baptism provides several optional formularies, local rituals may add other formularies of the same kind."[58] The permission first appeared in the introduction to the Rite of Marriage published in 1969: "When the Roman ritual has several optional formularies, local rituals may add others of the same type."[59]

There is an important condition attached to this permission, namely that the new formularies should be of the same type as those contained in the *editio typica*. The reason is obvious. In the process of composing new formularies there is a real risk that the rites may lose their original meaning due to an eventual superimposition of texts with estranged meaning. The church's teaching on baptism should not be lost in the process of adaptation. For this reason the type of creativity contemplated here needs to be inspired by the formularies of the Roman ritual, especially with respect to their theological and spiritual doctrine, the meaning they give to the rite they accompany, and their use of biblical typology. Among the formularies that permit new alternative texts we can mention the prayer of exorcism, the formula for the blessing of the baptismal water, the words of renunciation, and the formula of blessing at the end of the rite.

The option to compose alternative liturgical texts is a welcome concession granted by the postconciliar reform to the local churches. It is a sympathetic response to their need for a liturgy that speaks their language fluently and suggestively. Translations, however free, have always a restraining effect on the free flow of a language and on its singular ability to evoke images as well as experiences. It seems obvious that an option of this kind has sense only on a local level. The composition of new formularies for use in the sacramental celebrations of a local church, like alternative eucharistic prayers, can hardly be an international joint venture.

2. The Passage from the *Editio Typica* of Adult Initiation

"A catechumenate, endorsed by the ancient practice of the church and adapted to contemporary missionary work throughout the world, was so widely requested that the Second Vatican Council decreed its restoration, revision, and adaptation to local traditions."[60] With the consent of the Congregation of Rites the catechumenate was practiced in some mission countries already before Vatican II, but it was the council that placed it at the disposal of every local church and restored its ancient shape consisting of several stages. After the council the Consilium was entrusted with the task of drawing up a revised rite and of determining the suitable adaptations, with proper attention to the needs of the churches in the missions.[61]

The introduction to the Rite of Christian Initiation of Adults distinguishes two types of adaptations: one by the conferences of bishops, the other by the bishop in his diocese. Regarding the first type the introduction speaks of a discretionary power granted to the conferences regarding the various ways, in addition to those mentioned in the general introduction, of adapting the *editio typica*.[62] The list, which refers mostly to the catechumenate, is scanty if we consider the pastoral needs and the socio-cultural reality of the local churches, especially in the missions. As they progress in the practice of adult catechumenate they will eventually be constrained to ask for a broader scope for adapting the rite. The point about this list is therefore neither the quantity of items it offers nor primarily the nature of each of them. The important consideration here is the principle behind each proposed adaptation, change, or modification.

What follows is an enumeration of the different ways of adapting the rites of adult initiation presented by the *editio typica*. In the course of our discussion some of them will receive fuller attention.

First, where it seems advisable, the conferences of bishops may establish some method of receiving "sympathizers" prior to the catechumenate. Sympathizers are "those who, even though they do not fully believe, show some inclination toward the Christian faith." The reception does not entail any ritual or liturgical celebration.[63] Second, where paganism is widespread, the first exorcism and the first renunciation may be inserted into the rite of entrance into the catechumenate. The exorcism and renunciation referred to here are those directed against false worship and the use of magical arts.[64] Third, in areas where physical touch may not seem proper the sign of the cross may be made before the forehead instead of tracing it upon the forehead. Fourth, in places where other religions have the practice of immediately giving a new name to initiates, the rite of giving the baptismal name may be transferred from the period of purification and enlightenment to the rite of entrance into the catechumenate. Fifth, subsidiary rites symbolizing the reception of catechumens into the community may be allowed according to local customs. Sixth, in addition to the liturgy of the word and minor exorcisms, suitable "rites of passage" may be celebrated during the period of the catechumenate. Seventh, the anointing with the oil of catechumens may be omitted, or transferred to the final preparatory rites, or used as a "rite of passage." And eighth, the text for renunciation may be formulated in a more specific and detailed manner.

Beneath these different ways of adapting the rites of adult initiation, with stress on the catechumenate, we can see three principles at work. They are theological, liturgical, and cultural. The theological principle may be stated in these words: "The catechumens, who have been welcomed by the church with a mother's love and concern and are joined to the church, are now part of the household of Christ; they are nourished by the church on the word of God and sustained by liturgical celebrations."[65]

This principle echoes the teaching of LG 14 which affirms that "catechumens who, moved by the Holy Spirit, desire with an explicit intention to be incorporated into the church, are by that very intention joined to her. With love and solicitude mother church already embraces them as her own." AG 14, inspired by St. Augustine, adds that the catechumens "are already of the household of Christ."[66] Because they are joined to the church, they share, though in a limited way, in the life of the church: they are nourished on God's word and sustained by liturgical celebrations.

In other words, the essential meaning of the various rites of the catechumenate lies in the truth that the catechumens are already part of the household of Christ, even if they have still to cross the waters of baptism, receive the outpouring of the Spirit, and share in the Lord's supper. The catechumenate is a transitional phase in the life of faith, a progressive movement toward the Easter sacraments. This reality is what constitutes the theological content of the rites of the catechumenate.

The liturgical principle deals with the ritual shape of Christian initiation, especially the catechumenate. Examining the different rites that make up the catechumenate, we come to the conclusion that its principal elements are the word of God and the liturgical celebrations of exorcisms and blessings. Hippolytus of Rome strongly recommends that the catechumens listen to the word for three years. If at the end of this period they do not show any signs of conversion, they are to be excluded "because they did not listen with faith to the word."[67]

The frequent celebration of the word of God during the period of the catechumenate aims to implant in the heart of the candidates the teaching they receive, to instruct them on the different aspects and ways of praying, to explain to them the meaning of the liturgical symbols, gestures, and seasons, and to lead them gradually into the worship of the whole church.[68] The liturgy of the word forms the catechumens in Christian values and the life of prayer: it teaches them the art of being a Christian. In the words of AG 14, the catechumenate "is not a mere exposition of dogmatic truths and norms of morality, but a period of formation in the whole Christian life." In short, the celebration of God's word, which is the chief liturgical form of the catechumenate, gives shape to the theological content which consists of a progressive movement toward full incorporation into the church. The word of God calls the catechumens to faith and conversion and leads them to the Easter sacraments.

Other liturgical celebrations accompany the candidates during the period of the catechumenate. These are the minor exorcisms and the blessings. The explanation given by the introduction deserves to be quoted, especially because of its relevance to adaptation and formulation of new texts: "The first or minor exorcisms, which are of positive content and composed in the form of prayer, place before the catechumens the real nature of Christian life, the struggle between flesh and spirit, the importance of self-denial for reaching the blessedness of God's kingdom, and the unending need for God's help."[69] The blessings, on the other hand, "are a sign of God's love and of the church's tender care."

In the time of Hippolytus of Rome the exorcism and laying on of hands enabled the bishop, in some mysterious way, to gauge the spiritual progress of the candidate.[70] Something of this remains in the practice of the "scrutinies" whose purpose is to reveal what is weak, defective, or sinful in the hearts of the candidate, so that it may be healed, and what is upright, strong, and holy, so that it may be strengthened.[71] The exorcisms and blessings not only assist the catechumens; they also permit the church to look into the hearts of those who frequently listen to God's word. Indeed no one can listen to it and remain indifferent, or as Hippolytus of Rome affirms, "it is not possible for a stranger to pretend at all times."

From the foregoing discussion we can draw the conclusion that the word of God and the prayer of the church for the catechumens are the elements that bring together into an orderly whole the different adaptations in the rites of adult initiation. There are several ways of adapting the *editio typica,* but there is one liturgical principle that fastens them together. Whatever advantages may be derived, for example, from shifting the position of some of the rites or from adding new ones should not be estimated apart from this principle. Adaptation should not undermine the basic liturgical shape of the catechumenate nor obscure the role of God's word and the church's mediation in the catechumen's growth in faith and conversion.[72]

The cultural principle enjoys a privileged position in the scheme of the rites of Christian initiation. SC 37's principle of respecting, fostering, and admitting into the liturgy the genius and talents of various races and peoples is given an amplified resonance by the *editio typica* of adult initiation. It is remarkable how the program of the *editio typica* to foster inculturation prompts it to explicitly suggest the omission of Roman elements that are not compatible with the cultural sensitivity of the people. In the area involving culture the conferences of bishops are given an extensive latitude. The instances when they can make adaptations are spread over a wide range in the *editio typica.* In other words, culture plays a significant role in the preparation of particular rituals. The following examples will try to show this.

Early on we mentioned in passing that in regions where false worship flourishes the first exorcism and the first renunciation may be inserted into the rite of entrance into the catechumenate. False worship is defined as the cult of spiritual powers, the invocation of the spirits of the dead, and the use of magical arts to obtain benefits.[73]

In connection with the first exorcism the celebrant is directed to breathe lightly toward the face of each candidate and to hold up the right hand toward the candidates while reciting the formula. However, in places where the breathing would be unacceptable, it is omitted, and the gesture with the right hand may be replaced with another more in keeping with local expressions. This might appear to be a form of overindulging in ritual minutiae, but at bottom the issue is no less than the sense of respect which the church holds for the culture of every people.

With respect to the first renunciation the principle that prevails is the spirit of dialogue with other religions. Hence, the formula to be used for the renunciation of false worship and magical arts should not be offensive to the members of those religions where such practices still exist. The idea is to balance the open rejection of error with sincere respect for the persons concerned.

Another cultural consideration is the act of touching. When candidates are admitted into the order of catechumens, they receive the sign of the cross on the forehead and then on the ears, eyes, lips, breast, and shoulders.[74] But where touching in public view is considered improper, the sign of the cross is made, as we noted earlier, in front of the forehead, while the signing of the other senses is omitted in whole or in part. It is interesting to note that St. Ambrose had to deal with a similar issue apropos of the rite of ephphetha or opening the ears and mouth. He explains that our Lord touched the ears and mouth of the deaf and dumb, but the bishop touches the nostrils, not the mouth, "because women are being baptized, and there is not the same purity on the part of the servant as with the Lord."[75]

For the sake of propriety the anointing with the oil of catechumens, which by tradition is on the breast, may be made on both hands or even on other parts of the body.[76] Also for the sake of propriety, instead of placing their hand on the shoulder of the candidate whom they are receiving into their care, the godparents may make some other gesture during the rite of election to signify this.[77] Cultural prohibitions can be so thoroughly worked into the fiber of social life that unless there is a question of sacramental requirement it seems reasonable to drop contrary Roman practices from local use.

A related question concerns the new name and the color of the baptismal garment. The conferences of bishops may allow catechumens to keep the name they already have, or take a traditional Christian name, or one that is familiar in their culture, provided this can admit a Christian interpretation.[78] The use of native names could become an imperative in places where traditional Christian names are so inextricably associated with the politics and culture of the western world that they tend to isolate their bearers from the rest of society.[79]

Some people object that native names are often names of animals, trees, flowers, and inanimate objects. But so are many traditional Christian names like Leo, Sylvia, Rose, and Peter. They are considered Christian because of the persons who bear them or because of the Christian virtues they signify. Perhaps we should speak here rather of baptismal name, not only because some catechumens were given a Christian name at birth, but also because receiving a baptismal name means more than receiving a Christian name. It signifies the added reality in the life of a person, namely conversion to Christ and rebirth into a new life through water and the Holy Spirit.

As for the color of the baptismal garment, which is traditionally white, "another color may be used if local conditions require this."[80] For in the color scheme of some cultures white is for mourning. Surely the baptismal reality of being a new creation and being clothed in Christ can be expressed by other suitable colors, and not only by plain-colored clothes but also by multicolored ones. But the matter needs to be carefully studied because of the question of color symbolism and its traditional association in some countries, especially in Asia, with socio-political systems and religious cults. At any rate, what St. Ambrose wrote about the white garment as a symbol of baptismal transformation is a fine example of how to develop in another cultural setting and on the basis of another color scheme an equally inspiring liturgical catechesis.[81]

From the Editio Typica *to Alternative Rites of Marriage*

1. The Passage from the *Editio Typica*

The Decree promulgating the Rite of Marriage, published on March 19, 1969, states that "the rite for celebrating marriage has been revised according to the norms of the Constitution on the Liturgy, in order that this rite might be enriched, more clearly signify the grace of the sacrament, and impart a knowledge of the obligation of the married couple."[82] In revising the rite the Consilium was guided by the principle which grants "for the preparation of the particular rituals of marriage and for adapting them, a greater freedom than what is allowed for the other sacraments."[83] The greater freedom spoken of by the Consilium is easy to perceive in the norms dealing with the preparation of a particular ritual on the basis of the *editio typica* and the drawing up of a completely new rite.

1. There are two things to consider when preparing a particular ritual of marriage. First, the *terminus a quo* is the *editio typica*. And second, the option to prepare a particular ritual based on the Roman rite should not prejudice the faculty to draw up a new rite of marriage.[84] Should a conference of bishops decide to compose its own rite, adapting the *editio typica* would, of course, be pointless. But if no new rite is to be drawn up, the conference must adapt the Roman rite so that it may be suitable to the customs and needs of the area.

The *editio typica* presents five ways of preparing a particular ritual for marriage. The first is by adapting or, as the case may be, supplementing the formularies in the Roman ritual, including the questions before the consent and the actual words of consent.[85] The term adaptation, which in itself is culturally neutral, acquires here a cultural connotation. Adapting the formularies, above all the words of consent, is not merely a theological and liturgical undertaking; it is undoubtedly also a cultural one. This means that one has to take account of the idiomatic expressions, proverbs, and maxims that the people use when speaking of marriage and married life. For they reveal the people's solemn convictions and collective wisdom about marriage and the values they attach to its institution. Adaptation means that the formularies of the Roman rite are reexpressed according to the language pattern of the people and enriched from their treasury of linguistic expressions.

The type of adaptation we have just described might not always yield the desired doctrinal enrichment of the formularies, especially if the original has a somewhat confined range of theological interest. Although the new *editio typica* is richer in doctrine than its predecessor, it is not expected to convey everything there is to say about the theology of marriage or to address the particular concerns of the local churches. A case at hand is the actual formulary for the consent. There is nothing distinctly Christian about these words—in fact they are the same words used in civil marriages; they are not biblically inspired, and the christological, pneumatological, and ecclesiological dimensions of marriage are conspicuously absent from their scope. Yet they are regarded as the words of covenant between husband and wife, the words that express in sacramental rite the love of Christ for his church.[86]

Another example of a confined formulary is the *editio typica*'s series of questions before the consent. These questions cover only those points concerning freedom of choice, fidelity, and the acceptance of children and of the responsibility for their upbringing. Because of cultural considerations some conferences of bishops might wish to bring up other matters of current interest like the equality between husband and wife and the question of mutual support. In short, in addition to cultural adaptation, which is not directly involved with the question of enriching the doctrinal content, there is the option to supplement the formularies of the Roman ritual by elaborating on what is insufficiently stated or supplying what is lacking.

The second way of preparing a particular ritual is by adding other formularies when the *editio typica* has several optional ones.[87] As we noted when discussing the rites of initiation, the new formularies should be of the same type as the Roman in order to insure that the essential meaning intended by the *editio typica* remains intact. We cannot overemphasize this point. Although we can be critical of not a few formularies in the Roman ritual, we cannot dismiss the fact that they give us the official interpretation, however incomplete or subtle this may be, of the various parts of the rite like its gestures and symbols. New formularies bearing a different message will inevitably change the original meaning of the rite. The theological content of the new formularies can surely be enriched by inserting biblical types and doctrinal statements regarding the sacrament of marriage, but the original sense of the formularies, especially when they interpret the meaning of the rite, must not be lost. In passing, one may argue that because of cultural considerations it might be advisable to compose new formularies, though the method of borrowing from other rituals should not be entirely neglected.

The third way is by rearranging the *editio typica*'s plan or structure of the celebration: "Within the actual rite of the sacrament of marriage, the arrangement of parts may be varied."[88] Some basic liturgical norms intervene in this connection. The liturgy of the word, for example, precedes the liturgy of the sacrament, because the word of God leads to faith, and faith is required by the sacrament. The celebration of marriage before the readings at Mass obviously violates this norm. The explanatory rites like the blessing and giving of rings come after the exchange of consent, because their role is to make explicit those aspects of the sacrament that are merely implied in the essential rite. However, "if it seems more suitable, the questions before the consent may be omitted as long as the assisting priest [or duly appointed witness] asks for and receives the consent of the contracting parties."[89]

There is some uncertainty with respect to the fitting place for the nuptial blessing in the structure of the rite of marriage. Should it be placed immediately after the consent even at nuptial masses? At present it is imparted after the consent and before the explanatory rites when marriage is celebrated without mass; otherwise it is recited traditionally after the Lord's prayer in place of the embolism. This second arrangement seems to derive from a desire to place the prayer of the church for the spouses as close as possible to the eucharistic prayer, and thus to show that the sacrament of marriage flows from the sacrifice of the cross. However, if the nuptial blessing is given after the exchange of consent, the connection between the sacramental contract and the prayer of the church becomes more evident.

The fourth way of preparing the particular ritual is by making adaptations in the area of ritual elements such as gestures and symbols. Coming from different cultures and epochs they are not always easy to understand. However, if one penetrates their meaning, one discovers that they actually offer a vivid profile of what different local churches taught and practiced in the course of centuries regarding the sacrament of marriage.[90] We can cite several examples: the joining of the right hands, the blessing and exchange of rings, the crowning or veiling of the bride, and in some places like the Philippines where the Toledan Rite of Marriage is still partly extant, the placing of the *arrhae* or coins by the bridegroom on the hands of the bride to symbolize material support, the covering of the head of the bride and the shoulders of the bridegroom with a white veil, the encircling of the couple with a cord, and the lighting of two candles.[91]

The question of adapting these and similar ritual elements of marriage is at bottom a cultural matter. For example, the joining of hands, which characterizes the Roman rite, and the exchange of rings might not correspond with the marriage traditions of a people. They might simply be alien to their cultural experience or in some places even regarded as a western imposition. In such situations "the conference of bishops may allow these rites to be omitted or other rites substituted."[92] We should caution, however, about the facile solution of simply omitting ritual gestures. We should bear in mind that one of the aims of the conciliar reform of the marriage rite is to enrich both the doctrinal and the ritual aspects of the celebration. Explanatory rites have an important role in sacramental celebrations. They illustrate the meaning of the rites and call attention to the obligation imposed by the sacraments. Without the explanatory rites the message of the sacraments will often pass unnoticed. Hence, instead of simply omitting them because of cultural considerations, it is preferable to replace them with fitting and meaningful dynamic equivalents.

The fifth way, which focuses on the missions, permits the incorporation of "the marriage customs of nations that are now receiving the gospel for the first time" into the particular ritual.[93] The conditions are those indicated by SC 37 and SC 40. Such customs must not be indissolubly bound up with superstition and error and must be able to express the perennial values of the marriage institution. They should undergo a critical evaluation and, if possible, should be preserved intact. "Such things may in fact be taken over into the liturgy itself, as long as they harmonize with its true and authentic spirit."[94] Following the example of the Roman church which assimilated the marriage customs of the Roman people into its liturgy, the churches in the missions should consider how they can insert into their particular rituals whatever is good and noble in the marriage rites of their people.

Marriage customs refer to the ritual and linguistic components of the native marriage rites. In practice the assimilation of ritual elements may mean adding more explanatory rites or replacing the actual ones with appropriate equivalents. The assimilation of linguistic elements, on the other hand, may mean utilizing key words and phrases that are traditionally found in the native marriage formularies. Other elements like the role of the families of the couple, especially in places where the system of extended family is deeply rooted, and the local customs concerning the time and place of the celebration need also to be examined and, if possible, inserted into the Christian rite of marriage. They are often as important elements of the marriage rite as the formulary or gesture for the marriage contract.

2. Early on we quoted the words of the Consilium regarding the "greater freedom" that the local churches can enjoy in matters related to the rite of marriage. The liberal norms for preparing particular rituals on the basis of the *editio typica* should sufficiently prove that claim. However, in some areas these liberal norms might be only relatively so. For this reason "each conference of bishops may draw up its own marriage rite suited to the usages of the place and people and approved by the Apostolic See."[95]

The preparation of a completely new rite of marriage is a creative venture. It is not a question of adapting, however radically, the *editio typica,* but of drawing up a new rite whose liturgical shape is in many ways original. The features of a new rite could very well be the particular way the celebration is planned, the ritual gestures it employs, and the originality of its texts. However, that is a rather idealistic sketch of how a new rite should look. A new rite need not, or perhaps will never, be original in every respect. In fact there is nothing to stop a local church from drawing inspiration from existing rites or borrowing different marriage elements and fusing them into a harmonious whole. The idea is not new. Around the year 596 Pope Gregory the Great directed Augustine of Canterbury to do the same for the church in England: "Choose from each particular church what is godly, religious and sound, and gathering all together as it were into a dish, place it on the table of the English for their customary diet."[96]

Syncretism, which is merely external, should by every means be avoided. Perhaps one way of doing this is by carefully assigning to each borrowed element a definite meaning and role within the theological and liturgical framework of the celebration.

In places, especially in the missions, where traditional rites of marriage still exist, the plan or structure, the place and the time frame, the formularies, and the ritual gestures of the new rite could be patterned after them. The texts, especially of the words of consent and the nuptial blessing, could have the style of the corresponding native formularies. The explanatory rites too could be inspired by, if not directly drawn from, the ritual elements that normally accompany the celebration of marriage. There is no need to repeat here everything that has been said about the process of critical evaluation and the quality of "connaturalness" such elements should possess. Wholesale and indiscriminate adoption of native marriage rites and ceremonies is alien to the principles of cultural adaptation.

For some areas outside the western sphere the exchange of consent, which is normally done orally, may present cultural difficulty as well as ritual inconvenience. The *editio typica* generously offers two different forms for the exchange of consent. One is in the form of a declaration whereby each one expresses one's consent to the marriage contract, and the other is in the form of question and answer between the official witness and the contracting parties.[97] However, the *editio typica* does not address a question affecting those places where the exchange of consent is traditionally expressed not with words but with symbolic gestures. Does a form of non-verbal consent meet the requirements of the law for validity? We are so accustomed to the verbal character of the Roman rite that we can miss the value and force of non-verbal communication in the liturgy.[98]

A question that is particularly relevant to local churches in the missions is the celebration of marriage at home. Missionaries have reported instances when Christians are pressured to observe, in addition to the church celebration, the prescribed wedding ceremonies of their tribe. The practice has led to a disturbing attitude which regards the Christian rite as a formality imposed by foreign missionaries on their converts. One might even suspect a lurking sentiment that the real marriage, even for Christians, is the one celebrated in the home.

This peculiar situation calls for a missionary strategy. And the strategy consists of imparting to marriage customs a Christian dimension through the word of God and liturgical catechesis, and to allow the sacramental rite to be celebrated in the home. For pastoral and cultural reasons the medieval discipline of holding the marriage rite *in facie ecclesiae* now gives way to the ancient practice of celebrating marriage in the home.[99] "Among peoples where the marriage ceremonies customarily take place in the home, sometimes over a period of several days, their customs should be adapted to the Christian spirit and to the liturgy. In such cases the conference of bishops, according to the pastoral needs of the people, may allow the sacramental rite to be celebrated in the home."[100]

2. The Passage to Alternative Rites of Marriage

The impellent reason for revising the Rite of Marriage was the worldwide clamor for a liturgy with a richer theological content and a nobler liturgical shape. However, the question of cultural adaptation has not been overlooked. The provision of SC gives much space to the issue. The *editio typica* itself is absolutely remarkable for its liberal attitude and flexibility. In the area of cultural adaptation it is difficult to ask for more.

What remains to be done is a challenge to the local churches. It is a demanding task that requires the conviction and support of church leaders, the expertise of local liturgists, and the professional assistance of experts in the related sciences. Because the matter is complex, many years will be needed to realize the conciliar dream of enriched and truly meaningful local rites of marriage. The council has sown the seed, and in a number of local churches the roots are stirring.

It is consoling to note that the attempts to produce alternative marriage rites are not wanting. And they are all done with serious thought and sound criteria.[101] But few have the distinction of having received from the Holy See the stamp of official approval. The first to receive it was the Tagalog Rite of Marriage for use in the Philippines.[102] The decree of promulgation issued by the Catholic bishops' conference of the Philippines supplies the basic background information: "We hereby decree that the Tagalog Rite of Marriage prepared by Father Anscar Chupungco and his collaborators, approved by the Episcopal Commission of Family Life for the CBCP, and confirmed after some amendments by the Sacred Congregation for the Sacraments and Divine Worship on April 20, 1983 in the letter

Prot. CD 559/82, shall begin to be in force from November 27, 1983, First Sunday of Advent."[103]

The new rite follows the basic outline of its Filipino predecessor which included a number of Toledan elements like the giving of the *arrhae* and the use of the veil and the cord. What distinguishes it from the previous rite is its linguistic and ritual adaptation to the socio-religious culture of the lowland Filipinos.

The language used by the Tagalog Rite is often idiomatic, at times also solemn and poetic. At the exchange of consent, for example, the couple declare to each other: "You alone shall I love and shall cherish as the extension of my life, now and forever." The phrase "extension of life" (*karugtong ng buhay*) is a Tagalog idiomatic expression for the biblical concept of one body in marriage. At the exchange of rings they solemnly promise: "Never shall I betray your love! Wear this ring and prize it, for it is the pledge of my love and faithfulness." The verb "to betray" (*pagtaksilan*) commonly refers to marital infidelity, while the noun "pledge" (*sangla*) signifies in this context the sacrifice and deprivation the spouse endures in exchange for love. And as the bridegroom offers the *arrhae* to the bride, he assures her with these words: "I shall never forsake you. I hand to you these *arrhae* as a sign that I will look after your and our children's welfare."[104]

Another feature of the Tagalog Rite of Marriage is its elaboration of theological themes such as the role of the Holy Spirit in married life, the connection between marriage and the sacraments of initiation, and the eucharistic dimension of marriage. The allocutions and prayer of the faithful develop these themes to some extent. On the other hand, the formulary for the exchange of consent makes a modest attempt to give to the marriage contract a theological perspective: "Before God and his people I enter into covenant with you to be your husband (wife) in poverty and riches, in suffering and joy. You alone shall I love and shall cherish as the extension of my life, now and forever."[105] "Covenant" translates the Tagalog *tipan* which is the accepted term for sacred scriptures: Old Testament (*Lumang Tipan*) and New Testament (*Bagong Tipan*). The word is also used in the narrative of the eucharistic institution: "the blood of the new and everlasting covenant (*tipan*)." By using it the formulary alludes to the doctrine of covenant and to the sacrificial and eucharistic aspect of the marriage contract.

A final consideration concerns the ritual elements. The Tagalog Rite retains all the explanatory symbols of the preceding rite: the joining of the right hands, the exchange of rings, the use of the veil and the cord, and the lighting of two candles. In addition the new rite proposes the observance of the *mano po,* a traditional sign of respect toward parents, godparents, and elders on the part of the couple, and suggests the festive ringing of the church bells after the exchange of consent, while the newlyweds kiss each other affectionately and the assembly expresses approval by an applause.

The Tagalog Rite of Marriage is one example of an alternative rite for a local church. Similar attempts are being made in other churches throughout the world, especially in the missions. We can hope that in good time marriage as a cultural institution and marriage as a sacrament will enter into wedlock for the enrichment of both culture and the church.

Note on the Rite of Penance

The cultural adaptation of the rite of penance was not discussed during any of the various phases of conciliar reform. The issue was first addressed by the Rite of Penance published in 1974 after seven laborious years.[106] In the *edi-*

tio typica the conferences of bishops are given the responsibility "to determine more precisely regulations about the place proper for the ordinary celebration of the sacrament of penance and about the signs of repentance to be shown by the faithful before general absolution."[107] Since the general absolution precedes individual confession, it is important that the penitents manifest through external signs the sense of repentance and the intention to receive the absolution. The *editio typica* suggests signs like bowing the head or kneeling.[108]

The provision for the signs of repentance should apply to the other two rites, but particularly to the second because of its communal celebration. Public penance during the patristic and the early medieval periods were marked by symbols and gestures corresponding with the cultural sensitivity of the times. Examples are the wearing of sackcloth, imposition of ashes, and prostrations. For the rite of reconciliation other symbolic gestures, besides the laying on of hands, were performed, like sprinkling the penitents with holy water and incensing them.[109] In time these liturgical signs were dropped from use because they no longer corresponded with existing cultural patterns. The task given to the conferences of bishops is to adapt into the rite of penance such contemporary symbols and gestures as are rooted in the people's sense of sin, repentance, penance, and reconciliation.

In addition to the ritual elaboration of the rite of penance, it is the responsibility of the conferences of bishops "to prepare translations of the texts adapted to the character of each people; also to compose new texts of prayers for use by the faithful and the minister, keeping the essential sacramental formulary intact."[110] The work of translating the texts or composing new ones presupposes a profound understanding and appreciation of the linguistic pattern, words, phrases, and formularies used commonly to express penance and reconciliation. Every culture has its penitential vocabulary, and this should be diligently tapped for the translation of the words of absolution or the composition of prayers like the act of contrition, litany, and the thanksgiving after reconciliation.

Before concluding this note on penance we should discuss briefly the question of method. We need to distinguish between the liturgical shape and the theological content of the rite of penance. The ancient shape prior to the seventh century consisted of confession, penitential discipline, and the act of reconciliation. In the course of time the order of these parts was rearranged to suit the prevailing pastoral practice and the theological reflection which stressed the need for confession and absolution in order to "confect" the sacrament. As a result the shape, as we know it today, normally consists of confession, absolution, and satisfaction. The theological content, on the other hand, may be defined as the process of reconversion which culminates in reconciliation with God and the church. This metanoia or reconversion of heart is what the liturgical rites and penitential discipline signify. In other words, it is their meaning and purpose.

In the light of this methodological consideration it becomes clear that the task of cultural adaptation is to reexpress the liturgical shape of penance, namely confession, absolution, and satisfaction, in cultural forms that will signify the meaning of the sacrament, that is to say, the process of reconversion that culminates in reconciliation with God and the church.

Note on the Rite of Anointing the Sick

In its section on adaptation the Rite of Anointing the Sick presents two methods of preparing particular rituals.[111] The first consists of admitting into the rite appropriate elements from the traditions and culture of individual peoples. This method echoes SC 40 and repeats the provision of the General Introduction to *Christian Initiation.*[112]

The elements referred to here are gestures, symbols, formulas, and material things that people make use of in time of illness in order to relieve the sick, to comfort them, and to bring healing. Some medieval rituals developed ornate celebrations that required the presence of a host of ministers who came processing to the house of the sick with cross, candles, and holy water. The prayers and chanting of the seven penitential psalms were interminable, and sometimes the sick person had to wear the penitential sackcloth and to kneel during the entire service. The rite could be repeated for several days until the sick recovered or died.[113] Unrestrained ritualization is certainly the last thing any sick person needs, yet a moderate amount of liturgical signs that are culturally significant and spiritually inspiring can bring encouragement and strength to the sick.

The second method is drawn from SC 77 which repeats the words of Trent about retaining praiseworthy marriage customs and ceremonies. As in the rite of marriage, the conferences of bishops may "retain elements in the rites of the sick that may now exist in particular rituals, as long as they are compatible with the Constitution on the Liturgy and with contemporary needs; or to adapt any of these elements."[114]

The rest of the section on adaptation deals with the different ways of adapting the particular rituals. We discussed them at some length in connection with the rites of initiation and marriage. It is sufficient to enumerate them here: translations should be prepared in keeping with the genius of different languages and cultures; the introduction may, if necessary, be adapted and enlarged in order to foster the active participation of the sick and the members of the household; the material of the *editio typica* should be arranged in a format that will be as suitable as possible for pastoral use; and whenever the *editio typica* gives several alternative texts, the particular rituals may add other texts of the same kind.[115]

The number of anointings and the parts of the body to be anointed are by and large dictated by cultural considerations. In the medieval rituals the tendency is to instruct the priest to anoint the traditional seats of the five senses together with the navel or, as some rituals direct, where it hurts most.[116] We discussed already the problem of touching with relation to the rites of the catechumenate and baptism. Here the problem becomes somewhat more complex because anointing supposes touching. The solution arrived at by the new rite is to confine anointing to the forehead and the hands, while permitting the number of anointings to be increased and the places to be anointed changed, depending on the culture and traditions of the local church.

As a final consideration we can briefly address the question of method. In order to make adaptations in the rite of anointing it is necessary to define the liturgical shape and the theological content of the sacrament. Although the sacramental formula and the manner of anointing underwent considerable modifications in the course of time, we can identify the essential elements of the liturgical shape, namely anointing with blessed oil and the church's prayer of faith.[117] Pope Paul VI himself set an admirable and inspiring example of cultural adaptation in relation to the oil for the sacrament. He writes: "Since olive oil, which has been prescribed until now for the valid celebration of the sacrament, is unobtainable or difficult to obtain in some parts of the world, we have decreed, at the request of a number of bishops, that from now on, according to circumstances, another kind of oil can also be used, provided it is derived from plants and is thus similar to olive oil."[118]

Beneath the liturgical elements of anointing and the

prayer of faith we can perceive the concern or solicitude of the whole church "which commends the sick to the suffering and glorified Lord so that he may raise them up and save them."[119] That concern reveals the heart of Christ himself who showed a special care for the sick. This is what the liturgical rite expresses and celebrates. The task of cultural adaptation is to give shape to this theological content in such a way that the sick will experience more convincingly the concern of the church. It will be recalled that in the liturgy the experience of faith takes place in the cultural setting of the local church.

Notes

[1] The proposed text reads: *Cum autem, decursu temporum, non sine fidelium detrimento, quaedam in ea irrepserint quae praedictae eorum naturae minus bene respondeant, Sacrosanctum Concilium ea quae sequuntur decernit. Schema Constitutionis de Sacra Liturgia,* henceforth *Schema,* Emendationes VII, Vatican City 1963, p. 10.

[2] Chapter III has three parts: theological principles (SC 59–61), adaptation (SC 62–63), and revision of the liturgy of the sacraments and sacramentals (SC 64–82).

[3] *Schema,* Emendationes VII, p. 20.

[4] A. Nocent: "I tre sacramenti dell'iniziazione cristiana," *Anàmnesis* 3/1, Genoa 1986, pp. 57–59.

[5] When Chapter III was being discussed, a council father complained that the proposal to revise the sacramental rites seemed to imply that something was wrong with them. For this reason several phrases like *funditus recognoscantur* and *ex integro recognoscantur* were softened to *pro opportunitate, ex more,* and *admitti liceat. Schema,* Emendationes VII, p. 9.

[6] A. Bugnini: "7 marzo 1965: passaggio dal latino al volgare," *La riforma liturgica,* Rome 1983, pp. 108–21.

[7] The relator P. Hallinan sums up the discussion: *Quoad ipsam extensionem usus linguae vernaculae in Sacramentis et Sacramentalibus Patres tres sententias proposuerunt: nullus vel rarus sit usus linguae vernaculae; omnia, ipsis formis Sacramentorum inclusis, lingua vernacula dicantur; via media: omnia dicantur lingua vernacula excepta stricte dicta forma Sacramentorum. Schema,* Emendationes VII, p. 7.

[8] The other *modi* asked that the vernacular be used only for the readings and commentaries, and that Latin be kept for exorcisms and prayers that make mention of the action of demons. *Schema,* Modi III, Vatican City 1963, p. 12.

[9] The relator, P. Hallinan, explains what the conciliar commission meant by simpler and more solemn rites: . . . *ad clarius significandam naturam huius recognitionis Commissio mentionem fecit de ritu ampliori ad modum catechumenatus priorum saeculorum ("solemnior") et de ritu breviori quando catechumenatus liturgicus Baptismum non praecedit. Schema,* Emendationes VII, p. 12.

[10] *Ordo Initiationis Christianae Adultorum,* henceforth *OICA,* Vatican City 1972, no. 240, p. 98; *DOL,* p. 753.

[11] *Ibid.*

[12] *Schema,* Emendationes VII, Appendix, p. 28.

[13] See, however, A. Kavanagh: *The Shape of Baptism: The Rite of Christian Initiation,* New York 1978, pp. 126–27. According to him "the General Introduction to all the reformed initiatory rites, including the Baptism of Children and Confirmation by Bishops, makes it clear that the premier rite is that of full initiation of adults" and that "the spirit and principles contained in the full rites of adult initiation are operative throughout the other initiatory rites."

[14] *Ibid.,* p. 13.

[15] *Ibid.*

[16] *Schema,* Emendationes VII, p. 13. See also Appendix, p. 28.

[17] A council father did not think it practical to celebrate confirmation within mass, while another stated that confirmation must always be separated from first communion. *Schema,* Modi III, p. 14.

[18] *Schema,* Emendationes VII, p. 14. For the historical devel-

opments that led to this problem see: A. Nocent: "I tre sacramenti dell'iniziazione cristiana," pp. 107–16.

[19] P. Gy: "La notion chrétienne d'initiation. Jalon pour une enquête," *La Maison-Dieu* 132 (1977) pp. 33–54.

[20] S. Marsili: *I segni del mistero di Cristo,* Rome 1987, pp. 143–45. Marsili notes that besides theological inconvenience of disrupting the sequence of the sacraments there is also an ecumenical difficulty, since Protestants tend to place less accent on the pedagogical aspect of such a sequence.

[21] The relator reports: *Plures Patres petierunt ut recognitio ritus Sacramenti Poenitentiae eius naturam praesertim socialem et ecclesialem clarius exprimat. Commissio censuit hanc emendationem recipiendam esse per insertionem verborum "naturam et" ante verbum "effectum." Schema,* Emendationes VII, p. 14.

[22] *Schema,* Emendationes VII, Appendix, p. 28.

[23] *Ibid.* See: V. Fiala: "L'imposition des mains comme signe de la communication de l'Esprit-Saint dans les rites latins," *Le Saint-Esprit dans la liturgie,* Rome 1977, pp. 102–03.

[24] *Schema,* Emendationes VII, pp. 26–27: *Praxis hodierna (can. 940, 2), post monitum Concilii Tridentini (Sessio XIV, Doctr. de Sacr. Extr. Unctionis, c. 3), vetat in eodem vitae discrimine hoc Sacramentum iterare. Sed unctionis iteratio, etiam in eadem infirmitate, fuit consuetudo Ecclesiarum usque ad saec. XIII. Nam aegrotus, maxime in diuturna infirmitate, saepius indiget solatio spirituali.*

[25] A. Duval: "L'extrême-onction au concile du Trent. Sacrement des mourants ou sacrement des malades?" *La Maison-Dieu* 101 (1970), pp. 127–72; I. Scicolone: "Unzione degli infermi," *Anàmnesis* 3/1, pp. 231–34.

[26] *Ordo Unctionis Infirmorum Eorumque Pastoralis Curae,* henceforth *OUI,* Vatican City 1975, no. 9, p. 15; *DOL,* p. 1056.

[27] *Schema,* Emendationes VII, p. 23.

[28] *Ibid.,* p. 15.

[29] *Schema,* Modi III, no. 60, p. 16.

[30] *Schema,* Emendationes VII, Appendix, p. 29.

[31] *Schema,* Emendationes VII, p. 16. See *Tradition Apostolique,* ed. B. Botte, Münster 1963, p. 24.

[32] In his report to the preparatory commission Cardinal Lar-

raona explained: *Constitutio de Sacra Liturgia consequi vult recognitionem elementorum ipsius ritus, 1) sive partem Ritualis romani ex integro ordinando, 2) sive singulis regionibus commendando ut ditiora elementa propria servent, iuxta monitum Concilii Tridentini, 3) sive demum concedendo ut ex ritu Ritualis romani singulae Conferentiae Episcopales alium magis proprium efforment. Acta et Documenta Concilio Oecumenico Vaticano II Apparando,* henceforth *Acta et Documenta,* Series II, 3, Vatican City 1961, p. 289.

[33] *Acta et Documenta,* Series II, 5, p. 87; II, 1, p. 140; II, 3, p. 289; II, 1, p. 480, and II, 5, p. 619.

[34] *De Reformatione* I, Sessio 24, *Mansi* 33, col. 153.

[35] P. Jounel: "La liturgie romaine du mariage," *La Maison-Dieu* 50 (1956) pp. 30–57; H. Schmidt: "Rituals and Sacramentality of Christian Marriage," *Studia Missionalia* 33 (1974) pp. 258–84; A. Nocent: "Contribution à l'étude du rituel du mariage," *Eulogia,* Miscellanea in honor of B. Neunheuser, *Studia Anselmiana* 68, Rome 1979, pp. 243–65; J.-B. Molin: "Un rituel italien du mariage au XVIe siècle," *Ecclesia Orans* II (1985/2) pp. 163–71; K. Stevenson: "The Marriage Rite from an Early Ritual-Votive Missal," *Ecclesia Orans* III (1986/2) pp. 181–93.

[36] *Schema,* Modi III, p. 17.

[37] *OCM,* no. 17, p. 10; *DOL,* p. 924. See Canon 1108,2, *Codex Iuris Canonici,* Vatican City 1983, p. 194.

[38] The preconciliar *Analyticus Conspectus* summed up the *consilia et vota* of the bishops in three propositions: 1. *Matrimonii sacramentum arctius cum Missa connectatur;* 2. *Consensus matrimonialis locum habeat inter Missarum sollemnia;* and 3. *Matrimonii ritus in Missa integretur, ut iam facta est in Rituali Neerlandico. Acta et Documenta,* Series II, 2, pp. 175–78.

[39] *Schema,* Emendationes VII, p. 17.

[40] B. Fischer–P. Gy, *Notitiae* 2 (1966) pp. 220–30. See A. Bugnini: "Rituale romano," *La riforma liturgica,* pp. 566–69.

[41] *De limitibus aptationis, de quibus agitur in art. 63 et 39, nihil dictum est in relationibus conciliaribus. Tota res relicta est Consilio post-conciliari. Non videtur a priori solvenda, sed post maturum studium in diversis casibus diversimode determinanda. Ibid.,* p. 221.

[42] *Ordo Baptismi Parvulorum,* henceforth *OBP,* Vatican City 1973, no. 4, p. 20; *DOL,* p. 729.

[43] Justin Martyr: *Apologies* I, 61, ed. L. Pautigny, Paris 1904, p. 126–28; Hippolytus: *Tradition Apostolique,* 21, pp. 48–50.

[44] *De Recognitione Ritualis Romani,* pp. 222–23.

[45] *De Initiatione Christiana,* General Introduction, nos. 30–33, pp. 12–13; *DOL,* pp. 724–25.

[46] *OBP,* nos. 23–26, p. 20; *DOL,* pp. 729–30. See A. Bugnini: "Battesimo dei bambini," *La riforma liturgica,* pp. 582–95.

[47] *OICA,* nos. 64–65, pp. 29–30; no. 66 for the adaptations by the bishop, p. 30; no. 276 for the simple rite, p. 113; *DOL,* pp. 747–48 and 754. See A. Bugnini: "Iniziazione cristiana degli adulti," *La riforma liturgica,* p. 570–81.

[48] *De Initiatione Christiana,* no. 30,2, p. 12; *DOL,* p. 724.

[49] *Ibid.,* no. 30,3.

[50] *Ibid.,* no. 30,4.

[51] On the question of translating the sacramental form the Holy See has issued apposite directives. See Congregation for Divine Worship: *Circular Letter "Dum toto terrarum"* and Congregation for the Doctrine of Faith: *Declaration "Instauratio liturgica." DOL,* pp. 298–99.

[52] *De Initiatione Christiana,* no. 30,5.

[53] C. Vogel (ed.): *Le Pontifical romano-germanique du dixième siècle,* 2 vols., Vatican City 1963; idem: *Medieval Liturgy. An Introduction to the Sources,* trans. and revised by W. Storey and N. Rasmussen, Washington, D.C., 1986, pp. 230–37, 249–51.

[54] *De Initiatione Christiana,* no. 30,6.

[55] Congregation for the Sacraments and Divine Worship: *Letter "Decem iam annos,"* no. 2, *DOL,* p. 301.

[56] *De Initiatione Christiana,* no. 31.

[57] *Acta et Documenta,* Series II, 5, p. 427.

[58] *De Initiatione Christiana,* no. 32.

[59] *Ordo Celebrandi Matrimonium,* henceforth *OCM,* Vatican City 1972, no. 13, p. 9; *DOL,* p. 923.

[60] *OICA,* no. 2, p. 15; *DOL,* p. 736.

[61] *De Recognitione Ritualis Romani,* p. 224: *Circa aptationes in terris missionum faciendas et iam pro parte in novo Ordine catechumenatus praevisas considerandum erit quaenam sint aptationes ordinariae, de quibus in art. 39, quaenam aptationes profundiores, de quibus in art. 40.* See: A. Bugnini: "Iniziazione cristiana degli

adulti," *La riforma liturgica,* pp. 570–80; A. Kavanagh: *The Shape of Baptism: The Rite of Christian Initiation,* pp. 126–49; A. Nocent: "I tre sacramenti dell'iniziazione cristiana," *Anàmnesis* 3/1, pp. 73–86.

[62] *OICA,* Introduction, no. 65, pp. 29–30; *DOL,* pp. 747–48.

[63] See *ibid.*, no. 12, pp. 17–18; *DOL,* p. 738.

[64] *Ibid.*, no. 78–81, pp. 34–35.

[65] *Ibid.*, no. 18, p. 18; *DOL,* p. 739.

[66] *In Iohannis Evangelium Tractatus* XI, 11, 4, *Corpus Christianorum,* Series Latina XXXVI, Turnholt 1954, pp. 111–12.

[67] *Tradition Apostolique,* no. 20, p. 42.

[68] *OICA,* no. 106, p. 45.

[69] *Ibid.*, no. 101, p. 44; *DOL,* p. 749.

[70] *Tradition Apostolique,* no. 20, p. 42: *Cum appropinquat dies quo baptizabuntur, episcopus exorcizet unumquemque eorum ut sciat an purus sit. Si quis autem non est bonus aut non est purus, ponatur seorsum, quia non audivit verbum in fide, quia impossibile est ut alienus se abscondat semper.*

[71] *OICA,* no. 25, p. 21; *DOL,* p. 741.

[72] A. Nocent cautions about introducing other rites, however useful and legitimate, because they could diminish the use and the dynamism of the essential rites. See "I tre sacramenti dell'iniziazione cristiana," *Anàmnesis* 3/1, p. 78.

[73] *OICA,* no. 78–81, p. 34–35.

[74] *Ibid.*, nos. 83–87, pp. 36–38.

[75] *De Sacramentis,* ed. B. Botte, *Sources Chrétiennes* 25bis (1961), I, 1,3, pp. 60–63.

[76] *OICA,* no. 130, p. 52.

[77] *Ibid.*, no. 147, p. 59.

[78] *Ibid.*, no. 88, p. 38.

[79] A. Chupungco: "Le texte de Lima. Indicateur pour le futur: une perspective culturelle," *La Maison-Dieu* 163 (1985) pp. 59–68.

[80] *OICA,* no. 225, p. 94. In the Philippines it is the common practice to give a light blue baptismal garment to male children and a pink one to female children.

[81] *De Mysteriis,* ed. B. Botte, VII, pp. 174–76.

[82] *Ordo Celebrandi Matrimonium,* Vatican City 1969, p. 5; *DOL,* p. 921. See A. Bugnini: "Matrimonio," *La riforma liturgica,* pp. 677–86; P. Gy: "Le nouveau Rituel Romain du Mariage," *La Maison-Dieu* 99 (1969) pp. 124–43; A. Nocent: "Il matrimonio cristiano," *Anàmnesis* 3/1, pp. 356–64. See also the papers read at the Second International Congress on Liturgy by the Pontifical Liturgical Institute on May 27–31, 1985: G. Farnedi (ed.): *La celebrazione cristiana del matrimonio. Simboli e testi,* Rome 1986.

[83] *De Recognitione Ritualis Romani,* p. 228.

[84] *OCM,* no. 12, p. 9; *DOL,* p. 923. For a study on the preparation of the particular rituals of marriage see: A. Augé: "Dal rituale 'tipico' ai rituali particolari del matrimonio," *La celebrazione del matrimonio,* Bologna 1977, pp. 236–62.

[85] *Ibid.,* no. 13, p. 9; *DOL,* p. 923.

[86] A. Bugnini: "Matrimonio," *La riforma liturgica,* pp. 682–83; See A. Duval: "Contract et sacrement du mariage au Concile de Trent," *La Maison-Dieu* 127 (1976) pp. 64–105.

[87] *OCM,* no. 13, p. 9; *DOL,* p. 923.

[88] *Ibid.,* no. 14, p. 9; *DOL,* p. 923.

[89] *Ibid.*

[90] *Ibid.,* no. 15, pp. 9–10; *DOL,* p. 924.

[91] *Liturgical Information Bulletin of the Philippines* Vol. IX, 3 (1974) p. 76.

[92] *OCM,* no. 15, pp. 9–10; *DOL,* p. 924.

[93] *Ibid.,* no. 16, p. 10; *DOL,* p. 924.

[94] *Ibid.;* see SC 37.

[95] *Ibid.,* no. 17, p. 10; *DOL,* p. 924; see SC 77.

[96] *Epist. 64,* Lib. XI, *PL* 77, col. 1187.

[97] *Ibid.,* no. 25, pp. 12–13.

[98] A. Chupungco: *Liturgical Renewal in the Philippines,* Manila 1980, pp. 45–70. The case refers to mountain tribes in the north of the Philippines (Ifugao, Benguet, and Kalinga).

[99] J. Évenou: "Le mariage," *L'Église en prière* III, Paris 1984, pp. 214–16.

[100] *OCM,* no. 18, p. 10; *DOL,* p. 924.

[101] See *Rivista Liturgica* 2–3 (1985): D. Borobio: "Matrimonio e inculturazione nella Chiesa ispanica," pp. 238–92; M.

Allard: "Inculturazione del Rituale canadese francofono del matrimonio," pp. 239–92; C. Fernández: "Il matrimonio cristiano nelle diverse culture dell'ambiente messicano," pp. 302–12; L. Mpongo: "Una sintesi africana per un Rituale del Matrimonio cristiano inculturato," pp. 313–25; and P. Puthanangady: "Inserimento della liturgia del matrimonio nella cutura indiana," pp. 326–38. See L. Mpongo: *Pour une anthropologie chrétienne du mariage au Congo,* Kinshasa 1968.

[102] *Ang Pagdiriwang ng Pag-iisang Dibdib,* Manila 1983. See R. Serrano's study of this rite which he presented to the Pontifical Liturgical Institute as a doctoral dissertation: *Towards a Cultural Adaptation of the Rite of Marriage,* Rome 1987.

[103] *Ibid.* The decree was signed by the CBCP President, Archbishop A. Mabutas, on June 24, 1983.

[104] The Tagalog text reads: *Ikaw lamang ang aking iibigin at itatanging karugtong ng buhay ngayon at magpakailanman; N., kailanma'y di kita pagtataksilan. Isuot mo at pakaingatan ang singsing na ito, na siyang sangla ng aking pag-ibig at katapatan; N., kailanma'y di kita pababayaan. Inilalagak ko sa iyo itong mga aras na tanda ng aking pagpapahalaga at pagkalinga sa kapakanan mo. Ibid.*, pp. 20, 23, and 24.

[105] The Tagalog text reads: *N., sa harap ng Diyos at ng kanyang sambayanan, tinitipan kitang maging aking asawa sa hirap at ginhawa, sa dusa at ligaya. Ikaw lamang ang aking iibigin at itatanging karugtong ng buhay ngayon at magpakailanman. Ibid.*, p. 20.

[106] *Ordo Paenitentiae,* henceforth *OP,* Vatican City 1974, nos. 38–40, pp. 24–25; *DOL,* pp. 968–69. See A. Bugnini: "Riconciliazione," *La riforma liturgica,* pp. 646–64.

[107] *OP,* no. 38b, p. 24; *DOL,* p. 968.

[108] *OP,* no. 35b, p. 22; *DOL,* p. 967.

[109] *De Recognitione Ritualis Romani,* p. 226: *Inter media apta ad hanc indolem [socialem et ecclesialem] conculcandam iam Commissio praeconciliaris in declaratione sua enumeravit restaurationem (in quantum possibile est) venerabilis impositio manus, qua ex antiquissimis temporibus communio cum Ecclesia in Paenitentia restituta significatur.* See: B. Poschmann: *Penance and the Anointing of the Sick,* New York 1964, pp. 87–91; A. Nocent: "Il sacramento della

penitenza e della riconciliazione," *Anàmnesis* 3/1, pp. 157–66; 179–86.

[110] *OP*, no. 38c, p. 24; *DOL*, p. 968.

[111] *OUI*, nos. 38–39, p. 21; *DOL*, p. 1060. See A. Bugnini: "Riti per gli infermi," *La riforma liturgica*, pp. 665–75; *De Recognitione Ritualis Romani*, pp. 227–28.

[112] *De Initiatione Christiana*, no. 30,2, p. 12; *DOL*, p. 724.

[113] E. Martène: *De Antiquis Ecclesiae Ritibus Libri*, I, ch. VII, art. IV, Hildesheim 1967, pp. 841–981.

[114] *OUI*, no. 38c, p. 21; *DOL*, p. 1060.

[115] *Ibid.*, nos. 38d–f and 39.

[116] E. Martène: *De Antiquis Ecclesiae Ritibus Libri*, pp. 842–43. See: A.-G. Martimort: "Prières pour les malades et onction sacrementelle," *L'Église en prière* III, pp. 145–46; I. Scicolone: "Unzione degli infermi," *Anàmnesis* 3/1, pp. 225–28.

[117] Pope Paul VI: *Apostolic Constitution "Sacram Unctionem Infirmorum," OUI*, p. 10; *DOL*, p. 1052.

[118] *Ibid.*

[119] *Ibid.*, p. 9; see LG 11.

Chapter Four

The Future Shape of the Liturgical Year

Theological Premise

1. The Form and Content of the Liturgical Year

The liturgical calendar developed in the milieu of the northern hemisphere. Many of its feasts, especially those that are rooted in the seasons of the year, are very much tied to their place of origin. For this reason, such feasts often do not relate to the seasonal experience of those who live outside the northern hemisphere. Two typical examples are Christmas and Easter. The hymns and symbols of these feasts so unmistakably evoke the seasonal phenomena of the north that they give the impression of being essentially winter and spring feasts. Celebrating them outside these seasons can cause the unsettling sensation of misplacement.

The adaptation of the liturgical calendar requires a close examination of the *terminus a quo* and the *terminus ad quem.* Regarding the *terminus a quo* two basic questions need to be studied. First, what is the theology of the liturgical year and how is it expressed ritually? And second, what is the historical background, theological content, liturgical form, and pastoral relevance of the liturgical feast to be adapted? As regards the *terminus ad quem,* the following questions require careful attention. First, what linguistic, symbolic, and ritual expressions connected with the seasons of the year in the other hemispheres can be absorbed by the liturgical calendar and feasts? And second, in the regions outside the northern hemisphere should feasts with a well-defined seasonal character be held during the corresponding season of the year? Or should new ones more suited to the seasonal experience of the local church be instituted?

A distinction may be made between the ritual shape of the liturgical year and its theological content. SC 102 defines the theological content of the liturgical year in terms of the saving work of the divine bridegroom, the Lord's resurrection together with his blessed passion, the whole mystery of Christ, and the mystery of redemption. Articles 104, 106, and 107, on the other hand, use the expression "paschal mystery." The church celebrates the paschal mystery every eighth day (SC 106); in the course of the liturgical year the faithful celebrate the mysteries of Christian redemption and above all the paschal mystery (SC 107); and by celebrating the feasts of saints the church proclaims the paschal mystery achieved in them (SC 104).

From these texts we may conclude that the paschal mystery, which enfolds the whole mystery of Christ from his incarnation to Pentecost and his second coming, permeates the entire liturgical year. The paschal mystery is the axis around which the liturgical year revolves, although the other mysteries that lead to or flow from it are also celebrated in the course of the year. All liturgical feasts, including those that commemorate the various aspects of Christ's life, like Christmas, center on this mystery.[1]

The liturgical year is celebrated principally through the mass, the liturgy of the hours, and other liturgical actions proper to the feast or to the liturgical season: "Each day is made holy through the liturgical celebrations of the people of God, especially through the eucharistic sacrifice and the divine office."[2] These are the liturgical forms whereby the paschal mystery and the mysteries related to it "are in some way made present in every age in order that the faithful may lay hold on them and be filled with saving grace" (SC 102).

What cultural adaptation aims to do is to give an appropriate cultural shape to the various liturgical forms for celebrating the paschal mystery in the course of the year and to allow this mystery to penetrate the most secret recesses of human culture and traditions. To achieve this aim the method of inculturation can fittingly be employed.

We speak here of inculturation in reference to the process of harmonizing the elements of the liturgical feasts with the local church's perception and experience of the seasons of the year. Through inculturation the texts, symbols, rites, calendar date, and the hour of celebration are, as it were, uprooted from their original hemispheric setting and rerooted in the other regions of the world. We should note that the process of uprooting and rerooting does not necessarily imply changing or shifting the date of a feast. Because the dates of Easter and Christmas are universally accepted, the inculturation of these feasts will have to be confined to the area of language and symbols. The calendar date of Easter, for example, has such a long history and deep theological meaning that to celebrate it in the southern hemisphere during its springtime will likely create more problems. However, this is not the case with rogation and ember days which are best celebrated during the seasons of planting and harvesting.

What then is the basic theological principle governing the process of liturgical adaptation? From the conciliar texts we have cited we may infer that the theological principle is the anamnesis of Christ's mystery in the course of the liturgical year. In the first chapter of this book we defined anamnesis as a ritual activity that recalls the paschal mystery through the performance of appointed rites. Liturgical rites consist essentially of ritual acts and formulas. We noted how by virtue of this ritual activity and by the power of God the death and resurrection of Christ become present in mystery or sacramental form. We may say that every liturgical celebration is anamnesis: a ritual activity that commemorates the paschal mystery and renders it present in the church.

Anamnesis in the context of the liturgical year refers to both the weekly and the annual cycles and hence has two types. One is weekly memorial and the other is anniversary. The very nature of anamnesis, whether weekly memorial or anniversary, requires the time of the liturgical celebration to coincide with or be as close as possible to the event being recalled. This is a rule which we normally observe when we celebrate birthdays and important anniversaries. When one is dealing with anamnesis which implies the presence of the mystery being commemorated, the time-coincidence becomes even more necessary.

To the weekly memorial belongs the Sunday celebration of the eucharist which is connected with cosmogony and the apparitions of the risen Christ.[3] The Sunday eucharist highlights these two events. By proclaiming the word, celebrating baptism, and breaking the bread on Sunday the church commemorates the paschal mystery and relives the day when Christ, risen from the dead, appeared to his disciples. SC 106 confirms this when it exhorts the faithful to gather together on the Lord's day in order to hear the word of God and take part in the eucharist.[4] Sunday is thus the appointed day for the weekly anamnesis of the paschal mystery. Since the weekly anamnesis is bound to Sunday, no other day of the week can replace this day. The adoption of a day other than Sunday, possibly because of the special significance it has in a people's culture, like Friday in predominantly Muslim countries, does not meet the requirement of weekly anamnesis.

The date of Easter, on the other hand, has to be viewed in a different light. It is not a fixed calendar date, but a composite of lunisolar elements, namely Sunday, full moon, and spring equinox.[5] These elements constitute the conjectured date of Christ's death and resurrection. According to the calendar reckoning of the early church this lunisolar date stood closest to these saving events. The long and vexed history of the Easter date demonstrates the unwearied endeavor of the church to establish the feast on its "historical" date.

The theological underpinning of the Easter controversy that raged during the second century is that the yearly anamnesis of the paschal mystery, which takes the form of an anniversary, should coincide, as much as possible, with the conjectured date of the event being recalled. Failure to do this will reduce the Easter anamnesis to an ordinary weekly memorial, and bring about a confusion between the yearly and the weekly cycles of feasts. It is true that patristic theology speaks of a weekly or even a daily Easter inasmuch as every eucharistic celebration is the presence-in-mystery of Christ's death and resurrection.[6] Nevertheless, in essence and origin Easter is a yearly feast, an anniversary.

The cosmic elements of spring, equinox, and full moon played a key role in the development of the Easter liturgy and theology. For the fathers of the church they symbolized the presence of the paschal mystery as well as the grace of rebirth, fullness of life in Christ, and enduring light. Our problem is that spring occurs in the northern hemisphere when it is summer in the equator and autumn in the southern hemisphere. As a result, the spring symbolism of Easter in these regions can be quite irrelevant.

Since we are dealing with a lunisolar calendar, we should regard spring primarily as the time indicator for the northern hemisphere to celebrate Easter. The same thing applies respectively to summer and autumn for the equator and the southern hemisphere. One may argue, maybe rather naively, that when Christ died, it was summer and autumn outside the northern hemisphere. In other words, the adaptation of the Easter feast does not involve a change of date but the assimilation, through the process of inculturation, of the linguistic, symbolic, and ritual expressions proper to summer and autumn. The churches outside the northern hemisphere need to unearth the Easter symbols and images hidden in the seasons of summer and autumn, in much the same way as the fathers of the church did in regard to spring.

Outside Sunday and Easter, with Pentecost as the culminating feast, the anamnesis of the paschal mystery in the course of the liturgical year is not tied to a particular day of the week or season of the year. The dates of Christmas and Epiphany, for example, do not indicate the respective historical date of Christ's birth and his baptism at the Jordan.[7] We know that the calendar date of these feasts, though not devoid of logical thought or pastoral motive, is arbitrary. Surely we cannot speak here of an anniversary in connection with an historical date. Nonetheless, the mysteries they commemorate are in some way made present to the celebrating assembly. The teaching of SC 102 indirectly confirms this: "Recalling thus the mysteries of redemption, the church opens to the faithful the riches of the Lord's powers and merits, so that these are in some way made present in every age in order that the faithful may lay hold on them and be filled with saving grace."

The presence of the different aspects of Christ's mystery in the liturgy can be explained in relation to the paschal mystery. In the incisive words of O. Casel, "the mystery of the church year is always one."[8] Every feast recalls the paschal mystery, or, in the doctrine of Casel, every feast of Christ celebrates the entire mystery of salvation seen from a different angle. At Christmas the liturgy proclaims the paschal mystery at its initial stage. It is the celebration and experience of the mystery to which Christ's birth leads: his death and resurrection. In conclusion we may say that the feasts of Christ in the course of the liturgical year lead to or flow from the paschal mystery.

The primacy of the paschal mystery is evident also in the feasts of the saints. SC 103 affirms that "in celebrating the annual cycle of Christ's mysteries, the church honors with special love Mary, the Mother of God, who is joined by an inseparable bond to the saving work of her Son." The memory of the martyrs and other saints is also joined up with the mystery of Christ. SC 104 points out that "by celebrating their passage from earth to heaven the church proclaims the paschal mystery achieved in the saints."[9] In other words, the Marian and sanctoral cycles are contingent on the cycle of Christ's mystery. We may even affirm that the feasts of Mary and the saints are celebrations of particular aspects of the paschal mystery. Their primary accent is on Christ himself. This explains why SC 108 ordains that the feasts of the Lord are to have precedence over those of the saints. And SC 111 directs that "lest the feasts of the saints take precedence over the feasts commemorating the very mysteries of salvation, many of them should be left to be celebrated by a particular church or nation or religious family."

By tradition the church commemorates the saints on the day of their martyrdom, natural death, or an important event related to their life or cult. Obviously the tradition is supported by the concept of anniversary which, in the case of the saints, refers to their passage from this world to the Father in imitation of Christ. Hence, the date of the feasts of the saints is not to be taken too arbitrarily. For practical reasons it is not always possible to celebrate their feasts on the day of their *transitus* or even of the *translatio* of their mortal remains. Nonetheless, the principle of anniversary should, as much as possible, guide the choice of the date for their feasts, in order to give importance to the time or the "hour" of their passage to eternal life, when the paschal mystery was definitively achieved in them.

2. Conclusions

The liturgical year unfolds the mystery of Christ from his incarnation to his second coming. The axis around which the different aspects of Christ's life and mission revolve is the paschal mystery. This remains the center of the calendar of feasts, even as care must be taken that in the course of the liturgical year the mystery of Christ is celebrated in its entirety, that is, under its different aspects.

The principal forms for celebrating the liturgical feasts are the mass and the liturgy of the hours. Through the liturgical texts, symbols, and rites performed at the appointed time, the mystery of Christ is unfolded, breaks into time, and enters into our culture and traditions. The basic consideration is how those elements of the liturgical year that originated in the milieu of the northern hemisphere could be reexpressed in the other regions of the earth in harmony with the cultural and seasonal experiences of the local churches. We should note in passing that besides the mass and the liturgy of the hours there are other forms of celebrating the feasts. The liturgy of the word, liturgical blessings, and processions are forms that can be developed more fully, using especially the methods of inculturation and creativity.

The liturgical form consists essentially of the ritual anamnesis of the paschal mystery in the course of the year. The anamnesis on Sunday and Easter is tied to a particular time and takes the form of weekly memorial or anniversary. The Lord's day can be kept only on Sunday, and the lunisolar date of Easter, which falls in spring in the northern hemisphere (and consequently in summer or autumn elsewhere), is the appropriate time to hold this kind of anamnesis. It is important to bear in mind that in the liturgical calendar spring designates primarily the lunisolar date of Easter which, by church reckoning, stands closest to the historical circumstances of Christ's passion and death. It is outside the scope of cultural adaptation to propose another day for the weekly observance of the Lord's day or another seasonal date for the annual celebration of Easter. In these instances the task assigned to cultural adaptation is of a creative nature, namely to shape a new set of language, symbols, and rites suited to the cultural needs and seasonal experiences of the local churches in every region of the world.

The presence of the seasonal phenomena and cosmological elements like the equinoxes, the solstices, light, fire, and water can be strongly felt in some liturgical feasts. Adapting such feasts will involve the method of inculturation whereby they are made to assimilate the language, symbols, and rites of parallel native feasts as well as suitable seasonal phenomena. When composing liturgical hymns, for example, one should take account of the current season of the year and the images and cosmic manifestations it displays. In this way, the Christian feasts will make their way to the people's perception and experience of times and seasons.

Some liturgical feasts were instituted in connection with particular seasons of the year, like rogation and ember days. They will be meaningful to the people who observe them if they are celebrated during the corresponding season and with liturgical forms that express the connection between the feast and the current seasonal phenomena and human activities.

The inculturation of the language, symbols, and rites connected with the seasons of the year might not entirely satisfy the need for a truly meaningful celebration of the Christian feasts. Even the change in the date of some feasts will not automatically solve the problem of how to harmonize the liturgical calendar with the seasons of the year.

Inculturation alone will not fully answer every need. Eventually Vatican II's program of adaptation to the culture and traditions of peoples will require creativity.

In particular situations it will be necessary to introduce new feasts into the calendar of a local church in order to mark the seasonal turning points, the rhythm of life and work, or the principal events in the life of the people. We refer to those situations where Christian feasts fail to relate to the culture of the people or where no Christian feasts address significant local events. The history of feasts like Christmas, Michael the Archangel, and the Chair of St. Peter shows that the church instituted new feasts in order to respond to the need of the people. In short, the basic theological premise of cultural adaptation is this: at every turning point of the year and at every critical moment in the cycle of a people's life and activity there should be a liturgical feast to assure the faithful of God's abiding presence.

The Celebration of Easter Sunday

1. The Place of Easter Sunday in the Easter Triduum

In the reform of the Easter triduum the lion's share went to the liturgical celebrations of Holy Thursday, Good Friday, and the Easter vigil. Although the triduum, which begins at the evening mass of Holy Thursday, runs through Easter Sunday, the reform gave no particular attention to this day, and the pertinent documents mention it only in passing.[10] According to the General Norms for the Liturgical Year and the Calendar, the Easter triduum "closes with evening prayer on Easter Sunday." For some reason this document places Easter Sunday in the section of the Easter season, and explains that "the fifty days from Easter Sunday to Pentecost are celebrated in joyful exultation as one feast day, or better as one great Sunday."[11] In effect, it links Easter Sunday to the Easter season. Hence, Easter Sunday is the conclusion of the triduum and the beginning of the fifty days of Easter.

The Easter triduum, according to the same document, "reaches its high point in the Easter vigil." Viewed from the framework of ritual organization, the Easter triduum has a crescendo-decrescendo arrangement that begins on Holy Thursday, reaches its climax on Easter night, and ends on Easter Sunday. A. Bugnini warned that this ritual crescendo should not suggest the mistaken notion that Holy Thursday and Good Friday are preparations for the Easter vigil.[12] At any rate, it is a perfect example of the dynamics of liturgical celebration which gathers intensity or momentum as it moves on its course. Having reached its high point in the Easter vigil, the triduum loses intensity. Consequently, the celebrations following the Easter vigil will be, in every respect, a downward movement.

If we agree to the principle that the Easter vigil is the high point of the Easter triduum, we have to accept the conclusion that in ritual expression the liturgy of Easter day should not compete with the liturgy of the preceding night nor should it engage the assembly in another spiritual venture. The intensity of the Easter experience should not be sustained psychologically and ritually beyond the Easter vigil celebration. The mass and vespers of Easter day are like a passage formally concluding a musical composition. They are not meant to repeat the experience but to bring it to a conclusion. This seems to be the reason underlying the simplicity of the Easter day liturgy. However, there are two kinds of conclusion, one that is plain and almost abrupt, and another that is winding and reminiscent. Because of its predilection for classical simplicity and sobriety the post-conciliar reform predictably opted for the first.

How is the Easter day related to the Easter vigil? St.

Augustine tells us that "this night is understood to belong to the following day which we call Sunday."[13] The Easter vigil does not belong to Holy Saturday but to Easter Sunday. In other words, Easter Sunday includes the vigil. We should remember, however, that Easter Sunday is made up not only of the night but also of the day. In fact, some patristic homilies seem to bring the day more than the night into focus. And this is understandable, because in the western manner of reckoning the emphasis is on the day rather than on the night. St. Jerome says that Easter Sunday, with the stress on day, is "the mother of all days," while St. Zeno of Verona calls it "the father of all ages." Nicetas of Remesiana, on the other hand, writes: "Sunday is the resurrection of days."[14]

This shows that in the tradition of some fathers of the church Easter day is not a mere appendage to the Easter vigil. It is a full liturgical day that deserves to be celebrated with mass and vespers, for "this is the day which the Lord has made." It is known for a fact that, besides the mass of the vigil, a mass of the day was also celebrated in Africa at least by the end of the fourth century, as the homilies of St. Augustine attest, and in Rome toward the seventh century.[15] Despite the primacy accorded to the Easter vigil mass by the reform of Vatican II, the Missal of Paul VI retains the formulary of *Ad Missam in die.* There is no doubt that the mass of the day is to be regarded as a traditional element of Easter Sunday. The question is what place it occupies today in the overall framework of the triduum.

A. Adam has proposed that "now that the Easter vigil has been restored to its place during the night, we must regard the eucharist celebrated during it as the true mass for the feast, even if it be celebrated before midnight."[16] Accordingly the second mass of Easter Sunday is of secondary interest, and this probably explains why it is celebrated with such sobriety. Except for the obligatory recitation of the sequence and, in some countries, the renewal of baptismal vows,[17] the liturgy of Easter day has no special ritual element to distinguish it from the other Sundays of the year. In places where the renewal of baptismal vows takes the place of the creed, one gets the impression that the mass of the day is for those unable to attend the Easter vigil. As Adam has noted, "in most parishes many who attend this mass have not participated in the foregoing liturgies of the Easter triduum."[18] And it is very likely that a rather insignificant number of those who come to the vigil return to church on the following day.

From the foregoing discussion the following points emerge. First, the crescendo-decrescendo structure of the triduum and the climactic nature of the vigil necessarily make the mass and vespers of Easter day a ritual comedown. This may be logical, but it is not sympathetic to the tradition of some patristic writers who normally refer to Easter day as a full liturgical day.

Second, to appreciate the structure of the present Easter triduum, it is a requirement to participate in it fully from the beginning to the end. In this way, one can experience its crescendo-decrescendo movement. Vatican II's reform of the Easter triduum is premised on this ideal of participation.

Third, and this is the heart of the matter, Easter day lacks the ritual elements to enhance it as "the day made by the Lord." For those who miss the foregoing celebrations of the triduum, the simplicity, sobriety, and ordinariness of the mass of Easter day do not provide a fitting conclusion to the forty days of the Lenten observance. And for those who follow the course of the triduum, the liturgy of Easter day does not figure as an overflow of the Easter vigil. It is a remarkably plain ending of a most engaging, often dramatic, triduum of liturgical celebrations.

Does it follow then that the liturgy of Easter day will be torn between the ritual framework of the triduum and the response to a pastoral need? The answer need not be an either–or. It is not a question of deciding between the logical structure of the triduum and a pastoral situation. It is rather a question of giving the Easter triduum a fitting conclusion. The celebration of the mass and vespers of Easter day needs considerably to be enriched. It is true that in the framework of the Easter triduum the role of mass and vespers is to conclude, but must every conclusion be so bare and deprived? The bottom line is how to enrich the liturgy of Easter day for the benefit of the faithful, without encroaching on the primacy of the Easter vigil and without transforming a conclusion into another high point.

2. Anamnesis and Mimesis on Easter Sunday

The Easter day liturgy was not always as sober as it is today. At different stages of its history various ritual forms were developed in order to enhance its solemnity. Examples are: the stational vespers of Easter Sunday; the papal ceremony at the Lateran during which the pope kissed the so-called acheiropite image of Christ, while chanting the verse "the Lord has risen from the tomb, alleluia"; the solemn procession for the papal mass at St. Mary Major with the singing, according to the Ordo Romanus 50, of the stupendous verses of *Salve festa dies* of Fortunatus; the *pascha annotinum* or the bringing to church of children baptized on the Easter vigil of the preceding year; the *depositio* of the cross or consecrated host on Good Friday and its *elevatio* on Easter night or early Sunday morning; the *visitatio sepulchri;* the *officium peregrinorum;* the dramatization, with the use of images, of the meeting between the risen Christ and his mother; and the blessing of the mixed drink of milk and honey and of mutton and meat of other animals. M. Righetti's treatise on the celebration of Easter Sunday offers a good picture of the different traditions connected with this *dies festus.*[19]

Our information regarding each of these rites and practices come from usages that vary from place to place and from century to century. For instance, the *visitatio sepulchri* was scheduled at different times. In some places it was held after Terce, while in others before Matins. The *pascha annotinum,* on the other hand, was moved in the course of time from Easter Sunday to Monday after Low Sunday. And the *officium peregrinorum,* which was normally held on Easter Sunday, was kept on Easter Monday or even Tuesday in some places. Moreover, there were variations not only in the schedule but also in the roles of the actors and in the script itself. Fortunately, the variations do not make it impossible to piece together such elements as are needed to draw up an essential description of each rite or practice.

It is outside the scope of this book to deal expressly with each rite or practice. The two volumes of K. Young, *The Drama of the Medieval Church,*[20] of which the first concerns our study directly, and the first five of the seven volumes of W. Lipphardt, *Lateinische Osterfeiern und Spiele,*[21] are an indispensable collection of medieval plays connected with Easter. A good number of studies exist, especially on the stational vespers, the *pascha annotinum,* the *visitatio sepulchri,* and the *officium peregrinorum.* Of the many studies the following deserve to be mentioned. On the stational vespers, P. Jounel's "Les vêpres de pâques";[22] on the *pascha annotinum,* B. Fischer's "Formen gemeinschaftlicher Tauferinnerung im Abendland";[23] on the *depositio-elevatio* and *visitatio sepulchri,* O. Hardisons's *Christian Rite and Christian Drama in the Middle Ages,*[24] together with B. Berger's *Le drame liturgique de pâque,*[25] and W. Lipphardt's "Der dramatische Tropus, Fragen des Ursprungs, der Ausführung und der Verbreitung";[26] and on the *officium peregrinorum,* R. Kurvers' unpublished thesis, *Ad Faciendum Peregrinum.*[27]

A brief description of some of these rites and practices will show how they, in their own way, enriched the liturgical celebration of Easter Sunday and met the demand for popular involvement. Although most of them are things of the past—indeed practically all of them belonged to the middle ages—they are not hopelessly irrelevant to our times. In many ways their medieval shape and apparatus will not suit modern liturgical or religious sensitivity. However, they have a theological and pastoral underpinning on which the liturgy of today, without necessarily assimilating their external form, can be reshaped.

The service of the stational vespers, for example, has a direct bearing on the matter in hand. Under the influence of Jerusalem this practice was introduced into the Lateran basilica in the seventh century where, until the thirteenth century, it was observed during the entire octave of Easter. An early witness to the practice is the Hadrian-Gregorian Sacramentary. It offers three orations everyday during the octave of Easter: *ad vesperas, ad fontes,* and *ad Sanctum Andream.*[28] The ritual aspect is supplied in great detail by the Ordo Romanus 27 which speaks of a procession to the sanctuary, to the baptistery, and to the chapel of the holy cross, named *ad Sanctum Andream.* At each station the psalms of vespers, the Magnificat, and an oration are chanted, so that the impression is given that the liturgy consisted of three stational vespers.[29]

By the eighth century the practice had spread to the Franco-Germanic churches and, with the appearance of Ordo Romanus 50, also to the other parts of Italy and to England. Amalarius described it as *gloriosum officium,*[30] and rightly, for it was remarkable not only for its solemnity and splendor but also for the liturgical theology it meant to express. The three stations were clearly anamnestic, even though the Magnificat antiphons and the orations do not seem to suggest a direct reference to the stations where they were chanted. The stations around the altar, in the baptistery, and in the chapel of the holy cross where the newly baptized were confirmed on Easter night offered to the church of Rome a unique opportunity to recall the paschal sacraments by visiting the places where they had been celebrated. The stational vespers of Easter Sunday can thus be regarded as a ritual recalling, an anamnesis *in situ,* of the paschal sacraments of baptism, confirmation, and eucharist.

The Easter day anamnesis was directed also to the apparitions of the risen Christ. To this type of anamnesis belong the liturgical plays that developed from the tenth to the thirteenth century, especially in monasteries. Various kinds of such plays are recorded: the *visitatio sepulchri* dramatizing the visit of the women to the holy sepulchre, the *hortulanus* or the meeting between Christ and Mary Magdalene, the apparition to the disciples in the cenacle which includes the scene with Thomas, and the *peregrinus* or the meeting with the disciples on their way to Emmaus.

These plays are considered liturgical for four principal reasons. First, their texts are tropes directly borrowed from the liturgy and later elaborated to suit the play. The trope of the *visitatio sepulchri* is a classic example: *Quem quaeritis, in sepulchro, O Christicolae? Iesum Nazarenum crucifixum, O coelicolae.*[31] Second, they were, at least originally, part of the liturgical celebration. The *visitatio sepulchri,* for instance, is integrated with Matins in the English *Regularis Concordia,* in the *Rationale Officiorum Divinorum* of Augsburg, and in the monastic breviary of St. Lambrecht. In the troparia of Piacenza and Novalesa the *visitatio sepulchri* is inserted between the office of Terce and the mass. The *officium peregrinorum,* on the other hand, was held either during or at the end of vespers. The versions of Beauvais, Durham, and Palermo place it in the sanctuary before the procession to the baptismal font.[32] Third, the different roles were always performed, at least until the thirteenth century, by the liturgical ministers themselves: the presiding priest, deacons, members of the monastic or boys' *schola cantorum,* and the choir itself. And fourth, the apparatus of these plays consisted of the liturgical furnishings such as the altar, the baptismal font, vestments, and the sepulcher which was sometimes built as a permanent monument in a separate chapel.[33]

In other words, these plays were performed as a dramatic illustration of one of the principal themes of Easter Sunday, namely the apparitions of Christ after his resurrection. Their place in the framework of the liturgy can be compared to the so-called explanatory rites of the celebration of the sacraments and sacramentals, except that they are in the form of drama.

The English *Regularis Concordia* explains that liturgical plays are meant "to strengthen the faith of the ignorant people and the neophytes."[34] The concern to catechize the uninstructed and the neophytes is probably the underlying reason why these liturgical rites are in the form of drama, and why the drama takes the form of mimesis. It is obvious that the visual, the representational, and the imitative form of communication is not only more appealing but is also easier to grasp. The characters of the various plays represent Christ, the angel, Mary Magdalene, and the disciples of Emmaus. The script of the plays confirms their imitative or mimetic character. We come across rubrical descriptions such as: "in imitation of the angel," "in the person of the disciples," "in imitation of Mary Magdalene," "walking slowly as if in search of something," "walking about looking sad," and so on. We may say that while the celebration of the stational vespers was an anamnesis *in situ* of the Easter sacraments, the liturgical plays of Easter Sunday were an anamnesis, through mimesis, of Christ's apparitions.

There is another type of Easter drama. It did not originate from the liturgy but from popular piety. In Spanish-speaking countries it is called *procesion de encuentro,* in Sicily *incontro,* and in the Philippines *santo encuentro* or *salubong.* Basically it consists of two processions, one carrying the image of the risen Christ, the other of the Blessed Virgin. Coming from different directions, they meet at the town square on early Sunday morning. The two images, by some mechanism, are made to bow to each other. In the Philippines a young girl dressed as an angel lifts the black veil of the Blessed Virgin as she sings the antiphon *Regina coeli.*

Although this drama belongs to the category of popular religiosity, in the Philippines, by decree of the Congregation for Divine Worship, it has become the entrance rite of the mass of Easter Sunday. Today it continues to enjoy popularity in places where there is a strong devotion to the Blessed Virgin. In a way it expresses the perception of Christian piety that after his resurrection Christ must have appeared to his mother. The *procesion de encuentro* completes the theme of the Easter apparitions.

These rites and practices bear witness to the richness and exuberance of the Easter Sunday celebration. When the Easter vigil lost the importance it had during the patristic times, Easter day gained ascendancy. Still there is no reason why we should lay Easter Sunday aside as a day of secondary importance. The history of Easter Sunday, even if that history began in Rome only in the seventh century, tells us to do otherwise. Medieval models, of course, are rooted in the culture of a past age and are not necessarily pertinent to the modern situation. But they do make a point: the celebration of Easter Sunday has not always been as sober as it is today.

3. Enriching the Easter Sunday Celebration

The question of enriching the celebration of Easter Sunday should be addressed in the light of the theology and liturgy of Sunday itself. Sunday is the day of the Lord, because on this day the Lord, risen from the dead, appeared to his disciples. This doctrine is expressed by the church principally through the Sunday celebration of baptism and the eucharist.[35] In baptism a person experiences the death and resurrection of Christ. But it is in the celebration of the eucharist that the church witnesses Sunday after Sunday the apparition of Christ and reexperiences his abiding presence. For in the proclamation of the word and the breaking of bread Christ appears again and again to his people, as once he did to the disciples on the way to Emmaus.

While every Sunday is the day of the Lord, Easter Sunday is that day par excellence. In liturgical tradition Easter Sunday is the yearly anniversary of Christ's Easter apparitions and, at least from the seventh century in Rome, also the solemn commemoration of the sacraments of initiation that the church celebrated during the Easter vigil. Although the celebration of the eucharist should theologically suffice to express the sacramental presence of the risen Lord, the church developed lateral services to give to that presence a visual and dramatic form. And although the eucharist is the culmination of initiation into the death and resurrection of Christ, the church made use of vespertinal processions and stations to recall the sacraments of baptism, confirmation, and eucharist. The mass and vespers of Easter Sunday are the most appropriate way to commemorate the apparitions of the risen Christ and our sacramental participation in his paschal mystery. Nevertheless, because of the cultural and pastoral needs of the faithful the anamnesis of Christ's apparitions may have to take the form of mimesis, while the commemoration of the sacraments of Christian initiation takes the form of stational celebration.

The foregoing reflection leads us to some practical considerations. It is obvious that mimesis can greatly enrich the celebration of the Easter day. However, dramatization is not the sole form of mimesis. In many places, especially where the encuentro is observed, the image of the risen

Christ on the sanctuary serves as a representational form of mimesis. On a more liturgical plane the paschal candle evokes the presence of the risen Christ. It is, in its own way, a representational form of mimesis because of its symbolic character. In short, the mimesis of Christ's apparitions on Easter Sunday can take the form of drama or play, of plastic art, or of a liturgical symbol.

The mass of the day, which, in the words of a circular letter issued by the Congregation for Divine Worship, should be celebrated "with great solemnity,"[36] has three elements that can be elaborated to enhance the solemnity of the liturgy. The first is the sprinkling with water blessed at the vigil. The circular letter encourages its observance at the mass of Easter day in place of the penitential rite.[37] The texts accompanying the rite of sprinkling clearly indicate that we are dealing here, at least during the Easter season, not with a form of penitential rite but with the memorial of baptism.[38] The second is the sequence *Victimae paschali laudes.* This sequence was included into the twelfth century *visitatio sepulchri* of St. Lambrecht, obviously because of the dialogue: "Speak, Mary, declaring what you saw, wayfaring." The third are the gospel readings from John 20:1–9 for the day mass and Luke 24:13–35 for the evening mass. In the middle ages these two readings gave rise to the liturgical plays *visitatio sepulchri, hortulanus,* and *officium peregrinorum.* These three mass elements, if carefully worked out, can effectively bring into focus the two principal objects of Easter Sunday anamnesis, namely baptism and the apparitions of the risen Christ.

For the celebration of vespers, the General Instruction of the Liturgy of the Hours recommends that "great care should be taken to maintain, where it exists, the particular tradition of celebrating evening prayer on Easter Sunday in honor of baptism [vesperas baptismales]. During this there is a procession to the font as the psalms are being sung."[39]

The circular letter of the Congregation for Divine Worship adds that, if appropriate, the tradition should be restored.

These then are some areas that can be explored in order to enrich the celebration of Easter Sunday. At this point it may be useful to recall certain principles we discussed early on. The Easter triduum is planned according to a crescendo-decrescendo movement. This implies that the Easter day liturgy must not be so elaborate as to become the center of the triduum. Yet it must not be so plain and ritually impoverished that it appears like any ordinary Sunday liturgy. For the faithful Easter Sunday as the conclusion of the triduum is the fitting occasion to reminisce about the Easter vigil and recall the Easter sacraments. As the day of the Lord and the anniversary of Christ's Easter apparitions its celebration should be for them a vivid reexperience of his enduring presence.

The sobriety of the Easter day celebration may be regrettable, but there is no reason why local churches should do nothing about it. Historical models offer concrete examples of what the church has done. Liturgical theology, on the other hand, defines the principles for adapting the celebration of Easter Sunday. What remains to be done belongs to the realm of adaptation, and this is something that must be addressed on the level of the local churches.

Culture and the Sunday Observance[40]

SC 106 exhorts that the Lord's day "should be proposed to the devotion of the faithful." Sunday should become an experience of faith, a day of encounter between the community of the faithful and the risen Lord present in word and sacrament. But experience and encounter are cultural categories. They take place in the setting of a people's culture and are deeply influenced by it. If Sunday is to become part of a people's life, it must be grafted on their culture.

The subject we intend to pursue is the cultural adaptation of Sunday. The question is how to do it. For Sunday is made up not of a single liturgical rite, but of a set of observances that reflect the Christian meaning of the day.[41] Besides, we are not dealing here with Sunday as a unit consisting of twenty-four hours (or some thirty in liturgical reckoning, if we include the first vespers), nor with the proposal to move the obligation to another day of the week.[42] By adaptation we refer to the process whereby the observance of Sunday as the day of the Lord and the other practices connected with it are given an alternative form that corresponds with the culture and traditions of each local church.

1. The Traditional Elements of the Sunday Observance

The Sunday observance is made up of strictly liturgical elements and of practices that reflect the meaning of Sunday as a day for public worship, rest, and festivity. In connection with the strictly liturgical elements, SC 106 urges the faithful to gather together on Sunday "so that, by hearing the word of God and taking part in the eucharist, they may call to mind the passion, the resurrection, and the glorification of the Lord Jesus and may thank God, who 'has begotten them again unto a living hope through the resurrection of Jesus Christ from the dead.' " From this conciliar text we may draw the conclusion that the word of God and the eucharist are the constitutive elements of the Sunday observance. For indeed "there is no Sunday without a worshiping assembly and no assembly without the word of God and the eucharist."[43]

The proposed text of SC 106 shows that its framers had

in mind the celebration on Sunday not only of the eucharist but also of baptism. The preparatory commission had suggested that, if possible, baptism should be held on Sunday. The final text of SC 106 does not explicitly consider baptism, though its reference to 1 Peter 1:3 implies it. The suggestion of the preparatory commission is received by the Rite of Baptism for Children: "To bring out the paschal character of baptism, it is recommended that the sacrament be celebrated during the Easter vigil or on Sunday, when the Church commemorates the Lord's resurrection." The Rite of Christian Initiation of Adults counsels that "as far as possible, the sacraments of initiation are to be celebrated on Sunday."[44]

The other elements of the Sunday observance are the liturgy of the word and the celebration of the chief hours of the day, especially vespers. The liturgy of the word is "particularly recommended in places where no priest is available" (SC 35,4). As regards the liturgy of the hours, "pastors are to see to it that the chief hours, especially vespers, are celebrated in common in church on Sundays and the more solemn feasts" (SC 100). After the council there have been calls for "the exertion of every effort toward restoring to the Sunday celebration its crowning liturgical touch, the celebration of vespers, the evening sacrifice of praise to Christ the Redeemer."[45]

Besides liturgical celebrations there are other Christian practices associated with Christ's resurrection and the celebration of baptism and the eucharist. SC 106 instructs pastors to teach the faithful the meaning of the Lord's day "in such a way that it may become in fact a day of joy and of freedom from work." It is well known that the observance of Sunday rest, proclaimed by Emperor Constantine in 321, was motivated partly by the obligation to participate in the solemn Sunday liturgy.[46] The conciliar commission on SC treated Sunday rest as a matter of secondary importance with respect to Sunday worship which is its primary purpose.[47]

Abstention from work does not belong to the essence of Sunday. Until the fourth century Christians worked on Sunday, although they must have set aside the time needed for the celebration of the eucharist which did not require a whole day of abstention from work. Today Sunday rest has become part of the weekly rhythm of work and rest, of the modern phenomenon called "weekend."[48]

Connected with the theology of the Lord's day was the prohibition in the early church to fast or kneel on Sunday. The prohibition to fast on Sunday was an affirmation of the Church's faith in the resurrection of Christ.[49] SC 110 encourages that the paschal fast "be observed everywhere on Good Friday and, where possible, prolonged throughout Holy Saturday, as a way of coming to the joys of the Sunday of the resurrection with uplifted and welcoming heart." As for the prohibition to kneel, the new liturgical books retain the custom of standing, except for the persons receiving the sacrament or blessing, at the litany of the saints on Sundays and during the Easter season.[50] Also connected with the theology of Sunday is the offering of gifts during the mass. The practice underlines the spirit of the eucharist, the spirit of sharing especially with the poor.

To complete the picture of the Sunday observance, we may mention those practices that have become part of the socio-religious culture of Christian countries. These practices traditionally take place on Sunday for social and religious reasons. Their connection with the observance of the Lord's day is not always apparent, especially in secularized societies where Sunday, as part of the weekend, is considered the most fitting day to fulfill one's social obligations. The following passage enumerates some of these practices: "It is up to those engaged in the pastoral ministry to lead the faithful to set high value on all those forms and considerations that enter naturally into the Christian meaning of Sunday. They are all bound up with the richness of the Sunday's paschal implications for faith, hope and charity: to make family life more intense and close; to expand the joys of friendship; to do the works of charity; to visit the sick; to go to pray in cemeteries."[51]

Through the various liturgical elements and socio-religious practices that constitute the Sunday observance the faithful are led to a deeper appreciation of the Lord's day set aside by Christian tradition for public worship, feasting, and caring. For the faithful they are expressions of faith, moments of encounter with the risen Christ, and occasions to experience what it means to be Church.

2. Toward Alternative Forms of the Sunday Observance

The future shape of the Sunday observance will depend on whether one is dealing with the traditionally Christian communities or, to use the expression of AG 19, the "young churches," especially in the missions. As concerns the traditionally Christian communities where secularization is kept at bay, some of the elements of the Sunday observance can still be classified as religious expressions of culture. In spite of the changes brought about by secularization, a certain atmosphere of festivity can be felt in many communities of the faithful. The secular character of the weekend is not necessarily incompatible with the theology and celebration of the Lord's day. The ringing of the church bells, special family meal at home or in restaurants, the Sunday walk, family visits, wearing the Sunday best: all this continues to keep alive the festive mood of Sunday.

But as the modern weekend, which can mean absence on Sundays from the liturgical celebration of the parish, gives birth to a new pattern of socio-cultural activities, the pastoral program of the church must attend to the question of integrating Sunday observance with the secular weekend. The Sunday celebration of the word, baptism, the eucharist, and the liturgy of the hours, as well as the exercises of piety and social concern, do not exclude the weekend rest and recreation, as in the past they did not exclude work on Sunday. The observance of the Lord's day should not create the impression of remoteness from human experience.

The question acquires a different slant when dealing with the "young churches." Should the traditional elements of the Sunday observance be grafted on their culture and traditions? How is this to be done? The answer is not simple and will not apply generally to all, because these churches differ from each other in culture, not to mention the socio-political, economic, and religious factors that separate them.[52] Moreover, Sunday is not kept as a holiday in every part of the world, especially where Christianity is not a state religion.

Article 19 of the Decree on the Missionary Activity of the Church has a great deal to say on this matter. Three passages of this article are particularly pertinent. First, "the assemblies of the faithful must evermore become conscious of themselves as living communities of faith, liturgy and charity." Second, "the faith should be imparted by means of a well-adapted catechesis and celebrated in a liturgy that is in harmony with the character of the people." And third, "the communion of the young churches with the whole church must remain intimate, they must graft elements of its tradition on their own culture, and thus, by a mutual out-pouring of energy, increase the life of the mystical body."

The third passage directly addresses the question of cultural adaptation. In so many words it recommends the use of the method of inculturation. Phrases like "grafting elements of its tradition on their own culture" and "by a mutual outpouring of energy" are other ways of saying in-culturation. All this may be read in the context of the Sunday observance among the "young churches," where inculturation can conveniently take the form of assimilation through dynamic equivalence, as we shall presently consider. In line with what the Decree recommends, we may describe inculturation as the act of grafting the traditional elements of the Sunday observance on the culture of these local churches. Through mutual assimilation so characteristic of the process of inculturation the Sunday observance itself will be enriched.

What follows is an attempt to translate the foregoing principles into concrete suggestions.

Sunday in Christian tradition is a day of rejoicing; it is a feast.[53] If it must be proposed to the devotion of the faithful, it should stand out as a day of festivity. In the missions, especially where Sunday is kept as a holiday, the local church will do well to foster the atmosphere of festivity. By tradition the joy of Sunday is expressed in the liturgy by ornamenting the church, sounding the pipe organ, using festive vestments, and observing the posture of standing. We find in every culture expressions of rejoicing which can equivalently signify the Christian joy. Feasts are celebrated with special dances and rhythmic movements, types and color of clothes and headdress, flower leis, and musical instruments that impart a festive mood.[54] Many of these expressions, if they are still part of living tradition, can give to the observance of the Lord's day a lively sense of festivity.

The proclamation of the word of God occupies a privileged place in the Sunday observance. It is evident that to adapt it successfully, serious attention must be given to the translation of the scriptural text adapted to liturgical proclamation. The character of the language carries considerable weight on the question of whether or not the scriptural readings are to be chanted. The Lectionary for Mass cautions that if the readings are chanted, the chant must not obscure but rather extol the words of sacred scripture.[55]

At mass the gospel book is carried in procession with lighted candles and burning incense. In every culture there are surely equivalent native signs to venerate the gospel book. The lectern, which should relate architecturally to the altar, may be decorated, although soberly, at least on solemn occasions. It stands on the sanctuary and is honored next to the altar.[56] In some cultures a special place in the assembly hall is reserved for solemn proclamation. May the lectern occupy such a place, even if it means that it will be outside the sanctuary? And lastly, the traditional art of communication used in various cultural groups differs markedly according to the occasion. Solemn proclamation is marked by the use of a special rhetorical form and by dramatic or symbolic gestures. Can cultural expressions of this kind be absorbed by the art of liturgical proclamation? Among the "young churches" the material for adaptation, whether for inculturation or creativity, is never lacking.

Sunday alludes to cosmic realities, to the changes of the seasons, and to the cycle of work and productivity. There is a link between human work and the celebration of the Lord's day: on Sunday we approach our creator with the fruit of our labor.[57] That is why the Sunday liturgy necessarily relates to the seasonal turning points and the activities connected with them. When the occasion presents itself, appropriate biblical readings can be chosen to reflect the seasons of the year, the time of planting and harvesting, drought and torrential rains. It is understood that adaptations of this kind should follow the existing liturgical norms and should not become a normal Sunday practice. Cultural adaptation does not jeopardize the full unfolding of Christ's mystery in the course of the liturgical year.

Approaching the creator with the fruit of one's labor is portrayed in a graphic way by the presentation of gifts. J.

Jungmann explains that "the approach toward God, this movement in which the body and blood were offered up, begins to include the presentation of material gifts which were thus drawn into the liturgical activity."[58] The presentation of material gifts for the poor illustrates the social message of the eucharist. The early church forbade fasting on Sunday because of its faith in the resurrection. Today in many parts of the world people go hungry on Sunday, not because of their lack of faith in the resurrection, but because of the scarcity of food. The Sunday offering of foodstuff to be shared by the community or to be donated to the poor marks the eucharistic celebration of many parishes, especially in the third world. It expresses mutual concern and strengthens the bond of charity in the community.

Sunday is a day of abstention from work, but in a Christian perspective, especially in poor and depressed areas, it does not mean abstention from the works of charity and social concern. The offering of material goods at mass has a counterpart in the professional service of physicians and lawyers given freely to the poor in the community. The Lord's day is a time of encounter with the risen Lord present particularly among those with whom he chose to identify himself in a special way. In situations of poverty the day of rest is a day of service. The Sunday assembly does not end in the church, but continues on in the parish clinic and classrooms. It is the day when lay leaders visit the sick and the aged in order to bring to them the community's eucharist and comfort.

3. Sunday Liturgy in the Absence of a Priest

The Sunday assembly at which lay catechists presided was first introduced in Burundi in 1898. In 1943 the practice was made obligatory in areas not frequented by the missionaries. Togo followed the example of Burundi in

1930, and thereafter most of the other African countries. During the last few years the practice spread rapidly to the countries in Asia and Latin America. Today it is not an exclusive missionary phenomenon. Several countries in Europe have known it for a good number of years.[59]

SC 35 put the official seal of approval on the practice: "Bible services should be encouraged, especially . . . on Sundays and holydays. They are particularly to be recommended in places where no priest is available." The Instruction *Inter Oecumenici* of 1963 shifted the accent from Bible services to "a sacred celebration of the word of God with a deacon or even a properly appointed layperson presiding." The Instruction adds that "the plan of such a celebration shall be almost the same as that of the liturgy of the word at mass."[60] When the Instruction *Immensae Caritatis* of 1973 allowed laypersons to give communion as special ministers,[61] the permission was readily applied to the Sunday liturgy in the absence of a priest. Thus the practice developed into a full liturgical celebration of the word and holy communion.[62] The Directory issued by the Congregation for Divine Worship in 1988 sums up the history and theology behind the practice, clarifies some of its problematical aspects like the homily, and offers suggestions on how to celebrate it properly and with pastoral advantage.[63]

Two principal reasons are cited in favor of the Sunday liturgy without a priest. The first is the shortage of priests, the second the theology of Sunday. Even when no priest is available, the community is exhorted to come together as a liturgical assembly in order to hear the word of God and receive the body of Christ. However, as Pope Paul VI cautioned, "Let all realize that these Sunday assemblies could never be enough to rebuild communities that are alive and outreaching amid a populace that is barely Christian or in the process of dropping the observance of Sunday." Accordingly, the goal of such assemblies "must always be the celebration of the sacrifice of the mass, the only true actualization of the Lord's paschal mystery."[64]

The Sunday liturgy in the absence of a priest supposes that the gathered community recognizes the necessity of being in full communion with the bishop, the parish priest, and the rest of the parish community. It cannot isolate itself from the rest of the church whose "preeminent manifestation is present in the full, active participation of all God's holy people in liturgical celebrations, especially in the same eucharist, in a single prayer, at one altar at which the bishop presides, surrounded by his college of priests and by his ministers" (SC 41).

Although the Sunday liturgy in the absence of a priest should not become an easy substitute for the Sunday mass nor an excuse for not fostering priestly vocations, it can eventually become a commonplace. Although it is by nature an interim solution to the shortage of priests, one can foresee that it will be around for many years to come. For this reason, it is important to discuss even briefly the liturgical principles that directly concern its adaptation.

First of all, at the Sunday liturgy in the absence of a priest the community is gathered not for collective devotion, but for a liturgical action. Integrating popular devotions with the celebration of the word and holy communion will tend to produce a hybrid of liturgical rites and devotional exercises. We should bear in mind that we are dealing here with a strictly liturgical function. Furthermore, since the celebration takes place on Sunday, it should display, in its own limited way, the characteristic traits of the Lord's day: the proclamation of the word and holy communion. For it is through these liturgical actions that the community encounters the risen Lord.

Since this form of Sunday liturgy is not to be mistaken for the mass, it should not include the elements proper to the mass like the offertory procession and the eucharistic prayer (even without the institution narrative). It is appropriate, however, to retain the normal plan of the liturgy of the word consisting of proclamation, explanation, and general intercessions, and to use the readings assigned in the lectionary. In this way, the faithful can follow the course of the liturgical year and listen to the word of God in communion with the rest of the church.[65]

Within these limits there is ample room for cultural adaptation and creativity. The structure of the celebration can be more flexible, while keeping the elements of word, thanksgiving prayer, and holy communion. New euchological texts can be composed and new rites and symbols can be introduced in keeping with the culture of the people and the theology of the Lord's day.

Liturgical Feasts in the Life and Mission of the Church

Every feast in the liturgical year proclaims the mystery of Christ. But every feast also witnesses to the church's incarnation in the cosmos and in cultures, in imitation of Christ's own incarnation. The history of several liturgical feasts draws the picture of a church deeply involved in the problems brought about by the seasonal changes, in the people's religious and secular traditions, in the cycle of human work, and in the ever changing political and ideological systems.

1. The Seasonal Turning Points

Among the feasts associated with the seasonal turning points, Easter, Christmas and Epiphany, the birthday of John the Baptist, and Michael the Archangel deserve a special consideration.

1. We noted earlier in this chapter that the church

scrupulously keeps the traditional Easter date, which is determined by the spring equinox and the full moon. Even after it had become a universal practice in the fourth century to celebrate Easter only on Sunday in contrast to the Quartodeciman usage, the church did not discard the equinox and the full moon for reckoning the Easter date. The patristic writings outside the Quartodeciman ambient are unanimous in affirming that Easter must fall during the season of spring when God, according to the rabbinic tradition, created the universe and led the Israelites out of Egypt, and when Christ, according to Christian tradition, celebrated his passover at the time of the equinox and the full moon.[66]

Connected with Easter is the observance of the fifty days or Pentecost. On this feast the church fathers have abundantly commented. The observance, they point out, corresponds to the Jewish harvest festival lasting seven weeks. While the Jewish Pentecost concluded with the renewal of the covenant (2 Chr 15:10–14), the Christian Pentecost was marked by the bestowal of the Holy Spirit, the first fruit of Christ's paschal mystery.[67]

The church, which inherited and reinterpreted these Jewish traditions, has kept their seasonal character. Easter and Pentecost are so rooted in the seasonal turning points that one who is oblivious of the season in which they occur is likely to miss their symbolism. A more difficult problem exists in those regions where these feasts are celebrated in other seasons of the year like summer and autumn. It would seem that there is no other solution than to review the symbolic elements of these feasts in relation to the seasonal phenomena such as the length of daylight, the physical appearance of nature, and the human activities related to the seasonal turning points. There are many traditional feasts associated with summer or autumn whose elements can vividly portray the themes of the Easter triduum. The rites and texts for kindling the new fire and for blessing the water could be revised in order to evoke the images projected by the current season of the year.

The problem is not confined to the equator and the southern hemisphere. The weather conditions in the northern hemisphere can also greatly influence the cultural adaptation of the Easter feast. In some places the new fire of the Easter vigil is sometimes put out by snowflakes, the Easter light does not come from the firmament, and the Easter blossoms can be seen only in the heated sanctuary.

2. Another seasonal turning point that has left a lasting mark on the liturgical calendar is the winter solstice during which two principal feasts, Christmas and Epiphany, are celebrated.[68] Although these feasts have different dates, they have essentially the same meaning: the coming and apparition of Christ, the light of the world. The Roman winter solstice on December 25 and the Alexandrian on January 6 designated the victory of the sun over the darkness of winter. From then on the days became longer and the nights shorter.

On January 5 and 6 pagan Alexandria celebrated the birth of Aion from Kore. A significant ceremony held during the feast was the drawing of water from the Nile. Around the year 120 the gnostic sect of Basilides gave this feast a Christian counterpart. On January 6 it commemorated the baptism of Jesus at the Jordan in the belief that the incarnation, and hence the apparition of the Word in human flesh, took place at the Jordan.[69] The interplay of light and water is quite evident: light washes and water enlightens. Christ, coming out of the water of the Jordan, showed himself to be the light of the world.

Around the year 336 the Christians of Rome began to celebrate on December 25 the birth of Christ in Bethlehem. In the Julian calendar the winter solstice fell on December

25 and was marked by the festival of the *Saturnalia* and, since the year 274, also by the *Natale solis invicti,* the birth of the unconquered sun, instituted by Emperor Aurelian to honor the Syrian god Mithra.[70] The introduction of Christmas in Rome was very likely an item in the church's agenda of counteracting pagan festivals and of eventually replacing them with Christian feasts.[71] Thus, the birth of the unconquered sun became the birth of the Sun of Justice. At the turning point of the year, at the winter solstice, the church held its own *rite de passage* from darkness to light by celebrating the birth of Christ.

The origin of Christmas and Epiphany tells us that the central message of these two feasts is the apparition of light, victory over sin, the dawn of salvation. This message should not be lost in the process of adaptation. Cold winter nights and snow (or white cotton placed on Christmas trees to feign snow!) are, at least originally, not symbolic of Christmas. The Roman Christmas marked the day when darkness began to retreat from light, when the night began to give way to the light of day. That in the southern hemisphere Christmas falls in summer might, after all, not be so deplorable. But then the language and symbols of the Christmas liturgy should keep in sight the seasonal phenomena in that part of the world.

The liturgy can help to eliminate the sensation of celebrating a winter feast in summer. Songs that exalt the white winter of Christmas remove the feast from the reality of a scorching sun and alienate it from the actual experience of the community. Songs and hymns have a notable role in liturgical celebrations. And Christmas is one feast of the year that has inspired innumerable compositions. The work of adaptation can begin with songs and hymns that evoke the seasonal experience of those who celebrate the feast in the heat of summer.[72] Likewise, Christmas cribs, which are inevitably found in churches though they are not part of liturgical furnishings, could exhibit a more local appearance. In short, when Christmas is held in summer, it is summer and not winter, and its liturgy must not be unmindful of this reality.

3. Another feast with a pronounced seasonal character is the birth of John the Baptist. The feast has been observed in the west since the second half of the fourth century.[73] That the Roman church assigned the birth of John in June, six months before Christmas, can be explained in the light of Luke 1:36. But that it assigned the feast on June 24, the day of the summer solstice, points unmistakably to a purpose. In one of his homilies St. Augustine of Hippo explains the choice of date for this feast: "Today John is born: from now on the days get shorter. On December 25 Christ was born: from then on the days got longer." And in his usual fashion he concludes: "For as John himself said, Christ must increase, while he must decrease" (Jn 3:30).[74]

The birth of John is clearly associated with the phenomenon of the winter solstice, when the sun retraces its course to give way to autumn and winter. The saying of John that Christ must increase while he must decrease, however naively it has been applied to the matter at hand, has a theological underpinning. As the birth of Christ accompanied the church during the turning point of winter, so does the birth of John at the turning point of summer. The symbolic interplay of the two solstices spells out the relationship between Christ and his precursor.

Connected with the birth of John were practices whose roots went deeper than those of the feast itself. Examples are the midsummer bonfires, processions with torches, and the burning of rubbish. Many of these practices lasted until the middle ages.[75] Today the feast is celebrated with little or no allusion to the summer solstice. Yet the coming of the summer solstice continues to be greeted with various "rites of passage." In places where festivals are held to welcome the solstice could some of their ritual elements or linguistic expressions be incorporated into this feast in order to link it to the seasonal turning point? Or should the local church institute a new feast that can express more fittingly the presence of God among his people at this time of the year?

4. Not only the spring equinox and the solstices but also the equinox of autumn caught the attention of the church. In the fifth century the Roman church commemorated the dedication of the Church of St. Michael the Archangel on the Salarian way. The Sacramentary of Verona offers as many as five formularies for the mass.[76] The date assigned to the feast is September 30, that is, after the autumnal equinox, when the sun decidedly set out on its downward course. For the ancient city of Rome this seasonal change could bring about the swelling of the Tiber, floods, and pestilence. To deal with the situation a *dictator* with extraordinary powers was named by the senate. Regarded as the general protector of the city, the *dictator* entered his office by fixing a nail to the right wall of the temple of Jupiter on the Capitoline hill. The gesture was meant to symbolize the control of illness and natural disaster.[77] It is possible that the church, inspired by the Roman practice of naming a city protector, introduced the feast of Michael the Archangel, the champion against evil forces, whose protection it invoked at this time of the year.

Thus, at the four cardinal points of the year liturgical feasts have been instituted to accompany the faithful during the critical moments of seasonal change. Except for Easter, the choice of feasts was made rather freely and as the occasion demanded. Christmas was influenced by a Roman winter festival, and the feasts of John the Baptist and Michael the Archangel by the seasonal turning points of summer and autumn. But there was logic in the choice. The birth of Christ at the winter solstice signals the dawn of salvation; the birth of John the Baptist at the summer solstice heralds the coming of a new age; and the feast of

Michael the Archangel after the equinox of autumn offers the assurance of his powerful protection.

These considerations have a practical bearing on the question of adapting the liturgical feasts outside the northern hemisphere. In regions where the only notable changes are between the wet and dry seasons, one cannot remain unimpressed by the mildness of nature or its chronic outbursts of violence. How are such seasonal manifestations reflected by the liturgical feasts? History shows that at every turning point of the year, at every critical moment in the life of the Christian people, the church instituted feasts to accompany them during the period of transition.

That concern is not buried away in history. It lives on in the efforts of local churches to adapt the liturgical calendar to the experience of their people. The aim then of adaptation is to reinforce the seasonal character of existing liturgical feasts so that the faithful may perceive the connection between the mystery they celebrate and the seasons of the year. Through inculturation the liturgical feasts are able to assimilate the linguistic and symbolic elements drawn from the seasonal changes and thus reveal the nearness of the mystery. Sometimes, however, a recourse to creativity, in the sense of instituting new feasts for the local church, might be needed in order to express more fully the presence of Christ's mystery in the course of the year.

2. Religious and Secular Traditions

When dealing with religious and secular traditions the church has followed until today a certain pattern. With secular traditions its attitude has been generally friendly, but not with pagan temples, rituals, and festivals from which it shied, especially during the early centuries. With the peace of Constantine and the gradual waning of paganism, at least in urban centers, the church began to show a tolerant disposition toward pagan religious practices, provided they could be purified of error and superstition. Some feasts of pagan origin were eventually admitted into the liturgy. A classic example of this is the feast of St. Peter's Chair in Rome.

The *Roman Chronograph* of the year 354 assigns the *Natale Petri de cathedra* on February 22. In February ancient Rome celebrated for eight days the festival of *Parentalia* in memory of the ancestors. Part of the celebration was a solemn meal, a funeral banquet called *charistia* or *cara cognatio,* at which the dead were represented by an empty chair.[78] The *cathedra* symbolized the authority that the ancestors enjoyed over the family. For the Christians of Rome the ancestors in the faith were the apostles Peter and Paul, and it is not improbable that originally they were venerated together.[79] Later on the *cathedra* came to be interpreted as the bishop's chair or as the symbol of his teaching office.

In today's Christian society pagan festivals with cultic overtones are a rarity, but secular ones proliferate. There is a great supply of feasts commemorating political personages and events, or celebrating society's ideals and traditions. Christians share with others feasts like Independence Day, Thanksgiving Day, Labor Day, and so on. In the past the church instituted feasts to mark important events in the life of the people. Many such events were interpreted as divine intervention in time of crisis. In 1571 Pope Pius V instituted the feast of Our Lady of Victory to commemorate the naval victory of Christians over the Turks at Lepanto. When the Turks were defeated again in 1716 by Prince Eugen at Peterwardein in Austria, Pope Clement XI extended the feast to the entire church and changed its title to Rosary of the Blessed Virgin Mary, because the two victories were attributed to the recitation of the rosary.[80]

Is it advisable to institute liturgical feasts to mark important events in the history of a people or a nation? The question has no easy answer. On the one hand, the church has done it; on the other, the introduction of such feasts could easily lead to the proliferation of the "feasts of ideas."[81] Introduced during the middle ages, these feasts do not focus on any particular events of salvation history but on doctrinal propositions. They were often occasioned by theological controversies, political issues, and popular piety. Some examples are the Holy Trinity, Corpus Christi, Sacred Heart, Christ the King, and Immaculate Heart of Mary. The Roman church is disinclined to introduce "feasts of ideas" because of the nature of the liturgical year which centers on saving acts rather than on doctrinal propositions. As regards the political changes to which a local church gives approval, it may be debated whether the liturgical feasts commemorating such occasions will not undesirably bind the church to a political option.

Another question is whether secular feasts should be celebrated in the liturgy in order that the Christian mystery may be interwoven, so to speak, in the fabric of secular life. Should there be a mass and office formulary for Independence Day, Thanksgiving Day, Labor Day, and so on? The Roman missal includes mass formularies for the nation or city and its leaders, but not for such occasions.[82]

In the event that liturgical feasts are instituted to accompany secular events, it would be helpful to consider the following points. Far-fetched Christian themes and loosely connected biblical images, like the exodus for Thanksgiving Day, can become a strain on typology which requires a certain "connaturalness" between the type and its antitype. Furthermore, both the language and the rites require a certain nobility and beauty. Expressions borrowed from comic strips and frivolities of life do not foster prayer but instead cause snickers in the assembly. And, lastly, the new liturgical feasts, even though interwoven in the secular life of the people, must always center on the mystery of Christ.

3. The Cycle of Work and Productivity

We read in the General Norms on the Liturgical Year and Calendar that "on rogation and ember days the church publicly thanks the Lord and prays to him for the needs of humanity, especially for the productivity of the earth and for human labor."[83] The document suggests that the date of rogation and ember days be adapted to the needs of workers and the agricultural situation of every region.

In regard to the rogation days, the liturgical calendar before the reform of Vatican II listed two types: those on the three days before Ascension Thursday and the one on April 25.[84] The first type was introduced by Bishop Mamertus of Vienne in 469 to invoke God's protection during a series of earthquakes that afflicted some regions of Gaul. It consisted of litanies chanted during solemn outdoor processions. We meet similar processions during times of great calamity, of which the black death in the fourteenth century is a most terrifying example. This type of rogations was introduced in Rome at the beginning of the ninth century.

The second type, commonly known as the major rogation day, was a Roman practice connected with the agricultural world.[85] On April 25 ancient Rome held the *Robigalia,* a feast in honor of the god Robigo whom the farmers invoked against mildew. A procession to the grove of Robigo at the Claudian Way was held and there sacrifices were offered to the divinity. In the sixth century the procession was observed by the Christians who kept to the same route, except that the procession ended at the Vatican. It seems that Pope Gregory the Great, who promoted it, intended therewith to replace the pagan feast.[86]

This somewhat combative spirit, so typical of the early church, should not make us overlook the genuine and keen sensitivity of the church to the needs of workers, especially in moments when the forces of nature threaten the fruit of their labor. At such times the liturgy can become a meaningful expression of their trust in God's protection. Although the reform of Vatican II suppressed the major rogation day "since it began as a strictly local rite of the church of Rome," the fact alone that such a liturgical feast was instituted gives a convincing proof of the concern of a local church for its people.[87]

While rogation days centered on litanies and processions, the ember days, called *Quattuor tempora* in Rome, stressed prayer, fasting, and almsgiving on Wednesday, Friday, and Saturday of the weeks that opened the four seasons. Pope Leo the Great mentions the observance of fasting in spring before Easter, in summer at the time of Pentecost, in autumn during the month of September, and in winter during the month of December.[88] A similar observance existed in Jewish tradition,[89] but the parallel Roman festivals held at seedtime, grain harvest, and vintage kept respectively in the months of November-December, June-August, and September-October seem to have influenced more immediately the development of the ember days.[90]

Instead of the external activities that accompanied the pagan festivals, the church chose to pass the ember days in prayer, fasting, and almsgiving. The agricultural character of the ember days of Pentecost and September survives in some farming communities where the first grain harvest is offered as a sign of gratitude to the Lord of harvest and of concern for the less fortunate. The following observation aptly sums up the meaning of ember days: "In our own day, when all are concerned with the problems of peace, justice and hunger, the ember days should be restored to their former importance as days devoted to penance and charity. It is fitting, therefore, that in any given region, when local needs and customs have been taken into account, a suitable way be found to preserve the liturgy of the ember days and to devote it to the ministry of love."[91]

The ember days are strongly characterized by community spirit. During these days the church appealed to Christians as a community in need of God's help and grateful for the blessings it had received. This aspect of the ember days can have a profound influence not only on the process of adaptation but also on the people's reception of the ember days. Other aspects should also be kept in mind, like the congruity of the ember-day observance with the spirit of the liturgical feasts or seasons. Fasting and other penitential practices, for example, have little relation to the Easter season. On the other hand, social projects for the benefit of the poor are an appropriate community undertaking during Lent. There is also the aspect of local traditions in connection with the agricultural cycle, like the offering and blessing of the first fruit. In order that the observance will not be only penitential but also properly liturgical, these traditions should become an integral part of the liturgy of ember days.

Rogation and ember days belong, by origin, to the agricultural world. The church has yet to address itself to the industrialized world with its rhythm of work and rest, production and consumption, strikes and negotiations. By instituting rogation days the church showed concern for the farmers, especially when the forces of nature threatened their work. Should not the church do the same for the industrialized world?

Economic crisis, retrenchment, and unemployment can be as cyclic as the four seasons. Every now and then, despite modern technology, disaster areas are declared. In times like these the liturgy can become a source of courage and inspiration for employers and employees alike as well as for those afflicted by natural violence. The liturgy can assure them that God is not absent from the human scene, much less in time of distress. The Roman missal provides Mass formularies for various needs and occasions, and no. 326 of the General Instruction explains that "the liturgy of the sacraments and sacramentals causes almost every event in human life to be made holy by divine grace that flows from the paschal mystery." This lofty principle has yet to be applied to the concrete situation of Christians in the industrialized world.

The ember days are related to planting and harvesting, but their message is relevant also to the industrialized world, especially where it is possible to define in broad lines the cycle of work and productivity. Traditionally the church appealed to Christians during the ember days for sobriety in the consumption of goods for the purpose of sharing them with the needy. The modern world has rediscovered not only the health and cosmetic value of fasting, but also its social meaning. One can still come across farmers who on ember days generously set aside a portion of their harvest for the poor. Surely the ember days have a message to give to the industrialized societies. How these days should be celebrated and what liturgical shape they should have are questions local churches need to address.

4. The Political Nuance of Some Liturgical Feasts

"Christ gave his church no proper mission in the political, economic, or social order. The purpose which he set before it is a religious one." With this affirmation, article 42 of the Constitution on the Church in the Modern World made it unequivocally plain that the church's role in the world is to structure and consolidate the human community according to the divine law. To accomplish this, explains the Constitution, the church must not bind itself to any particular form of culture, nor to any political, economic, or social system. The mission of the church is a religious one, even though this is carried out in the political, economic, and social sphere.

In the course of history, however, both the clergy and political leaders often conveniently forgot this principle. This resulted in the unhappy marriage between the church and the state and the begetting of two undesirable offspring known as caesaro-papism and the temporal power of the popes. During the Constantinian era the clergy were decorated with civil dignity and together with it the use of some imperial paraphernalia. In the middle ages the church reciprocated liturgically by composing a rite for the solemn coronation of emperors and kings, and by reciting special prayers for them after the mass.

Politics is by nature a contingent reality, and the assimilation of its elements imprints on the liturgy a quality of transitoriness. With the change in the political climate the liturgical feast instituted in a particular political situation easily loses its pertinence. Nonetheless, liturgical feasts with political nuance are a faithful description of the Christian people's involvement in the ever changing political systems. Liturgical feasts permit them to celebrate as church the independence day and other important events in the life of their nation. But liturgical feasts allow them also to express censure of or anxiety over political developments related to such burning issues as racism, national security, terrorism, territorial occupation, and so on. The Roman missal provides mass formularies for the progress of peoples, for peace and justice, for reconciliation, and in time of war or invasion.[92] But the church also instituted liturgical feasts with obvious political overtones.

The feast of Christ the King was instituted by Pope Pius XI in 1925 as a weapon against what he described as the "destructive forces of our age."[93] The year marked the sixteenth centenary of the Council of Nicea which upheld that Christ was of the same substance as the Father. The pope saw in this doctrine a fitting basis for Christ's kingship. He chose the last Sunday of October in view of the feast of All Saints on November 1. Christ, he declared, triumphs in his saints and elect. The pope justified the introduction of the new feast, saying that "the yearly celebration of the sacred mysteries is more effective in instructing the people about faith and in bringing them the joys of spiritual life, than the solemn declarations of the church's teaching. Documents are often read only by a few learned people; feasts move and teach all the faithful."[94]

The Catholic world welcomed the feast with great enthusiasm and celebrated it with a eucharistic procession whose pomp and splendor was matched only by that of Corpus Christi. The public consecration to the Sacred Heart proclaimed to the world the victory of Christ over the destructive forces in the world.

But what were those "destructive forces" referred to by the pope? In 1917 the czar of Russia was deposed and the Bolsheviks took over; in 1922 the fascists marched into Rome, and Mussolini became prime minister and dictator; in 1924, with the death of Lenin, Russia was beset by a power struggle that led to Stalin's assumption of full power in 1928; in 1925 Hitler reestablished the National Socialist German Workers' Party, and by 1933 he was hailed by Germany as chancellor and führer. The pope must have watched also with concern the developments across the Atlantic. He must have seen the threat of materialism in the so-called "roaring twenties" with its easy credit, technological progress, and economic boom. The feast of Christ the King was clearly contingent upon this political and socioeconomic situation. It represented the stand of the church at that particular moment.

But times changed. Pope Paul VI's liturgical reform transferred the feast to the last Sunday of the liturgical year and framed it in an eschatological context. The readings present Christ's kingship in biblical images that give the feast a more spiritual orientation. Christ judges on the basis of love; he shepherds his people with solicitude; he offered his life for all, and now leads all to paradise; his kingdom is not of this world.[95]

Another feast with political nuance is the Immaculate Heart of Mary or the Most Pure Heart approved by Pope Pius IX in 1855 for Spain and several dioceses in the world. The feast was introduced in Rome in 1880. With the liturgical reform of Pope Pius X the feast practically disappeared in Rome, though it was kept in the Roman missal as an optional feast to be held on the Saturday following the feast of the Sacred Heart. The calendar reform of 1969 designated this day for its memorial.[96]

One of the reasons cited by Pope Pius IX for the approval of the feast was the remarkable number of conversions brought about by the devotion to the heart of Mary. But other factors as well favored the development of the feast. On October 31, 1942 Pope Pius XII, on the occasion of the twenty-fifth anniversary of the apparitions at Fatima, consecrated the church and the entire world to the immaculate heart of Mary. The outbreak of the Second World War occasioned a further development. On December 8, 1942 the pope, moved by the "serious calamities that afflict the Christian people on account of the great war," repeated the act of consecration and decreed that the feast be celebrated by the entire church on August 22.[97]

Through the feast of the Immaculate Heart the church invoked the protection of the Mother of God during the turmoil of war, "so that peace may be given to every nation, and liberty to the church of Christ." The feast served as the church's liturgical prayer for world peace. It responded to the plea at Fatima to pray for conversion and peace, and offered the vision of the future kingdom. But again times changed, and the feast was reduced to an optional memorial in 1969.

A third example of feasts with political overtones is St. Joseph the Worker, introduced as a solemnity by Pope Pius XII on May 1, 1955. The feast carried the title "Patron of the Working People."[98] The reason for the choice of May 1 is obvious. Workers have long been celebrating May Day to honor labor and promote the rights of the working class. May Day, however, was associated with Marxist ideology. Through this feast the pope hoped to counter the Marxist influence by presenting St. Joseph as the patron and model of Christian workers.

The revised calendar of 1969 reduced the feast to an optional memorial. The Commentary on the Roman Calendar explains that "while this is a day dedicated to the dignity of work in some countries, other countries observe it at another time and so it seemed best to have May 1 as an optional memorial."[99] Elsewhere the document further comments: "The solemnity of Joseph the Worker was introduced in the Roman calendar in 1955. It is now an optional memorial since it is mainly a secondary commemoration of Joseph connected with Labor Day."[100] One thing is certain: the feast no longer enjoys the ideological relevance it had in the 1950's.

5. Conclusion

The history of the liturgical feasts shows that the church has always been sensitive to everything that touches the life of the faithful. The seasonal changes, popular traditions, the cycle of human work, and the political systems and ideologies: all these aspects of human existence belong to the realm of the church's mission. The liturgical feasts, which reflect the life and activities of the people, express the church's profound interest in what goes on in the world. They also reveal the church's missionary concern. For the liturgical feasts possess an evangelizing power: through them the divine breaks into human history and weaves itself into the fabric of human life. That is why the church, which is always attentive to the changes that take place in the world, continues to seek ways of affirming through the liturgical feasts that the Lord of history is truly present in the life and activities of his people.

Notes

[1] O. Casel: *Das christliche Kultmysterium,* Regensburg 1960, pp. 90–99; see M. Augé: "Teologia dell'anno liturgico," *Anàmnesis* 6, Genoa 1988, pp. 11–34; A. Adam: *The Liturgical Year,* New York 1981, pp. 19–33.

[2] *Normae Universales de Anno Liturgico et de Calendario,* henceforth *NUALC, Missale Romanum,* Vatican City 1975, no. 3, p. 100; *DOL,* p. 1156.

[3] S. Marsili: "La teologia della domenica," *I segni del mistero di Cristo,* Rome 1987, pp. 441–45; A. Nocent: "Le jour du Seigneur: théologie du dimanche," *Célébrer Jésus-Christ* IV, Paris 1977, pp. 21–31.

[4] A. Chupungco: "The Place of Sunday in the Liturgical Year: a Re-reading of SC 106," *Ecclesia Orans* I (1984) pp. 133–51.

[5] N. Denis-Boulet: *Le Calendrier chrétien,* Paris 1959, pp. 10–25; J. Van Goudoever: *Biblical Calendars,* Leiden 1961, pp. 155–63; W. Rordorf: "Pasqua," *Dizionario patristico e di antichità cristiane,* henceforth *DPAC,* Vol. II, Casale Monferrato 1983, pp. 2691–95; A. Chupungco: *The Cosmic Elements of Christian Passover,* Rome 1977.

[6] Origen: *In Genesim Homiliae* X, 3, ed. L. Doutreleau, *Sources Chrétiennes* 7 (1944) p. 189; St. Augustine: *Incipit de Sancto Pascha* I, ed. G. Morin, *PL Suppl. II,* p. 724. See J. Van Goudoever: *Biblical Calendars,* pp. 164–75.

[7] B. Botte: *Les origines de la Noël et de l'Épiphanie,* Louvain 1932. See also A. Adam: *The Liturgical Year,* pp. 121–25; J. Jounel: "Le temps de Noël," *L'Église en prière* IV, pp. 91–111.

[8] *Das christliche Kultmysterium,* pp. 96–97. Casel gives the example of the feast of Epiphany: *Also ist Epiphanie auch das ganze*

Erlösungsmysterium, nur unter einem andern Gesichtspunkt gesehen. He concludes saying, *Also eins ist immer das Mysterium des Kirchenjahres.*

[9] P. Jounel: "Le culte de Marie dans la liturgie rénovée," *Le renouveau du culte des saints,* Rome 1986, pp. 233–43; idem: "Culto dei santi," *Nuovo Dizionario di Liturgia,* ed. D. Sartore–A. Triacca, Rome 1984, pp. 1338–55. See M. Augé: "Le feste del Signore, della Madre di Dio e dei santi," *Anàmnesis* 6, pp. 223–59; A. Adam: *The Liturgical Year,* pp. 199–211.

[10] *NUALC,* nos. 19–21, p. 103; *DOL,* p. 1158; *De Initiatione Christiana,* no. 6, pp. 8–9; *DOL,* p. 721; *Caeremoniale Episc rum,* Vatican City 1984, no. 371, p. 104.

[11] *NUALC,* no. 22, *DOL,* p. 1158.

[12] A. Bugnini: *La riforma liturgica,* p. 316.

[13] *Nox quippe ista ad consequentem diem quem dominicum habemus, intelligitur pertinere. Guelf. V, Tract. de nocte sancta,* ed. G. Morin: *S. Augustini Sermones post Maurinos reperti, Miscellanea Agostiniana* I (1930) p. 457. See: A. Chupungco: "Easter Sunday in Latin Patristic Literature," *Notitiae* 164 (1980) pp. 93–103; B. Studer: "Das christliche Fest, ein Tag der gläubigen Hoffnung (zur Festtheologie Gregors von Nyssa)," *Traditio et Progressio,* Miscellanea for A. Nocent, *Studia Anselmiana* 95, Rome 1988, pp. 519–23.

[14] St. Jerome compares Easter Sunday to Mary: *Quo modo Maria virgo mater Domini inter omnes mulieres principatum tenet, ita inter ceteros dies haec omnium dierum mater est. In die dominica Paschae* I, *CCL* LXXVIII, 2, p. 545. St. Zeno of Verona: *Tract. LI, de Pascha VII,* PL XI, col. 503A; Nicetas of Remesiana: *De Ratione Paschae,* ed. A. Burns, Cambridge 1905, p. 104: *Dominica vero dies resurrectio est dierum.*

[15] P. Jounel: "Le cycle pascal," *L'Église en prière* IV, p. 64; A. Adam: *Liturgical Year,* pp. 75–77; see: P. Weller: *Selected Easter Sermons of St. Augustine,* London 1959.

[16] A. Adam: *Liturgical Year, p. 83.*

[17] With the approval of the Congregation for Divine Worship this practice was introduced in the Philippines in 1975. A. Adam is wary of this practice: "Efforts to repeat some parts of the

Vigil at 'High Mass' on Easter Sunday may easily work to the disadvantage of the restored Vigil." *The Liturgical Year,* p. 84.

[18] A. Adam: *The Liturgical Year,* pp. 83–84.

[19] *Manuale di storia liturgica II,* Milan 1946, pp. 187–95.

[20] Oxford 1933 (reprinted in 1951).

[21] Berlin 1976–81.

[22] *La Maison-Dieu* 49 (1957) pp. 98–111.

[23] *Liturgisches Jahrbuch* 9 (1959) pp. 87–128; see idem: "Formen der Tauferinnerung in der Geschichte des privaten christlichen Morgen- und Abendgebets," *Mens concordet voci,* Miscellanea for A.G. Martimort, Paris 1983, pp. 569–76.

[24] Baltimore 1965.

[25] Paris 1976.

[26] *Dimensioni drammatiche della liturgia medioevale,* Città di Castello 1977, pp. 17–31.

[27] Pontificio Istituto Liturgico, Roma 1982.

[28] J. Deshusses (ed.): *Le Sacramentaire Grégorien,* Vol. 1, Fribourg 1971, nos. 405–06, pp. 196–97.

[29] M. Andrieu (ed.): *Les Ordines Romani du haut moyen âge,* Vol. III, Louvain 1974, nos. 67–77, pp. 362–66; cf. P. Jounel: "Les vêpres du pâques," pp. 97–102.

[30] *De Ordine Antiphonarii,* I.M. Hanssens (ed.): *Amalarii Episcopi Opera Liturgica Omnia,* Vol. III, Vatican City 1950, p. 82.

[31] Cf. B. Berger: *Le drame liturgique de pâques,* pp. 139–145; W. Lipphardt: "Der dramatische Tropus," pp. 17–31; R. Jonsson: "L'Environnement du trope 'Quem quaeritis in sepulchro.' Aperçu des tropes du propre de la semaine paschale," *Dimensioni drammatiche della liturgia medioevale,* pp. 53–73. The unpublished thesis of R. Kurvers brings to light the use of liturgical sources in the texts of the *officium peregrinorum.*

[32] The texts of both the *visitatio sepulchri* and the *officium peregrinorum* have been edited by K. Young: *The Drama of the Medieval Church,* Vol. I, and by W. Lipphardt: *Lateinische Osterfeiern und Osterspiele,* Vol. V.

[33] See: B. Berger: *Le drame liturgique de pâques,* pp. 261–65.

[34] K. Young: *The Drama of the Medieval Church,* Vol. I, p. 249.

[35] See: Hans Hollerweger: "Der Sonntag in der vom II. Vatikanum erneuerten Liturgie," *Der Sonntag. Anspruch–Wirklichkeit–Gestalt,* Miscellanea for J. Baumgartner, Freiburg 1986, pp. 99–112; A. Chupungco: "The Place of Sunday in the Liturgical Year," *Ecclesia Orans* I (1984) pp. 133–51.

[36] *Circular Letter "De Festis Paschalibus Praeparandis et Celebrandis," Notitiae* 259 (1988) p. 104.

[37] See *Missale Romanum,* Appendix, p. 917: *Huiusmodi ritus [benedictio et aspersio aquae] locum tenet actus paenitentialis initio Missae peragendi.* The *Caeremoniale Episcoporum,* no. 133, p. 44, encourages it on Sundays: *Die dominica, loco consueti actus paenitentialis, laudabiliter fit benedictio et aspersio aquae.*

[38] *Missale Romanum,* pp. 917–18: *in nostri memoriam baptismi; suscepti baptismatis memoria.*

[39] *Institutio Generalis de Liturgia Horarum,* IV, no. 213, *DOL,* pp. 1123–24.

[40] Numbers one and two of this section appeared in German translation, "Der Sonntag und die Kultur. Ein Beitrag zur Feier des Herrentags in den Missionen," in *Der Sonntag. Anspruch–Wirklichkeit–Gestalt,* Miscellanea for J. Baumgartner, Freiburg 1986, pp. 225–35.

[41] Cardinal J. Villot: *Letter to Bishop C. Manziana* on the occasion of the 28th Italian National Liturgical Week in 1977, henceforth, Card. J. Villot: *Letter.* The letter enumerates various Christian practices related to the observance of Sunday. *DOL,* pp. 1179–81.

[42] During the conciliar discussion on SC 106 it was proposed that those unable to fulfill the Sunday obligation be permitted to do so on another day of the week. *Schema Constitutionis de Sacra Liturgia,* henceforth *Schema,* De anno liturgico, Emendationes 11. See J. Baumgartner: "Herrentag–Herrengedächtnis–Herrenmahl. These zur Sonntagspflicht," *Heiliger Dienst* 27 (1973) pp. 4–12; L. Mougeot: "Recherches actuelles sur le dimanche," *La Maison-Dieu* 124 (1975) pp. 64–68.

[43] Card. J. Villot: *Letter,* p. 469; *DOL,* p. 1180.

[44] *Ordo Baptismi Parvulorum,* Vatican City 1973, no. 9, p. 17; *DOL,* p. 727; *Ordo Initiationis Christianae Adultorum,* Vatican City 1972, no. 59, p. 29; *DOL,* p. 747.

[45] Card. J. Villot: *Letter,* p. 471; *DOL,* p. 1181.

[46] W. Rordorf: *Der Sonntag. Geschichte des Ruhe- und Gottesdiensttages im ältesten Christentum,* Zurich 1962; idem: "Domenica," *DPAC,* Vol. I, pp. 1010–11; M. Rooney: "La domenica," *Anàmnesis* 6, pp. 71–85.

[47] *Schema,* De anno liturgico, Modi V, no. 9.

[48] U. Altermatt: "Vom kirchlichen Sonntag zum säkularisierten Weekend," *Der Sonntag,* pp. 248–89.

[49] P. Cobb: "The Calendar. The History of the Christian Year," *The Study of Liturgy,* London 1979, p. 405.

[50] *Caeremoniale Episcoporum:* ordination of a deacon, no. 507, p. 133; of a presbyter, no. 529, p. 136; of a bishop, no. 580, p. 143; dedication of a church, no. 899, p. 207; of an altar, no. 943, p. 218; blessing of an abbot, no. 685, p. 163; of an abbess, no. 706, p. 167; consecration of a virgin, no. 730, p. 170; religious profession, no. 758, p. 176 and no. 799, p. 181. See B. Neunheuser: "Les gestes de la prière à genoux et de la génuflexion dans les Églises de rite romain," *Gestes et paroles dans les diverses familles liturgiques,* Conférence Saint-Serge. XXIV Semaine d'Études Liturgiques, Rome 1978, pp. 153–65.

[51] Card. J. Villot: *Letter,* p. 471; *DOL,* p. 1181.

[52] See G. Wainwright: *Doxology,* New York 1980, pp. 362–87; D. Jala: *Liturgy and Mission,* Rome 1985; López-Gay: "Missioni e liturgia," *Nuovo Dizionario di Liturgia,* pp. 855–63. See also: K. Müller–Th. Sundermeier, ed.: *Lexikon missionstheologischer Grundbegriffe,* Berlin 1987.

[53] P. Grelot: "Le dimanche chrétien," *La Maison-Dieu* 124 (1975) pp. 40–42.

[54] G. Fontaine: "La pastorale liturgique," *Notitiae* 220 (1984) pp. 843–44; see also the papers read by various delegates to the Meeting of the Presidents and Secretaries of National Liturgical Commissions, 23–28 October 1984: *ibid.,* pp. 787–94 and 814–15. During my visit to Samoa Pago-Pago and Samoa Apia in July 1987 I was deeply impressed by the festive atmosphere of Sunday: people wore white clothes and flower leis for mass, drank together the ritual *kava,* shared the Sunday meal with

relatives and friends amidst singing and dancing, took the afternoon siesta, and gathered in church for the evening service.

[55] *Ordo Lectionum Missae,* Vatican City 1981, no. 13, p. xviii; see no. 17, p. xix.

[56] *Ibid.,* no. 17, p. xix; nos. 32–33, p. xxiii. See: I. Scicolone: "La proclamazione della Sacra Scrittura nella liturgia," *Gli spazi della celebrazione rituale,* Milan 1984, pp. 155–61; C. Valenziano: "Ambone e candelabro," *ibid.,* pp. 163–220.

[57] P. Grelot: "Le dimanche chrétien," pp. 47–50.

[58] J. Jungmann: *The Mass of the Roman Rite,* p. 316.

[59] O. Nussbaum: *Sonntäglicher Gemeindegottesdienst ohne Priester. Liturgische und pastorale Überlegungen,* Würzburg 1985; see also P.-A. Liégé: "Accompagnement ecclésiologique pour les assemblées dominicales sans célébration eucharistique," *La Maison-Dieu* 130 (1977) 114–28; M. Brulin: "Assemblées dominicales en l'absence de prêtre," *ibid.,* pp. 80–113.

[60] *Instruction "Inter Oecumenici,"* no. 37; *DOL,* p. 95.

[61] *Instruction "Immensae Caritatis," DOL,* pp. 650–52.

[62] R. Kaczynski: "Sonntägliche Kommunionfeier," *Der Sonntag,* pp. 213–24.

[63] *Directory "De Celebrationibus dominicalibus absente Presbytero," Notitiae* 263 (1988), pp. 366–78. See also the presentation of the document by P. Tena: *ibid.,* pp. 362–65. Regarding the homily the Directory declares: *Cum homilia sacerdoti vel diacono reservetur, optandum est ut parochus homiliam a se antea praeparatam tradat moderatori coetus, qui eam legat. Serventur vero ea quae a Conferentia episcoporum ad hoc sint statuta. Ibid.,* no. 43, p. 376.

[64] *Address to the Bishops of Central France, DOL,* p. 1178.

[65] *Directory,* nos. 35–49, pp. 374–77. The Directory mentions the following as the normal parts of the celebration: opening rites, liturgy of the word, prayer of thanksgiving, holy communion, and concluding rites.

[66] O. Casel: "Art und Sinn der ältesten christlichen Osterfeier," *Jahrbuch für Liturgiewissenschaft* 14 (1934) pp. 1–78; see A. Chupungco: *The Cosmic Elements of Christian Passover,* pp. 39–71.

[67] J. Van Goudoever: *Biblical Calendars,* pp. 182–94; R.

Cabié: *La Pentecôte. L'évolution de la Cinquantaine pascale au cours des cinq premiers siècles,* Tournai 1965.

[68] A related feast is the Presentation of the Lord, fixed on February 2 by Emperor Justinian in 542. Pagan Rome celebrated during the first week of February a procession called *Amburbium,* which J. Jungmann suspects to be the origin of the procession on February 2. *The Early Liturgy,* pp. 145–46; A. Nocent: "2 febbraio: presentazione del Signore," *Anàmnesis* 6, pp. 203–05. See N. Turchi: *La religione di Roma antica,* Bologna 1939, p. 121.

[69] H. Rahner: *Greek Myths and Christian Mystery,* London 1963, pp. 134–54.

[70] P. Jounel: "Le temps de Noël," p. 92; H. Rahner: *Greek Myths and Christian Mystery,* pp. 145–54.

[71] J. Jungmann: *The Early Liturgy,* pp. 147–48.

[72] An example of Christmas song related to the tropical climate is the composition of R. Santos (music by B. Maramba) for the Benedictine Abbey in Manila: *Ako'y may dalang pamaypay, para sa sanggol na Diyos, sapagka't dito sa Silangan, ay mainit ang araw* ("I bring a fan for the divine Child, because here in the East the sun burns"). *Kapaskuhan,* Manila 1977, p. 8.

[73] P. Jounel: *Le renouveau du culte des saints,* pp. 144–46; A. Adam: *The Liturgical Year,* pp. 232–35.

[74] *Sermo 287, PL* 38, col. 1302; see E.O. James: *Seasonal Feasts and Festivals,* New York 1961, pp. 225–26.

[75] E.O. James: *Seasonal Feasts and Festivals,* p. 226.

[76] *Sacramentarium Veronense,* ed. L.C. Mohlberg, Rome 1966, nos. 844–59, pp. 106–08; see P. Jounel: *Le renouveau du culte des saints,* pp. 198–91.

[77] N. Turchi: *La religione antica di Roma,* pp. 98–99.

[78] D. Baldoni: "Natale Petri de cathedra," *Ephemerides Liturgicae* 68 (1954) pp. 97–126; P. Jounel: *Le renouveau du culte des saints,* pp. 109–11.

[79] J. Kirsch: "Die beiden Apostelfeste Petri Stuhlfeier und Pauli Bekehrung im Januar," *Jahrbuch für Liturgiewissenschaft* 5 (1925) pp. 48–67.

[80] P. Jounel: *Le renouveau du culte des saints,* pp. 194–95.

[81] I. Scicolone: "Il senso liturgico delle feste," *Paschale*

Mysterium, Miscellanea in honor of Salvatore Marsili, *Studia Anselmiana* 91, Rome 1986, pp. 176–92; A. Adam: *The Liturgical Year,* pp. 25–26.

[82] *Missale Romanum,* nos. 17–20, pp. 819–20. The Roman missal for the use in the dioceses of the United States contains a complete mass formulary for Thanksgiving Day on the fourth Thursday of November. *The Sacramentary,* New York 1974, pp. 541 and 747. It is interesting to note that the preface uses the exodus as type of the pilgrim fathers' journey to America: "It happened to our fathers who came to this land as if out of the desert into a place of promise and hope."

[83] *NUALC,* no. 45, *DOL,* p. 1161.

[84] *Roman Calendar. Text and Commentary,* Washington, D.C. 1975, pp. 25–26. See A. Nocent: "Le rogazioni," *Anàmnesis* 6, pp. 267–69; A. Adam: *The Liturgical Year,* pp. 190–92.

[85] N. Turchi: *La religione di Roma antica,* p. 85.

[86] J. Jungmann: *The Early Liturgy,* p. 145.

[87] *The Roman Calendar. Text and Commentary,* p. 25: "The great litany is suppressed, since it began as a strictly local rite of the church of Rome. By the institution of this type of procession the popes hoped to replace an ancient pagan practice with a Christian observance"; p. 76: "The greater litany is abolished, since it duplicates the lesser litany on the rogation days."

[88] A. Chavasse: "Le quatre-temps," *L'Eglise en prière,* Paris 1961, pp. 738–46. P. Jounel: "Le dimanche et la semaine," *L'Eglise en prière* IV, pp. 40–41; A. Nocent: "Le quattro tempora," *Anàmnesis* 6, pp. 263–66.

[89] J. Van Goudoever: *Biblical Calendars,* pp. 211–12.

[90] A. Chavasse explains the development of ember days from three to four seasons in his article "Le quatre-temps" cited above.

[91] *The Roman Calendar. Text and Commentary,* p. 26.

[92] *Missale Romanum,* nos. 21–23, pp. 824–26.

[93] *Encyclical Letter "Quas primas," Acta Apostolicae Sedis* 17 (1925) pp. 593–610. See A. Adam: *The Liturgical Year,* pp. 177–80; M. Augé: "Le solennità del Signore nel tempo per annum," *Anàmnesis* 6, p. 227.

[94] *Ibid.,* p. 603.

[95] *Ordo Lectionum Missae*, p. 88.

[96] P. Jounel: *Le renouveau du culte des saints*, p. 136.

[97] See *Acta Apostolicae Sedis* 37 (1945) pp. 48–51 for the mass and office formularies approved by the pope and the Decree of Promulgation by the Sacred Congregation of Rites.

[98] P. Jounel: *Le renouveau du culte des saints*, p. 127; A. Adam: *The Liturgical Year*, p. 231.

[99] *The Roman Calendar. Text and Commentary*, p. 51.

[100] *Ibid.*, p. 77.